THE COMPLETE BOOK OF TAILORING

For Women Who Like to Sew

THE COMPLETE
BOOK OF
TAILORING

For Women Who Like to Sew

ADELE P. MARGOLIS

Illustrated by Nathan Margolis

DOUBLEDAY & COMPANY, INC.
GARDEN CITY, NEW YORK

To my grandsons,
JOHN and PETER
who "suit" me very well, indeed

Contents

and dimensions for making some of the equipment—
some general hints and helps for pressing all fabrics—
how to press woolens, worsteds, cottons, linens, silks, rayons, and synthetics—shaping and blocking, the use of
press pads—pressing fabrics with nap or pile—pressing
and shaping the collar and lapels—shrinking and shaping
the sleeve cap—pressing buttonholes, bound pockets, applied pockets, flaps, yokes, lapped seams, the zippered
area, hems, waistbands—pressing pleats and other types
of fullness—how to shrink and shape the tape—final
pressing before inserting the lining—pressing the lining
—right side touch-up—first aid

The regulation zippered closing, the slot-seam zippered
closing—button placement—easy-to-follow directions for
the narrow two-strip bound buttonhole, a wider two-strip
bound buttonhole—finishing the underside of the buttonhole—handworked buttonholes—how to locate and sew
the buttons on—other types of fastenings—pick a pocket
for prettiness or practicality—types of pockets and how
to make them: patch pockets, bound pockets, welt pockets, flap pockets—designing with zippers, buttonholes,
and pockets

The progress of the work thus far—arranging the outer
fabric, the interfacing, the underlining, and the lining in
units of work—pin fitting the shell—stitching each fabric
unit of jacket, coat, skirt, dress—stitching each unit of
interfacing, underlining, and lining—joining garment
fabric and understructure—finishing the skirt—perfecting
the fit—eliminating the interfacing from the seams—setting the collar—establishing the roll line on collar and lapels—determining the placement of buttonholes and

pockets—and the position of the sleeves on the shoulders
—making the buttonholes and pockets—applying the
tape—pad stitching—completing the collar and the lapel
—the collar joins the garment—the collar and lapel join
at the gorgeline—attaching the cuffs—setting and stitching the sleeves—sewing kimono and raglan sleeves—attaching the shoulder pads—setting and making the hem
—fastening the facings—removing the tailor bastings and
the final pressing

Introduction

When I was a little girl, in those far-off times just before the First World War, my mother, like everybody else's mother, made all the family clothing—dresses, coats, hats, lingerie, my brothers' suits. She was even known to have made Pop's trousers. Though Mom was considerably more skilled than a lot of mothers, her motivation was the same. Mom had to! Ready-to-wear clothing was in short supply and too expensive for our family's limited means. We lived in an economy of scarcity.

Right up through my teens Mom continued to sew. I suppose no mother ever sews to the satisfaction of an adolescent daughter and, talented as mine was, she was no exception. The dresses were never tight enough, the skirts never short enough. The fabrics were noted more for their immortality than their beauty. The styles, I thought, were babyish. In the days of "flaming youth," I was still wearing organdy ruffles.

There was something much more devastating, however. Other girls' mothers had given up sewing. Their dresses were *bought* at a store. For, by the twenties, the production of ready-to-wear clothing had become a major industry. Furthermore, there was a good deal more money around to spend. The "bought" dress became a status symbol in the jazz age, along with the Stutz Bearcat, the Spanish-type furniture, and privileged admittance to a night club. In my home-made clothing, I felt that I had been left behind along with the horse and buggy.

Here we are in the early sixties. Literally millions of women and teen-age girls are once more sewing at home. Sewing-machine companies, pattern companies, piece goods and notions departments are doing a booming business. This means that a large proportion of clothing production has shifted back to the home.

Though beautiful clothes in prices for everyone's pocketbook are plentifully available and multimillion-dollar mass media exhort you to buy-buy-buy, why sew at home? I put this question to some of my classes. Here are a few of their most frequent replies:

I don't want to see myself coming and going. I want to look a little different.

I can't afford the high-style high-priced clothes I love. If I sew for myself I can have them.

I'm paralyzed when I see a rack of dresses—dozens in the same style and same color. They can keep them. I go home and sew.

I love the excitement of creating a new outfit. I'm off from the moment I see a new style or a new fabric or a new pattern.

I guess I'm hooked. I can't pass a fabric counter without succumbing.

I have no need and certainly no room for all the stuff I make but I just keep right on making them because I love to.

Economy will always be a big reason for sewing. My own experience with home sewers leads me to believe that the most compelling reasons, presently, for personal sewing are a need for self-expression, a joy in creativity, and an assertion of individuality in an increasingly automated and standardized world.

Home sewing, yes. But with a difference! Today's sewer has the time and the money to concern herself with style and creativity. She sews in an economy of abundance.

This is a book for the fashion-minded sewer who has reached that point in her sewing experience when she is ready to move on to an area she has up to now left to the professionals—tailoring. Anyone who can "sew a fine seam" and follow some simple directions doesn't have to be an expert to tailor her own coat, suit, or ensemble.

This book is a compilation of classic techniques, new methods, simplified directions, and some short cuts. The first is the result of study; the second, the result of observation; the third, sheer self-defense in teaching; the last, this sewer's experience after much trial and even more error.

Whether you sew for economy, for fashion, or for fun, it is the author's hope that tailoring will be from this moment on a happy as well as a creative experience for you.

Philadelphia, Pennsylvania   *Adele Pollock Margolis*
1964

CHAPTER I

Suit Yourself

What does the word "tailor" call to your mind?

If you are like most, you visualize an aging little man with a grayish patch of thinning hair. He's always a little man. Who ever heard of a tall tailor? He is dressed in baggy trousers and a wilting shirt, whose open collar and rolled-up sleeves emerge from a vest stuck full of pins. He is forever slaving away in some back room over some mysterious handwork or over a steaming ironing board.

Everyone has known or heard or read about such a tailor. Time was when fine-tailored clothes for women were always made by him. When you went to a tailor for a suit or coat you knew exactly what you were going to get. No surprises in style or fabric. He made one thing only —a man's coat or suit—except that yours buttoned right over left. You could count on amazing construction, pressing that you marveled at, and expert workmanship. Perhaps there were a few little details thrown in to please you but it showed its masculine origin all too clearly.

Fortunately for most of us, Fashion has given this strictly tailored little number back to the male members of the family. After all, how many Marlene Dietrichs are there who can look devastatingly feminine in a severely man-tailored suit? The era of the "little tailor" is gone. Gone too, alas, is the little tailor—and without replacement.

A whole new breed of suits and coats has emerged. The old suit formula still prevails—skirt, blouse, jacket—but what a difference! The overcoat is still here but in a softened version. The new tailoring has retained many of the fine features of construction of the old tailoring but something new has been added—the feminine touch.

While the prospect of making a traditionally tailored garment seemed absolutely forbidding to home sewers, the new tailoring with its dressmaker details and fabrics is something that any woman who sews can aspire to. From the moment one joyously decides to make something new there are a string of delicious decisions which must be made. All of them add to the excitement and pleasure of tailoring your own suit or coat.

A LITTLE SISTERLY ADVICE ON WHAT TO SEW

What's New?

There is certainly no dearth of information on what's new. The news fairly leaps at you in news flashes, advertisements, fashion columns, women's magazines, store-window displays, and just plain feminine chatter.

Concerning what's new: Here are a few suggestions.

Keep an open mind about new styles. Don't hop on the bandwagon of ridicule, mostly male. Remember that laughter often has an economic base. It's easy to discourage you from buying or making the new by labeling it a monstrous style or implying that it will look monstrous on you.

Extremes are just as important in fashion as they are in all art forms. They temper the stodgy and dismiss what has already had its day. For all the bitter denunciation of the chemise dress, it did serve a noble purpose. It brought an abrupt halt to the sausage-tight sheath and ushered in a new design period with more relaxed lines. While a particular fashion may not be for you in its avant-garde form, adapt it or modify it to suit your figure needs.

Choose an incoming style rather than an outgoing style. Contrary to popular notion, styles do not change overnight. Fashion is evolutionary rather than revolutionary. If you are fashion conscious you can sense a necessity for change and you can see a new look coming several years before it catches on.

If you want to get maximum wear out of what you make and still look à la mode throughout the duration of a fashion, choose an incoming rather than an outgoing style.

Try something new each season. Does everyone expect you always to show up in blue? Try arriving in something green. Can you be counted on to appear at a party in a sirenish sheath? Try something with "shift" lines for a change. Do you generally choose something safe and staid? Switch to something bold and see what a lift you feel.

Try something different each season whether it be a line, a color, or a fabric. It gives your wardrobe a fresh look. You may be delightfully surprised to find the new look a just-for-you look.

Distinguish between fad and fashion. Fashion is timeless; fads are of the moment. How can you tell in advance what is going to be timeless or of the moment? If it's gimmicky, you can be pretty sure it will be only a fad. It may be appealing but it will quickly pall. If it's a style made famous by a well-known public figure, too many people will adopt it. If everyone is going to wear *a* style it cannot help but tire you to see it. While in itself it may be good fashion, its very prevalence and uniformity guarantees its early demise. A big but short run—that's a fad!

If a style is so different as to be attention arresting, it may capture your immediate interest but soon become boring. Showy things don't wear well.

Have the courage to be a little independent of the news. This in itself can be news. The year when every show window is displaying purple, put away your purple suit even though it is one of your best colors and you always have something purple in your wardrobe.

When every news report shouts, "Pink," buy or make something small and unimportant in that color just to get it out of your system. But don't appear in public in pink. Wear that lovely beige instead.

Being independent does *not* mean that when skirts are lightly bypassing the kneecap you wear yours down to the ankles or vice versa. Such a departure will make you look queer. Be different but within the prevailing style. Be independent of fashion clichés but avoid the bizarre. To look current, individual, and yet not freakish, this is the neatest trick of all.

Patterns and Pictures

If you are a true-to-form sewer, fashion-conscious variety, you probably have piles of pattern and fashion books which you yank out from time to time to study. You also have a stack of patterns, more or less organized, which you also study from time to time. You lovingly examine those well-thumbed magazines over and over again. ("I'd still love to have this suit." "I'm glad I never made that one.") You hesitate to part with any of the patterns. They do have details you may want some day. No such occasion has presented itself in the past twenty years and that fine, undiminished stack still sits there in the corner.

But never mind. Both magazines and patterns are just great. They come under the heading of research and development. They steep you in fashion ideas. They accustom you to the new. They sensitize your eye to line, color, shape, and texture. They make you weigh the merits of one design against the other. They make you impatient with the trite. They teach you to prefer the subtle. They are a backlog of ideas. They cannot help but influence your choice either consciously or unconsciously. The patterns and pictures are dream stuff. But they are most important dream stuff since they help to cultivate your taste.

Fabric Is Half the Fun

Buying fabrics is one of the small vices and great joys of sewing. A fabric collector is always quite willing to un-plastic-bag and un-demothball any amount of her not-so-secret cache if anyone (usually another sewer) shows the slightest interest in seeing it. So great is the aesthetic pleasure of just looking at and handling beautiful fabric that making a garment of it is frequently an anticlimax.

What if you come upon fabric you love but have no immediate plans for using? By all means, buy it. How much should you buy? This varies with style but you can make simple garments from the following yardages. Yardage is given for size 14.

1 to 1½ yards of 54″ will make a skirt
1½ to 2 yards of 54″ will make a dress
1½ to 2 yards of 54″ will make a jacket
3½ to 4 yards of 54″ will make a dress and jacket
2½ to 3 yards of 54″ will make a suit
3½ to 4 yards of 54″ will make a coat
1½ to 2 yards of 39″ will make the lining for the jacket
2 to 2½ yards of 39″ will make a long-sleeved blouse
3 to 3½ yards of 39″ will make a jacket lining and blouse

Additional fullness takes more yardage, as does fabric with nap, design motifs, stripes, plaids, or checks which need matching.

Before storing the fabric, pin a paper label to it noting the width of the fabric and the yardage. This will do away with the necessity for measuring each time you wonder if you have enough to make up a particular style. Or better still, keep a record of what you have on hand. Many women have found it helpful to keep a small notebook with them at all times containing a small swatch of fabric and a notation of its yardage. This simplifies the purchase of dressmaking supplies whenever you are close to the source. It also gives you the opportunity to take advantage of unexpected finds in millinery, shoes, bags, and other accessories.

If the amount you have to spend for fabric is limited, there is always the conflict of practical considerations versus "love that fabric and that color." There are, I presume, sensible ways to make a selection. But fashion is far from sensible. If you insist on being judicious you may end up wearing sturdy walking shoes and cast-iron tweed.

Is This the Year?

If your closet is anything like most, you very likely don't *need* much. You could undoubtedly coast along for a few seasons without making anything new. This would be bad for business and very bad for your morale.

What does a search of your closet reveal?

What fashions are still good?

Which clothes need repair or replacing?

Which should be retired or given away?

What do you really need?

A replacement for a successful but now worn item?

An outfit for some special event coming up?

Where were you caught short last year? An exciting invitation and you without *the* dress with which you hoped to impress? An unexpected trip and you without a suitable suit? It is well to have your closet, like your pantry, contain a few staples for emergencies.

What do you want?

Which of the new fashions fire your imagination?

What new items will freshen your wardrobe and make you content with the rest?

What have you wanted for a very long time?

For home sewers what one wants is more often the determining factor than what one needs. Since the cost is comparatively little, we can indulge our desires. Now comes the time to haul out that trusty file of pictures, patterns, and fabric. Your research may finally pay off. This may be just the year to realize some of those long-cherished dreams.

So You're Going to Make a Suit! or Coat! or Ensemble!

Let's talk a bit about what you are going to make.

A coat, perhaps? I remember how surprised I was when I discovered that one person could have more than two coats. (I am referring to cloth coats, of course. I have not quite gotten over the wonder of one woman having more than two fur coats). I was raised on the formula of one coat for "every day" and one coat for "good." The "good" coat, nine times out of ten, turned out to be a safe "little black basic coat." This was supposed to go over everything. What folly!

One coat or even two coats can no more satisfy your coat needs than one dress or two dresses. Think of the clothes they must be worn over—the slim ones, the full ones, the short ones, the long ones, the light colors, the dark colors, the bright colors; the spring, summer, fall, and winter clothes. Think of the many times a first impression of you is in a coat. Day after day, night after night, season after season, and sometimes even year after year, this most over-worked item in your closet sees duty.

This year, instead of starting with a dress and planning a coat to go over it, start with the coat and think of a dress to wear under it. Coats are the big stars of many a fashionable wardrobe. If you add a new coat each season, it won't take long before you have just the variety you need. This could cost a small fortune if you had to buy your coats. Aren't you lucky that you can make them!

If you are just a beginner in tailoring you will find a coat easier to make than a suit. Generally a coat requires less fitting than a suit. You will eliminate a big problem if you choose an unfitted or semi-fitted style.

Could you use a new suit? Suits are such a happy answer to the many needs of contemporary living. Little wonder that practically every wardrobe includes its share of suits. Not only the classic wool, but linen, cotton, silk, velvet, satin, and brocade are now used for suits. Every color appears—from white through grays to black, from pastels through jewel tones to darks. And how versatile they are! Suits can be severe, tailored, feminine; fitted, semifitted, unfitted; furred, jeweled, or utterly simple. So suited are they for everything from trudging through the country to dinner and the theater, that they have given rise to a whole new way of dressing.

If you are making a suit for the first time, choose an unfitted or semifitted style, the "Chanel" type. Fortunately, such suits are high fashion at the present.

An ensemble? If the skirt-blouse-jacket look is not flattering to your figure but you still like "dressing in layers," make an ensemble instead. A dress and jacket or dress and matching coat give a wonder-fully co-ordinated look. This may be the answer to your wardrobe needs as well as your figure needs. It could see you through the many demands of a day-evening-work-play schedule. Indeed, many notably fashionable women use this as their formula for the many-purpose costume.

When you learn how easy it is to tailor beautifully, you will undoubtedly make all three—coats, suits, and ensembles.

THE PATTERN

With the large and growing number of home sewers in this country (40,000,000 at last count), patterns have become big business. Since the competition is keen, all the pattern companies offer a wide selection of styles, designed to cover a wide range of sewing experience. The bulk of the patterns are designed for the average sewer. An average sewer is one who has some basic knowledge of sewing, can follow pattern directions carefully and who has completed half a dozen successful garments.

All of the pattern companies claim their patterns are easy to follow. For the beginners, however, they make special patterns. McCall's has its "Easy" patterns, Vogue its "Easy-to-make," Butterick its "Quick'n Easy," Advance its "Sew-Easy" patterns. Perhaps the easiest line of patterns is Simplicity which offers attractive but simple designs with few pattern pieces.

Experienced sewers are lured with patterns by big-name designers. The most difficult and also the most exciting are the Vogue Paris Original Models. Spadea's entire line is its International and American Designer series. McCall's and Advance also feature designer patterns. Those who find this extensive array still not quite what they are looking for can be their own designers and learn to make their own patterns.

If tailoring is new to you, don't multiply your tailoring problems by choosing a difficult pattern. The fewer the pattern pieces, the fewer the problems. Remember that the loveliest clothes are most often of simple design, beautiful fabric, fine fit, and exquisite workmanship.

Get the pattern you like even if it does cost a little more. The cost of the pattern is a very small item in the total cost of the garment. An extra dollar or even two may make the difference between an ordinary design and a superb one. If you were buying your coat or suit, would an extra dollar or two discourage you from buying an original design or even a very good copy?

What Size Pattern?

Most of the pattern companies use the measurements approved by the Measurement Standard Committee of the Pattern Industry (page 12). The exception to this is the Spadea Company whose patterns are designed in what they term ready-to-wear sizes (page 14). However, these are Spadea's ready-to-wear sizes. The clothing industry has never adopted uniform sizing. In fact, there is a good deal of anarchy in this area. An expensive Size 10 may equal an inexpensive Size 14. The higher-priced firms sell flattery as well as merchandise. Many manufacturers gain their reputations on a particular cut and fit for what they consider a standard size. For home sewing it is safer not to go by ready-to-wear sizes. Consult the measurement chart for size. If you use a Spadea pattern consult their measurement chart.

Today's patterns are designed in sizes to fit many figure types: girl, chubby, pre-teen, sub-teen, junior, junior petite, petite, misses, women's, and half-sizes. Spadea's ready-to-wear sizes are designed for the following figure types: juniors, half-sizes, tall sizes, diminutive, and mature figures. Of course there are not all styles in all sizes. Each style is designed for specific sizes. So you will need to consult not only the Standard Measurement Chart for size and type, you will also have to study each pattern.

Practically no one is a perfect size. Choose that standard-size pattern which most *nearly* meets your measurements and make such changes as are necessary. Since the bodice is most difficult to fit, let that determine the size. For most figures the bust measurement is a good guide. But you must also take into consideration the build of the neck, shoulders, and chest, since these areas are difficult to fit. It is usually better to choose a smaller pattern which fits these areas, and then adjust the bust, waist, or hips. It is easier to start with a smaller size and grade it up than to start with a larger size and try to make it smaller. If the discrepancy between bodice and skirt is very great (more than one size), buy two patterns: the correct size for the bodice and the correct size for the skirt.

Personal-Measurement Chart

(To help determine your size and any necessary alterations)
Use this chart to compare your measurements with the measurements of the pattern you are using. See page 104 for directions.

Unless you are making a bathing suit or a fitted evening dress, your clothes need *ease*. This is an amount added to the body measurements in *length* and *width* to allow for body movements and comfort in wearing.

The best measurements are taken wearing a slip over the bra and girdle (if any) you intend to wear under the garment you are making. Wear shoes with heel height similar to ones you will wear with the garment.

You will need some help in taking the hard-to-get-at measurements.

Item	Me	Ease for slim dress	Ease for suit jacket	Ease for fitted coat	Total needed	Pattern measures	Desirable changes + or −
1. Bust—taken over the high point of the bust and across the shoulder blades in back		plus 3″	plus 4″	plus 4″ to 5″			
2. Waistline—taken snugly in the hollow of the waist or where you would like your waistline to be		plus ½″	plus 1½″	plus 2″ to 2½″			
3. Hips—taken generally about 7″ below the waist or around the fullest part of the hips; if this is lower or higher than the 7″, note it on the chart		plus 2″	plus 3″	plus 3″ to 4″			

Now, tie a piece of string snugly around your waist. Push the string into the position you want for your waistline. This will give you a fixed point from which and to which you may measure.

Item	Me	Ease for slim dress	Ease for suit jacket	Ease for fitted coat	Total needed	Pattern measures	Desirable changes + or −
THE BODICE							
4. Center front, from the hollow between the collar-bones to the string		plus 0 to ½″	plus 0 to ½″	plus 0 to ½″			
5. Center back—bend head forward and locate the bone at which the head bends; straighten and measure from this bone at the neckline to the string		plus 0 to ½″	plus 0 to ½″	plus 0 to ½″			
6. Bust-point height—from the highest point of the bust to the string		plus 0 to ½″	plus 0 to ½″	plus 0 to ½″			
7. Bust-point width—from bust point to bust point		plus 0 to ½″	plus 0 to ½″	plus 0 to ½″			
THE SKIRT							
8. Center front length—from waistline string to floor; subtract the number of inches the skirt is worn from the floor		NO EASE NEEDED					
9. Center back length—from waistline string to the floor; subtract the number of inches the skirt is worn from the floor		NO EASE NEEDED					

(Ease in length — indicated between columns 5, 6, and 7)

For waist and hip measurement see page 10.

Item	Me	Ease for slim dress	Ease for suit jacket	Ease for fitted coat	Total needed	Pattern measures	Desirable changes	+ or −
THE SLEEVE								
10. Overarm length—from shoulder point, to elbow, to wrist at little finger, with the arm bent		the bent arm provides the ease						
11. Shoulder to elbow—while tape is still in position, note this measurement		the bent arm provides the ease						
12. Girth—around the heaviest part of the upper arm; usually about midway between elbow and shoulder		plus 2″	plus 2½″	plus 3″				
13. Elbow to wrist—the difference between the overarm measurement and the shoulder to elbow measurement		plus ½″	plus ½″	plus ½″				
14. Knuckle circumference—around the fullest part of the hand as you would slip the hand through a sleeve		plus ½″	plus ½″	plus ½″				

These measurements are just a few of the list of possible body measurements. But they should be sufficient to make simple changes in your pattern.

Revised Measurement Chart for All Pattern Companies

Approved by the Measurement Standard Committee of the Pattern Industry

Select your size by the bust measurements on this revised chart. That size is your correct size for all patterns. These are actual body measurements, not garment measurements.

Misses	10	12	14	16	18	20	
If bust is	31	32	34	36	38	40	
Waist	24	25	26	28	30	32	
Hip	33	34	36	38	40	42	
Back waist length	15¾	16	16¼	16½	16¾	17	

Junior misses	9	11	13	15	17		
If bust is	30½	31½	33	35	37		
Waist	23½	24½	25½	27	28½		
Hip	32½	33½	35	37	39		
Back waist length	15	15¼	15½	15¾	16		

Teens	8	10	12	14	16		
If bust is	29	30	32	34	36		
Waist	23	24	25	26	28		
Hip	31	32	34	36	38		
Back waist length	14½	14¾	15	15¼	15½		

Children	½	1	2	3	4	5	6
If chest is	19	20	21	22	23	23½	24
Waist	19	19½	20	20½	21	21½	22
Hip						25	26
Back waist length							10½

Girls	7	8	10	12	14		
If bust is	25	26	28	30	32		
Waist	22½	23	24	25	26		
Hip	27	28	30	32½	35		
Back waist length	11	11½	12¼	13	13¾		

Sub-teens	8s	10s	12s	14s			
If bust is	28	29	31	33			
Waist	23	24	25	26			
Hip	31	32	34	36			
Back waist length	13½	13¾	14	14¼			

Women	40	42	44	46	48	50	
If bust is	42	44	46	48	50	52	
Waist	34	36	38½	41	43½	46	
Hip	44	46	48	50	52	54	
Back waist length	17⅛	17¼	17⅜	17½	17⅝	17¾	

Half sizes	12½	14½	16½	18½	20½	22½	24½
If bust is	33	35	37	39	41	43	45
Waist	27	29	31	33	35	37½	40
Hip	37	39	41	43	45	47	49
Back waist length	15¼	15½	15¾	16	16¼	16½	16¾

Skirts, slacks, and shorts

Teens			8	10	12	14	16			
Waist			23	24	25	26	28			
Hip			31	32	34	36	38			

Junior misses			9	11	13	15	17			
Waist			23½	24½	25½	27	28½			
Hip			32½	33½	35	37	39			

Misses & women	10	12	14	16	18	20	40	42	44	46
Waist	24	25	26	28	30	32	34	36	38½	41
Hip	33	34	36	38	40	42	44	46	48	50

Boys' and men's clothing

Boys	1	2	3	4	5	6	8	10	12	14	16
Chest	20	21	22	23	23½	24	26	28	30	32	34
Waist	19½	20	20½	21	21½	22	23	24	25½	27	29
Hip					24	25	27	29	31	33	35
Neck-base girth						11½	12	12½	13	13½	14

Men										
Chest	32	34	36	38	40	42	44	46	48	50
Waist	28	30	32	34	36	38	40	42	44	46
Neck-base girth	13½	14	14½	15	15½	16	16½	17	17½	18
Shirt-sleeve length	33	33	33	33	34	34	34	35	35	35

Spadea's Ready-to-wear Size Charts

Regular sizing								
Sizes	6	8	10	12	14	16	18	20
Bust	32	33	34	35	36½	38	40	42
Waist	22	23	24	25	26½	28	30	32
Hip (5″ below waistline)	33	34	35	36	37½	39	41	43
Length (nape of neck to waist)	16	16¼	16½	16¾	17	17¼	17½	17¾

For mature figures							
Sizes	14	16	18	20	40	42	44
Bust	36½	38	40	42	44	46	48
Waist	27½	29	31	33	35	37	38
Hip (5″ below waistline)	37½	39	41	43	45	47	49
Length (nape of neck to waist)	17	17¼	17½	17¾	18	18¼	18½

For diminutives (short figures, 5'5" and under)

Sizes	8	10	12	14	16	18	20
Bust	33	34	35	36½	38	40	42
Waist	24	25	26	27½	29	31	33
Hip (5" below waistline)	34	35	36	37½	39	41	43
Length (nape of neck to waist)	15¾	16	16¼	16½	16¾	17	17¼

For tall girls

Sizes	8	10	12	14	16	18	20
Bust	33	34	35	36½	38	40	42
Waist	23	24	25	26½	28	30	32
Hip (5" below waistline)	34	35	36	37½	39	41	43
Length (nape of neck to waist)	17	17¼	17½	17¾	18	18¼	18½

For half sizes

Sizes	12½	14½	16½	18½	20½	22½
Bust	35½	37½	39½	41½	43½	45½
Waist	27½	29½	31½	33½	35½	37½
Hip (5" below waistline)	35½	37½	39½	41½	43½	45½
Length (nape of neck to waist)	15¾	16	16¼	16½	16¾	17

For junior sizes

Sizes	5	7	9	11	13	15	17
Bust	31½	32½	33½	34½	36	37½	39
Waist	21½	22½	23½	24½	26	27½	29
Hip (5" below waistline)	32½	33½	34½	35½	37	38½	40
Length (nape of neck to waist)	15½	15¾	16	16¼	16½	16¾	17

Coats (capes, stoles, aprons)

Sizes	Small	Medium	Large
Bust	33–34	35–36½	38–40
Waist (used if garment has waistline)	23–24	25–26½	28–30
Hip (5" below waistline)	34–35	36–37½	39–41

Important—Patterns are available only in the size range and category noted with each illustration.

A matter of "Ease"—What you need and what you get in a pattern. The question of ease is a puzzling and confusing one for many home sewers. Just what ease is necessary? What ease can one expect when buying a pattern? Does the ease affect the size?

In the ease column of your personal-measurement chart, the amount suggested is an average amount necessary for movement and comfort. Ease is also a matter of personal preference. You may use a little more if you like your clothes more relaxed, a little less if you like them quite snug. Add the ease to your body measurements. In working with a pattern, compare *the total amount of your body measurements plus ease* with the actual measurements of your pattern which already includes the correct amount for the size and design.

The basis of all designs is the "staple" (or basic pattern) from which all pattern-making is done. This is based on standard body measurements plus a standard amount of ease as set by the Bureau of Standards. Therefore size and ease are uniform in most patterns though produced by various pattern companies. These measurements are revised from time to time to keep up with the fashion trends.

All style patterns are drafted or draped from these basic patterns. It is the designer, now, who chooses just how much additional ease there is to be in any particular style. The designer being a very creative fellow need not be governed by or adhere to an average amount of ease.

Even a designer in deciding the amount of ease required in a garment must consider the following factors:

1. The type of garment: the dress to be worn for golf obviously needs more ease than a slinky cocktail dress.

2. The style of the garment: a shift pattern has more ease at the bust and waist than a fitted sheath. A dinner dress with a low neck will have less than standard ease around the bust and across the chest, or the neckline will gap.

3. What is fashionable: skirts and slacks fit much closer now than they did in former years.

Sometimes, even if your measurement differs slightly from standard measurements, the ease in a design will accommodate the difference. That is why you can often wear a smaller size than actual body measurements call for.

Use the same size for suit or coat as you would for a dress. All the necessary additional allowances have already been made in the pattern. Take into account the fullness inherent in the style.

Having gone to such trouble to determine it, insist on the correct size. Stores which carry patterns stock but a few in each size. A complete line in all sizes would take considerable storage space. If your size is not on hand, have it ordered for you or order it yourself from the pattern company.

It is frustrating to get all set to sew in an unexpected bit of free time only to discover that the pattern of your choice in your size is not available. The temptation is to take the pattern on hand and try to alter it for size. This is inviting trouble. It is not just a case of taking it in or letting it out a pinch or two here and there. Every pattern piece needs corresponding grading to keep the design in scale. Pattern grading is a very specialized skill too difficult for amateurs. Don't settle for any but the right size.

Before You Buy Your Pattern

A dozen things to think about before you buy your pattern.

1. Choose simple patterns in the beginning. The designer patterns are for the more advanced sewers.

2. The fewer the pattern pieces, the fewer the problems.

3. Choose an incoming style rather than one that has already seen the peak of its popularity. This should give you five or six years of fashionable wear—a reasonable lifetime for your coat or suit.

4. The shaping of your garment is accomplished by the darts and seams. The more darts and seams, the more places to fit.

5. Shaped seams originating at the shoulder or armhole offer excellent opportunity for fitting. This is particularly true for narrow-shouldered, heavy-bosomed figures.

6. The darts and seams should be consistent with the fabric used. Solid colors in medium-weight fabrics with a smooth surface make

the choice of pattern limitless. All seams, darts, and details are clearly visible with no distortion of the surface design of the fabric. They may be straight or curved, vertical, horizontal, or oblique.

7. The style lines and darts are lost in rough-textured, napped, or nubby fabrics. Painstaking work and intricate seaming won't even show. Save yourself the time. Choose a pattern of simple lines.

8. When plaids, checks, or stripes are used choose straight rather than curved style lines; choose designs with either horizontal or vertical darts which can be balanced on the straight lines of the fabric design.

9. The length of the jacket depends not only on the current style but on the proportions of the figure. Choose a style with a jacket length becoming to you or alter a desirable style to that length.

10. Double-breasted styles will make you look heavier.

11. Generally, vertical style lines make you look slimmer; horizontal style lines make you look heavier.

12. Kimono and raglan sleeves are easy to wear and easiest to fit but give a broader line to the shoulders. These sleeves are by nature bulky. They appear even bulkier in wool, especially heavy wool. This is a disastrous choice when the jacket is short and the wearer's figure is a short, heavy one. Kimono or raglan sleeves look much less top-heavy when the bulk of the shoulders is balanced by the length of a coat.

FABRIC

Time was when one would really have to search for handsome fabric. Now, the chief problem is which of the many enticing yardages to choose and when to stop buying. Inexpensive as well as expensive lines offer a vast array of exciting colors, textures, and designs. It is almost impossible to make a bad choice. What one must aim for is an inspired choice.

A tailored garment is a long-term investment. A good suit or coat of fine fabric and excellent lines should last for at least five or six years. Women who spend a great deal for custom-made clothes often wear them much longer. (Consider the case of Mrs. Joseph P. Kennedy who wore the same dress to her son's inauguration as President in 1961 that she wore when presented at the Court of St. James's in 1938. This was hardly because she could not afford a new one. The dress was timelessly beautiful.)

Before You Buy Your Fabric

Things to think about before you buy your fabric:

1. Solid colors permit unlimited pattern selection.

2. Light, bright colors make your figure appear heavier. Heavy, bulky, nubby, looped fabrics make your figure appear heavier, too.

3. Beginners will find that woolens are easier to handle than worsteds.

4. Medium-weight wool is easier to handle than sheer, bulky, or heavy wool.

5. Black and navy are difficult for beginners to handle, they require particular care in pressing.

6. Black woolens pick up lint.

7. Plaids, stripes, checks, and some design motifs require matching. Be sure to buy sufficient fabric depending on the size and direction of the repeat and how many seams have to be matched.

8. Naps, piles, and directional-design motifs require pattern layout with all pattern pieces going in one direction (neck to hem). Buy sufficient fabric.

9. Allow enough fabric to take care of straightening the grain, sponging or shrinking when necessary, alterations to the pattern, matching and directional cutting.

10. Sharp pleats require firm, close weaves; unpressed pleats are better in soft fabrics.

11. Soft, limp, or stretchy fabrics must be completely underlined for tailored garments.

12. When the sleeves are set in, you will find that soft, loosely woven wool is easier to "ease" than hard, stiff, or closely woven fabrics.

13. Hard-to-stitch fabrics are: ribbed fabrics like ottoman; heavy coatings; napped or fleece fabrics; and corduroy or velveteen which "creeps" in stitching.

14. Fabrics which require special pressing techniques are: gabardine (very difficult for beginners); ottoman and other ribbed fabrics; twills; velvets, corduroys, and velveteens.

A Few Do's and Don't's

Since the fabric is so fundamental to the beauty and success of your tailored garment, you will find numerous references to it throughout this book. However, it would be well before making a choice to read the following: Chapter II, The Pattern, the Fabric and You, and Chapter VII, Pressing Problems.

DO choose a color or texture that you will enjoy working on. If it doesn't give you a "lift" in the making, chances are it won't in the wearing.

DO choose a fabric that will not present too many problems in layout, sewing, or pressing if you are a beginner.

DON'T compromise on the quality of the fabric. The same effort and labor go into inferior fabric as into good fabric. It just isn't worth while to put a great deal of work into something that will come apart at the seams the first time you wear it. On the other hand, don't put it to every test. It is equally not worth while to work on something sturdy that you don't enjoy. You must love what you are making while you are making it to carry you through the hours of work and the discipline of sewing. Most tailored garments require small yardages between 2½ to 3½ yards. The saving is comparatively small. A few extra dollars per yard of fabric will reward you with a truly expensive-looking suit or coat.

DON'T skimp. Get the yardage you need. A few extra inches may save you hours of time and effort in laying out and cutting your pattern. Not enough fabric may force you to change a design you love to something that doesn't have quite the flair of the original. Allow sufficient yardage for straightening the grain, sponging the fabric, any alterations to the pattern; placing, spacing, and matching of surface-design units, stripes, checks, plaids, and for the directional placement of naps, piles, design motifs, or bias cut.

DON'T succumb to novelty fabrics *unless:* you can afford to indulge yourself in time as well as labor and money, they present a challenge to you, you will have a lot of fun making them up, or you must get the "whimsy" out of your system even if you have to give the garment away afterwards!

MORE NECESSARY MATERIALS

Select a Lining

Perhaps you've always thought of a lining as a mere cover-up for all the internal works of a tailored garment. Its usefulness doesn't preclude its decorativeness. Linings are like eyeglasses in this respect; if they have to be, why not make them beautiful! Let them be seen and enjoyed!

If the outer fabric is a solid color or has a solid-color effect, you have unlimited choice—colors that match, colors that blend, colors that contrast, prints, stripes, plaids, and weaves. A surprise lining adds interest. If the outer fabric is elaborate in weave or printed surface, then your lining is best limited to a solid color.

If you are making a coat, consider the color of the dresses or suits over which it will be worn. (Remember that one coat can't go over everything.) Choose a color for the lining which picks up the color of the outer fabric and yet blends with the clothing over which it will be worn.

A coat with lining and dress that match or a suit with lining and blouse that match can make a costume out of what might otherwise be just another wardrobe item. This "made for each other" look has many advantages. It produces a unified, harmonious over-all appearance, it simplifies the selection of accessories, and it lends itself to bold accents.

Lining is best when of some soft fabric which facilitates slipping the garment on and off. It is usually lighter in weight than the outer fabric. Soft or light-weight satin, satin-backed crepe, crepe, soft taffeta or peau de soie, surah, China silk, tub silk, soft cottons—these all make fine linings. When stiff, heavy, quilted, or fur linings are used, the sleeve lining is usually made of some soft lining fabric.

With the perversity of all fashion, linings sometimes defy the rules. A silk garment with a wool lining can be useful as well as startling. Wool with a contrasting wool lining makes a snug as well as beautiful coat.

The lining should be opaque so that it really covers the inner construction.

If the lining will show through a loosely woven outer fabric, choose one that matches in color. Or, back the coat fabric with an opaque underlining (page 201). This will leave you free to choose any contrasting or figured lining.

Every skirt needs a lining. If you are making a straight, wool skirt, it should be lined to prevent it from bagging in the seat. In most instances it is necessary to line the back only from waist to mid-thigh length. The fabric should be firm and have no "give" to be effective. Soft rayon taffeta is best for this purpose. Bemberg (men's suit lining), sheath lining, cottons, crepes, and China silks are also used.

In Size 14, ½ yard of 39″ skirt lining will do for the back of the skirt. One yard will line the skirt front and skirt back to mid-thigh length. If you wish to line the entire skirt, see the pattern envelope for the necessary skirt yardage.

Perhaps an Interlining

Interlining is used for adding warmth to a winter suit or coat. Lamb's wool, chamois, outing flannel, wool-backed satin are all used —lamb's wool most frequently. It comes in gray, white, beige, and black in several weights. It is 54″–60″ wide. The yardage will depend on the style of the garment and how much of it is to be interlined. If you are the type who never thaws out till the end of May, interline the entire coat and sleeves, full length. If you live in a very cold climate or if you have to wait for public transportation on cold, windy highways, there is no reason why you cannot put a double or even a triple interlining through the body of your coat or sleeves to ensure adequate warmth. Sometimes chamois is used as a windbreaker.

Bought coats never seem to be adequately interlined. Here is your chance to make your coat really warm enough for you.

The Shape of Fashion

One of the questions most frequently asked by fashion-conscious sewers is "What gives it that shape?" The use of interfacings and underlinings to sustain the present subtle shape of fashion is one of the most important aspects of tailoring to be considered. There is a bewildering array of interfacings and underlinings on the market. Which to choose? There is no simple answer. For this reason the entire matter has been dealt with at length in Chapter V. Read the whole "inside story" before you decide which will be best for your purpose.

Shoulder pads. The amount and kind of shoulder padding changes with fashion. We have just come through a period which used little or no padding (much to the delight of many). Undeniably, there are times when tailored garments look better with some *light* padding.

The design of the shoulders and sleeves determines the type of shoulder pad to be used. There are pads for set-in sleeves, kimono sleeves, and dropped shoulders. Your pattern will indicate which type to use. You can either make (see page 207 for directions) or buy the appropriate kind. If what you can buy is too thick for your personal taste, remove some of the padding.

Hold that line! Tape is used as a stay in those areas of your garment where it is essential to preserve a measurement or shape. It can also be used to prevent bulk in a seam. Half-inch cotton tape is easy to handle and shape. It comes in black and white. The amount you will need varies with the use of it. It is economical to buy a roll of tape if you do much sewing. When you have mastered the technique of applying tape you may want to try the ¼" tape which is used in fine custom work.

A Few Findings

Thread. It is important that you choose the right thread for your fabrics. The characteristics of the thread should match the characteristics of the fabric in elasticity and strength. Use cotton thread for cotton fabrics. They are both vegetable fibers. Use synthetic thread for synthetic fabrics. They are both man-made fibers. Use silk thread for silk or wool fabrics. They are both animal fibers. Silk thread is also good on linen fabric. Though rightly this is a vegetable fiber, it is more like silk in strength.

In tailoring wool use silk thread for all construction seams; it provides the necessary strength. Use mercerized thread for all handwork or topstitching. Its dull finish blends better with the dull finish of the wool in those places where the stitching may be visible.

Since thread works up a bit lighter than it appears on the spool, it is generally correct to select a color which is just a shade darker than the fabric. However, if light striking the fabric produces a sheen and makes the color appear lighter (as in satin), select a color of thread which is a shade lighter than the fabric.

When it has been standing around for a while, silk thread sometimes dries and becomes brittle, breaking easily while stitching. Dampening restores its resiliency. Wrap the spool of silk in a damp cloth for several hours; then allow it to dry naturally.

The amount of thread to buy will depend on the amount of stitching to be done. Four 50-yard spools of silk should see you through a so-called "average" suit or coat. It is often necessary to use more. For ease in purchasing additional thread, note the color number on the spool.

Zippers. A 7-inch zipper is generally used on skirts. It may be placed in any convenient seam—side, side front, side back, back, or front. There is no orthodoxy about this. The design and the construction of the garment controls the placement. Suits with short jackets expose the zippered closing to view. Why not try two shorter-length zippers, one on each side seam which will not be visible below the jacket? Two four-inch zippers work just as well as one 7-inch one.

Seam binding. Use straight seam binding for a straight hem; bias seam binding for curved hems. Seam binding should be shrunk before using unless it is bought preshrunk. Immerse the binding in water for ten minutes. Dry and press.

Grosgrain ribbon, belting, or interfacing. The waistline of a skirt needs some stay to prevent stretching. Grosgrain ribbon, belting, interfacing, seam binding, or tape may be used. Choose the one which is consistent with your fabric and your personal taste. (Some women don't care for too much stiffness around their waists.)

Unbleached muslin. Unbleached muslin in a weight approximating that of the garment fabric is used for a trial muslin to check the style and fit of the coat or jacket. See the pattern envelope for necessary yardage.

Special Findings

Special findings for a particular design are listed on the back of the pattern envelope. If you live in an area which has a dressmaker's supply store, it is well worth a visit. You will find notions and gadgets you never dreamed existed—all planned to make sewing easier and the finished product more beautiful.

Buttons. Buttons are often the chief decorative feature of an otherwise simple garment. Gone are the days of standard bone buttons for strictly tailored suits or coats. Fashion welcomes and stores offer wood and metal buttons; buttons of plastic, pearl, and horn; rhinestone buttons and jeweled buttons; crochet and ribbon buttons. There are many to choose from.

Your button box may yield up its treasure. If you don't actually use your old buttons, they may be helpful in deciding what kind of new ones to get. Try them on your fabric for color, size, sheen, and surface.

If you have any doubt about the color, the suitability, the effectiveness of any particular button on your fabric, use a self-covered button which is always in good taste. These can now be made in a variety of interesting shapes and combinations. Another way to get a perfect color match in an interesting button is to make a crocheted button, using yarn unwoven from the garment fabric. There are always enough scraps of fabric left in cutting to use for this purpose. Use a wooden mold or a covered button as the base.

The opening extension of each garment is planned for a specific width of button. Measure the distance from the center front to the front seam line; this is the size button which the designer planned (Fig. 1a). It provides the right amount of space to properly set off your button like the jewel it is. When the button is stitched on the center front line, there is half a button's width between the rim of the button and the finished edge of the garment (Fig. 1b).

You may use a slightly smaller button in this same space. For larger or outsize buttons, this is the rule: the distance from center front to front seam line is equal to half the button's width plus ½″ (Fig. 1c).

It is better to use the size of button indicated on the pattern than to attempt to make pattern changes on the opening extension. (Unless, of course, you know pattern making.)

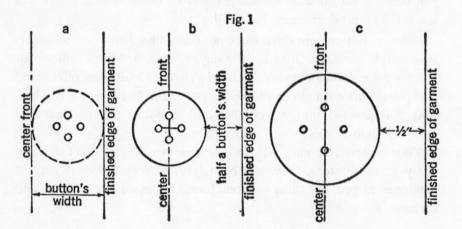

Fig. 1

THE EQUIPMENT YOU NEED

"On Location"

It is grand to have a sewing room where you can work and store all the sewing equipment. Next best is a little corner of your home just for you. Even a closet will do. There should be some place where you can shut the door on that vast pile of fabrics, trimmings, supplies, gadgets, and sewing equipment which all sewers need and seem to accumulate.

A good deal of the equipment needed for tailoring is somewhere in that pile. Some used specifically for tailoring will be new to you. These can be purchased at a tailoring or dressmaking supply store, a department store or a variety store. Some can be made at home.

Any work can be made easier with the proper tools. It is hard to convince resourceful and economical women of this. They are apt to make anything handy do—a bobby pin, a paring knife, a spoon.

If you want to do a professional job in sewing, get the tools with which a professional job is done. Even if you splurge and buy everything you need, you will still not be spending very much. You can probably make up the entire cost in the amount saved by making your first coat or suit. Think of the larger purchases as being amortized over the years. If you can just resist buying that one extra length of enticing fabric which you may not sew up for years anyway, you'll have the money needed for most of the tailoring equipment. However you rationalize it, you will still be financially far ahead of women who buy their clothes.

Permanent Equipment—Tools You Absolutely Need

A good cutting surface should be flat, firm, large enough for the 54″ width of woolen fabrics. A dining-room table, a metal folding table, a cutting board—any of these will do. A bed will *not* do; it is not firm enough. A floor is better if you have no other suitable surface.

Sewing machine. Any one of the numerous good machines, either portable or table model, new or used. Tailoring requires only a simple model in good working order. Fancy gadgets are not used.

Yardstick is absolutely essential.

12" or 18" ruler should have inches marked off in ⅛".

Tape measure should be of the sturdy nonstretchable type.

Gauge. A small metal one is convenient. If it is not available, make a gauge using the cardboard on which seam binding is wound. Mark off inches in ⅛" measurements.

Scissors and shears should be used only for fabric and thread. Keep the points and edges sharp. Use an old pair of scissors for paper cutting. You will need 3" scissors for clipping and trimming seams, 5" scissors as a good all-around tool, and 6" to 8" shears for cutting woolens.

Pins. No. 16 dressmaker pins are a good size. These have fine sharp points which won't injure the fabric. It is economical to buy pins in a half-pound box. (Whatever happens to all those pins one is continually buying?)

Pincushion is handy for pins and needles.

Needles. No. 8 crewel needles have sharp points and large eyes. These are good for general sewing. The No. 10 crewel needle is smaller and finer and is also needed. Good needles are imperative for the considerable handwork in tailoring.

Thimble makes hand sewing much easier. It should fit the middle finger of the hand comfortably.

Marking materials are used for transferring the pattern markings to the fabric.

Tailor's chalk, in assorted colors. The chalky kind is preferable to the waxy which needs cleaning fluid to remove it. Who wants to use cleaning fluid on a garment that hasn't even been worn yet?

Dressmaker's carbon paper. A package contains sheets of assorted sizes and colors.

Tracing wheel. Blunt type.

Basting thread. In assorted colors. Use any colored thread from previous projects. Silk thread is frequently used for basting because it slides into the fabric easily and is less likely to leave marks.

Stitch ripper. You know the old gag about "As ye sew, so shall ye rip." Well, this tool makes it easier.

Skirt marker. This is an adjustable rule mounted on a stand. The most accurate is one that uses pins rather than chalk.

Mirror. A full-length mirror is essential for checking fit.

Dress form which duplicates *your* figure is best of all. Either make one or have it made for you. A standard-size dress form is no more help than fitting your clothes on someone else.

*Basic pattern.** A pattern made to your measurements and used for adjusting standard-size patterns to your individual requirements. Make one for yourself.

Pressing equipment. A great part of your permanent equipment is used for pressing. This is discussed at length in Chapter VII, Pressing Problems. To acquaint you now with some of the things you will need for pressing, here is a list:

iron, ironing board, press board, sleeve board, sleeve press board, clapper or pounding block, hardwood press block, edge and point presser, needle board, cloth press mitt, press cloths, steam-iron cover, brown wrapping paper, tissue paper, small basin of water, dampening devices, tailor's ham, assorted rolls, and press pads.

Chapter VII contains descriptions and illustrations of all this equipment and directions for making some of it.

Very Nice Extras to Have—(hints for families and friends)

Sewing table especially constructed for you. A large plywood board mounted on a trestle of the correct height is a simple, inexpensive way of solving the problem if you have the space. Have it constructed wide enough and at your best working height. A sewing area with built-in table which can be folded out of sight is ideal.

Zigzag attachment. Handy for joining interfacings.

45° triangle.

---

* Complete directions for making a basic pattern will be found in PATTERN WISE by this author, a Dolphin Handbook published by Doubleday & Company, Inc.

Tailor's square. Both this and the triangle are useful for determining grain, for making changes in the position of the grain, and for making pattern alterations.

Left-handed shears. If you are left-handed, you will find these much more convenient to use.

Pinking shears are fine for seam finishes. They are *not* used in cutting woolens.

Extra-fine pins are toilet pins with colored-glass heads. These are somewhat larger than dressmaker pins but they have very fine points and slide into the fabric very smoothly. They are especially good for fabric which bruises easily.

Wrist pincushion. A pincushion which can be worn on the wrist is very convenient.

Bodkin. This is a long, blunt needle with a large eye. Use it for turning casings, tubings, and cording buttonholes.

Mirror installed in sewing area. This is most convenient for work. A three-way mirror gives you the whole picture (if you can take it).

CHAPTER II

The Pattern, the Fabric and You

What a wonderful state of affairs when the pattern and the fabric look as if they were "made for each other" and both are just right for you! To achieve such a happy union you must know something about patterns, something about fabrics, and something about what's for you.

SOMETHING ABOUT PATTERNS

Which First—the Pattern or the Fabric?

This is like that ancient question about which comes first, the chicken or the egg? The arguments are endless.

You have a hoarder's drawerful of beautiful, unusual, never-to-be-found-again fabrics. This could be the year to make up one of these lengths. Obviously, the fabric comes first.

A new fashion magazine arrives. You postpone making the beds, settle yourself with that second cup of coffee and you're off! You must find a pattern for that perfectly divine suit. The fabric can come later.

Sometimes your ideas are built around a particular fabric; sometimes around a particular design; sometimes (happy day!) both simultaneously.

Great designers and dressmakers can drape fabric into beautiful clothes. This takes much skill—and considerable fabric. Most of us depend on patterns to provide the results we want.

There is a rather widespread assumption that the mere act of using a pattern endows one automatically with the wisdom to know how it works and how to adjust its parts. This is just as untrue as assuming that because one drives a car one can understand how it works and how to repair it when it doesn't.

However, women who sew would benefit greatly from even an elementary knowledge of pattern making. It is so much simpler to put a pattern together when you understand how it got that way. It is so much easier to fit yourself when you know why your pattern fits as it does. Pattern alteration seems less of a mystery when you know what to change.

The following discussion will explain very briefly how the pattern works.* It will help you see the pattern in relation to the fabric of your choice.

DART CONTROL—WHY, WHERE, WHEN, AND HOW MUCH

A flat pattern and a curved you.

A pattern is flat. You are not. A pattern contains all the information and all the magic necessary to convert a flat length of fabric into a garment that follows the contours of your body in a flattering manner. How is this done?

The pattern maker has to consider the curves both concave and convex which produce the bulges and high points of a woman's body.

The Eight Bulges

There are eight such bulges to consider (Fig. 2):

1. Bust
2. Abdomen or front hip bone
3. Side hip curve
4. Buttocks—back hip
5. Upper shoulder blades
6. Lower shoulder blades
7. Elbow
8. Dowager's hump (found in mature or round-shouldered figures)

* How to Design Your Own Dress Patterns also by this author published by Doubleday & Company, Inc., presents complete, simple, step-by-step instructions for creating your own patterns.

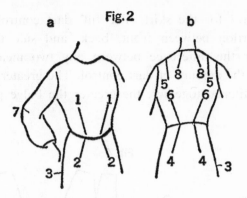

Fig. 2

As you think about this you will realize that these are places where patterns have darts or seams (Fig. 3).

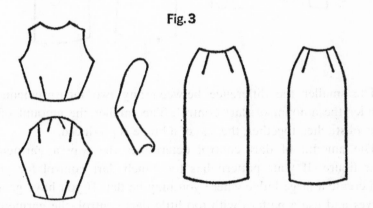

Fig. 3

Enough material must be included in the pattern to cover these bulges or high points. At the same time, the adjoining smaller areas require less material. One flat piece of fabric must be so worked as to accommodate both. The difference between the larger measurement and the smaller measurement comes out in what is called "dart control."

For instance, a Size 14 pattern is designed for a figure with a 34″ bust and a 26″ waist. The difference between these two measurements is 8″. This is the dart control for the bodice. The skirt is designed for a 26″ waistline and a 36″ hip. This 10″ differential is the dart control for the skirt. The full dart control is divided in proper proportion between front, back, and side (Fig. 4).

The greater the difference between any two measurements, the larger will be the amount of dart control. The greater the amount of dart control stitched together, the greater the bulge produced.

Fig. 4

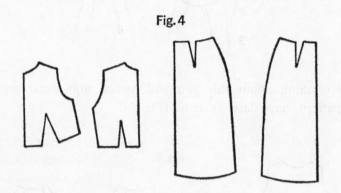

The smaller the difference between any two measurements, the smaller the amount of dart control. The smaller the amount of dart control stitched together, the less of a bulge is produced.

The amount of dart control determines the way a garment fits your figure. If your pattern has too much dart control for you, it will create a large bulge where you may be flat. If you have generous curves and use a pattern with too little dart control, the garment will span the figure in one place, permit the fabric to droop in another, and distort the grain. Dart control always represents a relationship —large measurement to small measurement wherever there is a body curve.

While the amount of dart control is constant, it may appear in a variety of places. The amount of bulge produced by stitching a control dart is always the same, no matter what the direction of the dart. It follows this rule: it starts from some seam and extends to or heads toward a high point. In the bodice front, for instance, darts may appear in any of the positions illustrated in Fig. 5.

Fig. 5

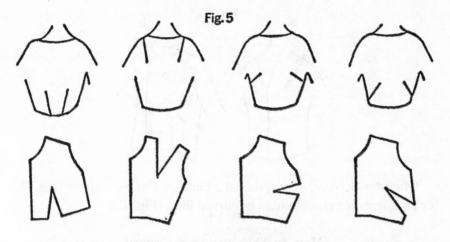

A dart from any position on the bodice front must always lead to the high point of the bust. If it leads anywhere else it will release the greatest amount of fabric in an area which does not require such fullness. What is true for the bodice front is equally true for the bodice back, the skirt front and back, and the sleeve. This being so, it is essential that you discover the *amount and proper placement of the dart control* for your needs. Alter patterns accordingly. A basic pattern is a good guide for adjusting commercial patterns to fit your particular needs.

Since the placement of the dart does not change the resulting bulge, darts may be shifted to many different positions in order to vary the design of the garment. So that what started out as a matter of structural necessity—the dart control—now becomes a matter of design interest by virtue of its placement on the garment (Fig. 6).

Fig. 6

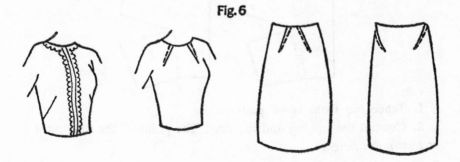

Fig. 7

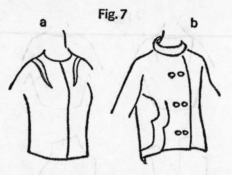

Often for decorative purposes the dart appears as a curve (Fig. 7a) or an interesting combination of curved lines (Fig. 7b).

How to Shift the Dart Control

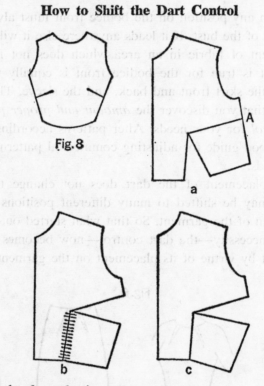

Fig. 8

1. Trace the front basic pattern.

2. Cut out the tracing and the dart. The point of the dart *must be at bust-point height.*

3. On the tracing, locate the point from which the new dart will enter the bodice. Mark this point A (Fig. 8a).

4. Draw a line connecting the point of the dart with A (Fig. 8b).

5. Slash on this line.

6. Close the original dart; pin or tape to position (Fig. 8b).

The new dart will appear in the new position. It will automatically contain the proper amount of dart control (Fig. 8c).

Fig. 9

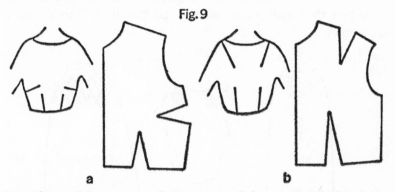

a   b

Sometimes the amount of dart control is too much for just one dart. So the dart control may be divided. On the bodice front, the dart control is frequently divided between waistline and underarm darts (Fig. 9a) or waistline and shoulder darts (Fig. 9b).

How to Divide the Dart Control

Fig. 10

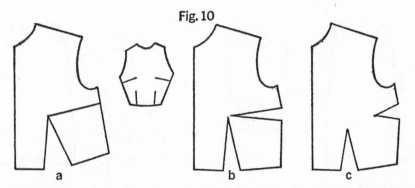

a   b   c

Proceed as in the previous exercise to Step 6, which takes us to Fig. 10a.

6. Close *part* of the original dart control, thereby shifting the rest to the new position (Fig. 10b).

In finished patterns the darts are always shortened (Fig. 10c). You will find directions for shortening darts on page 97.

Dart Control as Design

Any interesting design or dressmaking device is legitimate. The only requirement is that it "take in" the amount needed to make the garment fit the small measurement and "let it out" to fit the larger measurement.

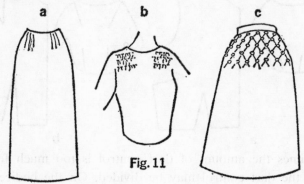

Fig. 11

The dart control does not need to be a dart. The same control is accomplished by gathering (Fig. 11a), shirring (Fig. 11b), or decorative smocking (Fig. 11c).

Fig. 12

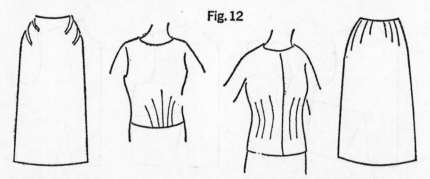

The dart control may be divided into several darts on the same seam line (Fig. 12). These are called multiple darts.

Fig. 13

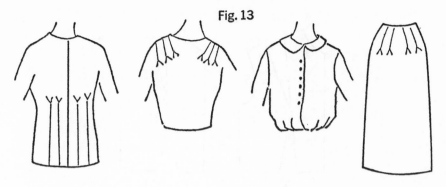

The dart control may also appear as dart tucks or pleats, either pressed or unpressed (Fig. 13).

You can begin to see the endless design possibilities from this elementary and basic concept of dart control.

The Control Seam

Fig. 14

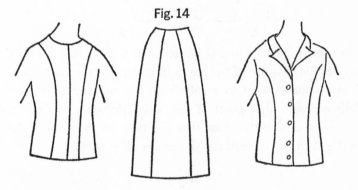

The illustrations in Fig. 14 show no darts (or their equivalent). Yet we know that dart control must be there. The dart control has been ingeniously hidden in a seam which is used as a decorative feature of the design. This style line is really a control seam.

The control seam is produced by dividing the dart control (Fig. 15a). Instead of stitching the two resulting darts which are shortened (Fig. 15b), the pattern sections are separated (Fig. 15c), then

Fig. 15

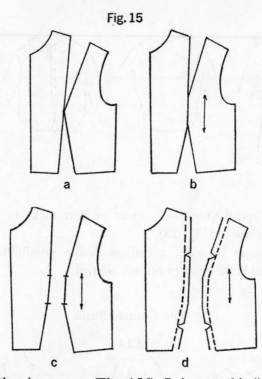

stitched together in a seam (Fig. 15d). It is now this "control seam" which does the shaping of the garment instead of the dart control.

When a seam is used as a substitute for the control dart, it generally falls across a high point of the body. However, the control seam may be moved *slightly* from this position either toward the center front (Fig. 16a) or toward the side seam (Fig 16b).

Fig. 16

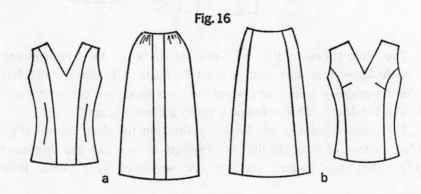

Dart Control and Its Relation to Fit

From the standpoint of fit, a control seam or a combination of darts is better than a single dart. A single dart produces a sharp bulge. Several darts or a control seam produce a more gentle shaping.

The more darts or control seams, the more places where one may fit the garment. The number and position of darts and seams must follow the laws of good design and good taste.

Dart Control and Its Relation to Fabric

Any dart or seam will interrupt the continuity of the fabric design. Therefore you must choose darts which will do so with the least disturbing effect. For this reason, too, almost any combination of darts is better than a single dart because the break in the fabric design is minimized.

When you are using a solid-color fabric you have much freedom in the choice of design or pattern. Your chief concern is deciding which style lines or shaping will look best on you. Some darts and some seam lines are more flattering to a particular figure than others.

When you are using a figured material—a spaced print of either large or small units; a stripe, a check, a plaid; a vertical, horizontal, or diagonal weave—then the choice of darts or control seams becomes more complex.

Here are a few pleasing effects showing a good use of control darts and control seams:

Fig. 17

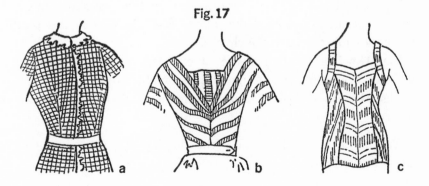

a   b   c

Fig. 17a Straight darts are balanced on the straight lines of the check. This is a good rule for plaids and stripes as well.

Fig. 17b Here is an ingenious use of a striped fabric where the dart control becomes the chief feature of the design.

Fig. 17c The style line of this bathing suit is the control seam. Note the clever use of the grain which adds to the interest of the design.

Here are a few common casualties. The incorrect use of control darts and control seams produces unpleasant breaks in the continuity of the surface design of the fabric.

Fig. 18

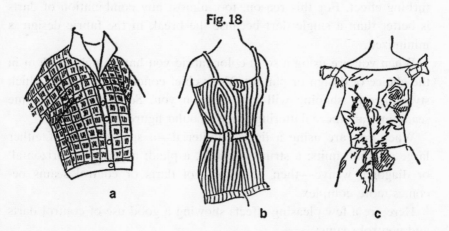

a   b   c

Fig. 18a The French underarm dart on this checked fabric produces a great distortion of the fabric. With the dart in this position it is impossible to match the checks.

Fig. 18b This particular use of exaggerated control seam on a striped fabric results in a design of questionable taste.

Fig. 18c An elaborate fabric design is mutilated by the control seams.

The moral is clear: Consider the shaping of your garment in relation to the fabric.

If You Have the Pattern First

If you have the pattern first, find a fabric with a surface design which will not be distorted by the control darts or seams. If you are at all uncertain, consult the back of the pattern envelope for the designer's suggestions. While your own choice may depart somewhat from these suggestions, they will give you a good idea of the type of fabric best suited to the design. Even more important, *do* observe the caution as to which fabrics are not desirable. When the advice is "Not suited for striped material," it is well to heed it. You can be sure that considerable experimenting was done to determine the co-ordination of style lines with fabric.

If You Have the Fabric First

If the fabric is a solid color, your choice of pattern is unlimited. All style lines either curved or straight, all darts, all decorative details will show clearly and effectively.

If the fabric has pile or nap, a raised or looped surface, intricate lines and painstaking work are completely lost in the depth of the surface. Choose a simple pattern with good lines but little detail.

If the fabric is richly figured or elaborately decorated, choose a simple pattern with the least possible number of darts and seams. This avoids cutting into or mutilating the design motifs of the fabric.

If the fabric is checked, striped, or plaid, choose a pattern whose darts can be placed and balanced within the straight lines of the fabric design; or, shift the darts to a preferred position.

Pattern and fabric must be considered together from the standpoint of the shaping of the garment.

Women who sew think and read a great deal about style selection. Indeed, it would be difficult to avoid it. Advice in this department is generous and many women profit by it. However, even expert style knowledge doesn't automatically lead to good results. In order to avoid some of the mistakes we have been discussing, one must become equally wise in the choice of fabrics and patterns suited to each other. Perhaps it is the general absence of information on pattern construction that shows up in sewing failures. Certainly more women err in the co-ordination of fabric and pattern than in the selection of a flattering style.

The foregoing discussion gives you just a tiny taste of pattern making. It is hoped that this will whet your appetite for more. You will find it a fascinating subject to pursue.

SOMETHING ABOUT THE FABRIC

One of the symptoms of the confirmed sewer is her utter inability to pass a fabric counter without buying something new to add to an already more-than-ample supply stashed away through the years. Every so often she goes through her hoard, fondles each treasured length, folds it up lovingly, then puts it away for another day's admiration. She cannot bring herself to cut into this fabulous fabric. No pattern seems quite worthy of it. Mere clothes are not reason enough. The fabric has its own intrinsic beauty and contemplation of it brings the same aesthetic delight as looking at a beautiful landscape or a handsome painting. For it is indeed a work of art.

The creation of beautiful fabric has been an art form since that long-ago day when man first decided to clothe himself. Each age has contributed its share to the wealth of decorative splendor—innovations of color, design, and texture. Every place under the sun where man has lived has added to the rich tradition of fabric design. Our own time and our own country have joined scientific genius and technical know-how with the cumulative artistry of the past to produce ever more beautiful fabrics. What is more, modern production methods have made them comparatively inexpensive.

Natural Fibers or Man-Made Fibers?

In producing his textiles, man has always used those natural sources, both plant and animal, which he found around him. From these he derived fibers of wool, silk, cotton, flax, jute, and hemp. The first three have had the longest and most persistent use—wool for warmth, silk for luxury, cotton for versatility and low cost.

Recent years have seen a rapid growth of man-made fibers. Despite the publicity given these new fibers and the unprecedented sums spent on research, advertising, and sales promotion, 70 per cent of United States consumption and about 85 per cent of world consumption is presently still of natural fibers.

The synthetic fibers possess many remarkable qualities suited to contemporary living. The natural fibers have qualities that, after centuries, still make them desirable. The future will undoubtedly see a group of fabrics that blend the best features of both. Meanwhile, each has its uses and each seems here to stay.

Natural fibers are deeply rooted in our culture. The source of much inspiration in the textile field is still the handwork of skilled craftsmen. Synthetics and blends are made to resemble natural fibers. Machine-loomed cloth of natural fibers strives for the effect of hand-loomed cloth. This is not without its significance. We may admire the mechanical ingenuity and chemical advances of our day but we still demand fabrics that bring us the aesthetic satisfaction of cloth of natural fibers.

Wool for Classic Tailoring

Wool continues to be the classic fabric for tailoring. It has tremendous variety ranging from sheer, lacy, lightweight, porous, to heavy, bulky, and dense. It is a versatile insulator protecting against cold, heat, and dampness. The wool fibers are alive and resilient. The cores of the fibers have a great affinity for dyes so that wool can be produced in many colors. The strength and wearing quality of wool are notable.

As for sewing wool, it is perhaps the easiest fabric to handle. It doesn't slide or slither. It is easy to stitch. It can be both eased and stretched. It can be pressed and shaped effectively.

Wool is the fiber taken mainly from the fleece of sheep or lamb. However, other specialty fibers are also classified as wool: camel's hair, vicuña, cashmere, mohair, angora, alpaca, and fur blends. Fur fibers add surface interest and warmth. Some of the pelts used are beaver, chinchilla, fox, angora hare, muskrat, nutria, opossum, raccoon, mink, marten, and sable.

Wool has long been used in combination with other fibers. The linsey-woolsey of the story books was a combination of wool and linen. Viyella flannel is a combination of wool and cotton; Alaskine, a combination of wool and silk. Recently wool has been successfully blended with orlon, nylon, Dacron, Dynel, and other synthetic fabrics.

Wool is labeled for your protection. Because the world supply of new wool is insufficient to meet all the demand, it is expensive. For this reason, too, some fabrics are made in part of reprocessed or used wool. To protect the consumer, Congress passed the Wool Products Labeling Act in 1937. Under this act wools must be labeled for content. The tag which comes with the fabric tells the story.

"Wool" means new or virgin wool which has never been used before. It applies only to wool fibers taken from the fleece of sheep and not reclaimed in any way. Fabrics classified as wool but containing specialty fibers must state the percentage of each fiber.

"Reprocessed wool" means wool that *has been reclaimed* from woven or felted products which have *never been used or worn before.* For example, clippings and scraps from garment factories or custom-tailoring shops.

"Reused wool" means wool that *has been reclaimed* from any type of wool fabric which has been *worn or used before.* For example, old clothing, blankets, etc. This was formerly known as "shoddy."

Woolens or worsteds for home tailoring? There are two types of woolens: those called woolens and those called worsteds (woosteds). These are classified, one or the other, according to the kind of fibers and the process of making them into yarns. (By the same process, cotton and synthetics can be made to resemble woolens and worsteds.)

Woolens are woven from yarns of short, fuzzy, uncombed fibers which are twisted together loosely. They cross and intermingle leaving protruding ends making a bulky yarn with a soft, fuzzy, fluffy surface (Fig. 19a). A few examples of fabric woven from these yarns are tweed, fleece, flannel, suede cloth, broadcloth, chinchilla, bouclé, and mohair.

Worsteds are woven from long fibers combed parallel before spinning, tightly twisted together to give a smooth, compact, firm, hard surface. The weaves are distinctly visible in worsteds (Fig. 19b). Wool gabardine, serge, and sharkskin, are examples of worsteds.

Fig. 19

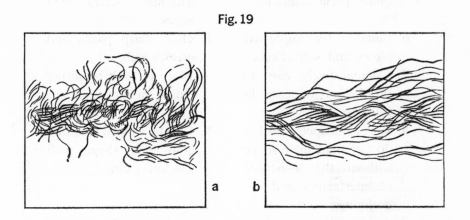

a   b

Worsteds are used primarily in men's clothing but they make handsome suiting for women as well. Woolens give a softer effect. They are more popular for women's wear. If you are a beginner, consider the relative merits of each with regard to your ability to handle the fabric.

Woolens	*Worsteds*
1. Look best when made up in easy relaxed lines.	1. Make stunning strictly tailored suits.
2. Show wear more readily than worsteds.	2. Can stand hard wear though they have a tendency to get shiny.
3. Porous surface makes them good insulators.	3. Firm, hard surface reduces their insulating quality.
4. Stitching, both machine and hand, is hidden in the fuzzy surface.	4. Machine and hand stitching is clearly visible on the smooth surface.

Woolens	*Worsteds*
5. Press well generally; nap or pile woolens require special handling.	5. Respond well to pressing but require force for flattening seams and edges.
6. Suitable for unpressed pleats and soft effects.	6. Hold sharp pleats and creases well.
7. Comparatively easy to shrink out or ease in fullness.	7. More difficult to shrink out or ease in fullness.
8. Can be shaped well but do not hold their shape without the assistance of interfacings and underlinings.	8. Can be shaped well and hold their shape with less interfacing.
9. Muss easily.	9. Resist wrinkling.

Home sewers find woolens easier to handle than worsteds which require more skill.

Since wool fiber is "alive," woolen garments should be treated in an almost-human manner. They require rest periods after they have seen action, so that wrinkles can hang out. Woolens like their "hair" brushed. Frequent brushing keeps them clean just as frequent brushing keeps your hair clean. Steam pressing will revive them as a warm bath will revive you. Treat them with care and they will last—well, almost forever.

Present-day fashion features many handsome suits and coats of linen, cotton, and silk as well as the classic wool. These require somewhat different handling but many techniques used in tailoring woolen garments are applicable. See Chapter X.

The Timeless Beauty of Silk

Silk has always been a prized fabric. The early mystery and difficulty surrounding its production and the limited supply available even today have made it a prestige cloth. Beautiful in luster and soft to the touch, silk always gives a feeling of luxury. Silk comes from the cocoon of the silkworm in long filaments. Though delicate in appearance and often woven into fragile fabrics, the fiber itself is very strong.

There are four kinds of silk fiber:

Cultivated silk comes from domesticated silkworms. The filaments are fine and even in size. Crepe, satin, peau de soie, chiffon, and other dress silks are made of cultivated silk.

Wild, tussah, or raw silks come from wild silkworms. The fibers are coarse and nonuniform, and dry to the touch. They come both lightweight and heavy. They may have some sheen but are usually dull. There is a randomness about the fibers which makes fabric of very interesting texture. These silks require a rather sophisticated taste but they do make handsome suits and coats.

Douppioni silk is the filament from cocoons which have grown together. As a result the fibers are joined at irregular intervals making uneven nubs. Douppioni silks are used in quality shantung and other slubbed fabrics.

Waste silk is the tangled mass of silk called noils, taken from the outside of the cocoons or from damaged cocoons. Noils are fuzzy and dull. Spun silk is made from this waste silk. Its irregular slubs, somewhat similar to douppioni, make it usable for less expensive shantung and other rough-textured silks.

Silks, like woolens, require labeling. If they contain no fiber other than silk they may be labeled "pure dye," "pure dye silk," "silk," "all silk" or "pure silk." When the fabric contains any metallic weighting, any loading or adulterating materials it must be labeled accordingly and the percentage noted.

Silk has excellent draping qualities. It is naturally resilient. It takes dye well. This, coupled with its natural luster, makes the color of silk a joy to behold. Many silks are colorfast but some are subject to fading. White silks tend to yellow with age. (This goes for white-silk thread, too.) Although the fiber is washable (and some silks are hand washable), most silks retain their original appearance best when dry cleaned. Silk is damaged by heat so great care must be taken in pressing.

Silk is the most difficult fabric to sew. It requires great care in pinning, cutting, stitching, and pressing. Despite the hazards of construction, the beauty of silk is such that it makes the effort involved worthwhile.

Linen, an Old Friend

Linen has always been an understandably cherished fabric. The combination of strength, beauty, absorbency, and washability have made it a treasured household item and a desirable fabric for clothing. Its natural luster and crispness give it beauty. Its long, strong, smooth, and pliable fibers give it practicality. The variety in the size of the fibers from very fine to very coarse makes it possible to produce a range of fabrics from sheer handkerchief linen to heavy suitings.

Linen has one drawback—its lack of elasticity. This makes it wrinkle easily. Crease-resistant finishes remove this difficulty but also remove the absorbency.

Linen is made of the fibrous material in the stem of the flax plant. Since flax must be imported and the production is expensive, a good quality linen is high in price. The characteristic linen weave is often copied to make inexpensive fabrics of rayon, nylon, or spun silk resemble linen.

To protect the consumer the Federal Trade Commission requires the labeling of linen as it does other fabrics. "Linen," "pure linen," or "pure flax" means that the fabric is made entirely of linen. If any other fibers are combined with linen, the percentage must be stated.

Irish linen has long been famous. In the past few years, Sybil Connolly, Ireland's great designer, has created gowns of such rare beauty as to inspire a whole new use of linen for fashion. Linen comes in a suiting weight fine for tailoring.

King Cotton

Relatively abundant and relatively cheap, cotton is the most commonly used of all fibers. Cotton is easy to wash, iron, and bleach. Like linen, it absorbs moisture—though not quite as well. Like linen, it has little elasticity and therefore is inclined to wrinkle easily. There are cool sheers like batiste and warm piles like corduroy; there are fragile cottons like voile and heavy-duty cottons like denim. Cottons take color beautifully. Some are colorfast; others, like madras, depend on "bleeding" for effect.

Recently cotton has been subjected to a number of treatments which make it resistant to wrinkles, shrinkage, flame, mildew, spots, stains, and perspiration. There are special finishes—articurl, glazed, permanent, and water-repellent. "Mercerization" adds luster to the finish and more absorbency.

Cotton is made of the soft, white, hairy fiber that grows on the seeds of the cotton plant. Its quality is judged by the length of the fibers, or "staples," and the ply. The finest fibers are the long staples —Sea Island, Pima, and Egyptian. "Ply" is the number of strands which are twisted together to make the yarn. Two-ply and three-ply cotton are stronger than one ply.

The cotton fiber is cleaned and straightened by carding. Combing after carding makes the fibers lie parallel. Combed cottons are high-quality fabric.

It is the winter-weight cottons which lend themselves best to tailoring. They resemble wool in texture, color, and weave. Many of them "handle" like wool. They are not as warm as wool but this can be one of their great advantages.

Man-Made Fibers

There are so many fabrics of man-made fibers and so many new ones continually being developed that even people in the field have trouble keeping up with them. There is no doubt that chemically developed fibers have revolutionized the textile industry. These new fabrics do things formerly only dreamed about: they are cool in summer, warm in winter, they are wrinkle resistant but can be permanently pleated, they are wash-and-wear, they are lightweight and crush-resistant (a boon to travelers), they even resist moths and bacteria. Since making the fiber is a controlled process, it can be developed for special purposes and in uniform quality.

The methods for making the hundreds of new yarns vary considerably. In general, they pass through these three stages:

1. Some basic material is transformed into a liquid.
2. The liquid is drawn out into fine streams.
3. The liquid streams are changed into solid filaments.

The solid filaments, like natural fibers, are then combined to make the yarns. These can be continuous or in short lengths—1″ to 6″ long, called staples.

The yarns are woven into cloth by the same processes as the natural fibers.

The tremendous competition between natural and man-made fibers has forced the textile industry, particularly that segment of it which deals with natural fibers, to re-examine its thinking and its techniques. The result has been an even more exciting array of fabrics of all fibers.

How Fabric Is Woven

The fibers derived from wool, silk, cotton, flax, or synthetics are twisted together by spinning. These twisted strands are called yarns. It is the yarns which are knitted or woven into cloth.

In principle, weaving is the same today as when man first began to weave cloth. One set of lengthwise yarns (warp) are placed side by side in a row on a loom. Another set of crosswise yarns (filler, woof, weft, or picks) are threaded over and under the warp yarns. The lengthwise yarns and the crosswise yarns are interlaced at right angles to each other. The advances in weaving have been in the method of separating or lifting groups of yarns in the pattern of the weave so that the filling yarn can be inserted with one motion of a shuttle.

Do you recall weaving paper mats or pot holders when you were a child? When you wove those strips or strands of contrasting colors so they looked like a checkerboard you were really producing the most commonly used weave, the plain weave (Fig. 20a). When your weave resembled that in Fig. 20b, you were making the pattern for a twill weave. As you grew more inventive you probably produced the design in Fig. 20c which is the satin weave.

Fig. 20

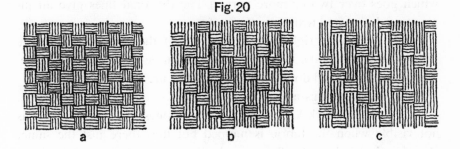

a   b   c

There is a seemingly endless variety of fabric derived from these three basic weaves. This is produced by:

1. variations within each type of weave
2. use of different fibers—wool, silk, linen, cotton, synthetic
3. different kinds of yarn—thick, thin, tightly twisted, looped, slubbed, etc.
4. use of different colors for warp or filler yarns
5. use of heavy yarns in one direction, light-weight yarns in the other, producing a ribbed effect either lengthwise, crosswise, or diagonally
6. printing of warp yarns before weaving
7. combinations of any of the above for more intricate or more elaborate designs.

The plain weave has no right or wrong side unless the cloth is finished differently on one side. The plain weave is nondirectional. Because it does not divert attention from the design it is the weave most often used for printed fabrics. Variations in weave come from using two or more adjacent warp yarns as one and an equal number of adjacent filling yarns as one.

The plain weave in a solid color is the easiest to use in sewing.

The twill weave produces a fabric with diagonal wales. These wales are made by either warp or filling floats which interlace in such a way that they progress one or more spaces to the right or left. (A wale is the line which appears on the surface of the fabric. A float is a yarn which goes over two or more yarns.) The diagonal lines give an interesting design and texture to the surface.

Twills *do* have a right and wrong side. If the wales go up to the right on the right side, they will go up to the left on the wrong side. They have no up and down except when they are napped.

Many wool suitings are made in the twill weave: gabardine, serge, covert, flannel, sharkskin, tweeds, herringbones. The twill weave is not visible when the fabric is napped but it is there just the same. Broadcloth, suede cloth, fleece, and velour are a few napped fabrics of twill weave. Surah is a printed silk-twill weave.

The diagonal wales of the twill weave are less prominent in some fabrics than others. Even when the twill weave is not too evident, it requires great care in layout. Wales in opposing directions at the center back seam of an under collar are a common error. This distortion is particularly objectionable in shawl-collar designs when the facings join at the center back to form the upper collar (Fig. 21a).

Fig. 21

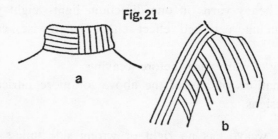

a

b

In kimono-sleeved garments the different directions of the diagonal wales appear on the shoulder and sleeve seams (Fig. 21b) unless skillfully cut from both right and wrong sides of the fabric. (See page 158 for layout of fabrics.)

When the diagonal wales are prominent the choice of design is sharply limited.

One could safely say that twill weaves are not for beginners.

The satin weave is related to the twill weave. The floats interlace in a progression mostly in a ratio of 4 to 1 and sometimes 7 to 1 (Fig. 22).

Fig. 22

float   float   float

⊙⃝⃝⃝⊙⊙⃝⃝⃝⊙⊙⃝⃝⃝⊙⊙

This avoids a twill effect. In silk, the floats are lengthwise (satin). In cotton, the floats are crosswise (sateen or polished cotton). Because of the long floats this is a weave that does not wear well. The floats may catch or break. But they do give a beautiful luster and smooth feel to the fabric.

The luster is due not only to the weave but to the fiber, the yarn, and the play of light on the long floats. The direction of the light affects the color and sheen of the fabric. *Directional layout of pattern pieces is essential for uniform color throughout the garment.*

Novelty Weaves

Novelty weaves are variations of basic weaves.

In velvets and other pile fabrics an extra yarn is woven through the cloth at right angles to it. Sometimes this yarn is looped over rods or wires having little knives in the ends. The loops are cut as the rods are withdrawn. Sometimes velvets are woven double and the pile is cut through the middle (Fig. 23). The pile may be left standing or it may be pressed in one direction (panne velvet).

Fig. 23

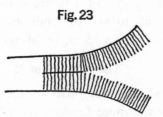

Matelassé is made by using crepe (tightly twisted) and plain yarns. Shrinking the crepe yarns causes the plain yarns to pucker producing a crinkled effect. *Matelassés* need care in ironing so that the puckered effect is not pressed out.

Plissé is similar to *matelassé*. It is made by shrinking part of the material in stripes or patterns.

In *seersucker* the crinkled effect is woven in rather than shrunken in. Here the puckered effect results when stripes of coarse warp yarns are loosely held in the loom while alternate stripes of fine yarns are held firm.

Table of Fabric Widths

Fabrics are usually woven in the following widths:

cottons and linens	35″
velveteens and corduroys	36″
silks, rayons, and nylons	39″–40″
	42″–44″
	45″
Italian shantung	36″
Hong Kong brocade	29″–30″
hand-woven wools	27″–29″
	30″
woolens	54″–56″

The Wrong Side May Be the Right Side

Silks and woolens are folded with the right side inside to protect the surface. So are expensive cottons. Generally, cottons and linens are folded with the right side outside.

Sometimes the wrong side of a fabric is more interesting than the right side. If it appeals to you or lends itself to a more interesting interpretation of your design ideas, by all means use the wrong side.

The "Hang" of It

The lengthwise and crosswise yarns are the grain of the fabric. You may know grain by the more familiar term "the straight of goods." The lengthwise and crosswise yarns are woven at right angles to each other. The fabric hangs true when it is in this position. Most fabrics are woven to hang with the vertical grain. For many fabrics it makes little difference whether they are used on the vertical or horizontal grain. What is important is to maintain the right-angular position of the yarns.

Sometimes in the finishing process, the fabric is pulled off-grain. The sewer must restore the true grain so that the pattern may be placed accurately on the fabric (page 132).

Every pattern piece, no matter how small or how large, has "the straight of goods" marked on it. Generally, it is laid on the fabric in such a way that the straight of goods is parallel to the selvage or finished edge. The selvage is the vertical grain. Sometimes for special effect (striped or plaid fabric) the pattern is laid with the straight of goods parallel to the horizontal grain. Sometimes fabric is used on the bias. The desired hang of any pattern piece and the design of the garment determine the straight of goods.

Fabrics persist in hanging with the grain whether you cut them properly or not. If you disregard the position of the grain in either pattern or fabric you may end up with an unanticipated and unpleasant result. For the proper layout of a pattern on true grain, see page 152.

Knitted Fabrics—A New Vogue for an Old Favorite

Women have long enjoyed the beauty and comfort of knitted garments. In the past several years, however, knitted clothes have reached a new high in popularity. It is easy to understand why. Being elastic, knits both shape to the body and yet permit ease of movement. They may be light-, medium-, or heavyweight. They are warm when of wool and cool when of silk. They do not wrinkle. In an age of travel, this quality becomes a very important consideration. The innovations in knits have been fascinating. Their high styling gives them great fashion appeal.

Fortunately, the home sewer can get in on this new fashion. Beautiful knitted fabrics are now available in many fibers, designs, weights, and colors. They come in flat or tubular form.

Most of us have either done some knitting or watched others. You will recall that the yarn was passed through a series of loops. The principal unit of any knitted fabric whether made by hand or by machine is the loop. A vertical series of loops is called a *wale;* a horizontal series of loops is called a *course.*

In knitting, when the yarn runs horizontally across the fabric in a series of loops, it is called a *filling knit* (Fig. 24). When the loops run vertically in knitting, the resulting fabric is a *warp knit* (Fig. 25). Interesting patterns can be made by the method of interlocking the loops.

In filling knits, the crosswise yarns are interlocked in a chain of stitches (Fig. 24). When the chain is broken, the fabric "runs" or "ladders." You will certainly recognize this as the knit of stockings. Cutting into knits is hazardous and requires great care to avoid "running." Filling knits are sometimes made as flat fabric but they are usually knitted on circular machines to make a tubular fabric. There is a right and wrong side unless it is made with a rib stitch in which case it is the same on both sides.

Fig. 24

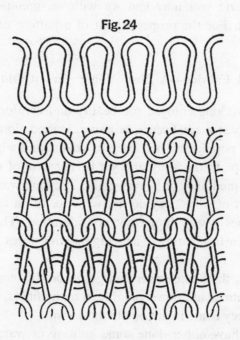

In warp knits the thread follows a zigzag path, forming a loop at each change of direction. These loops interlock with the loops formed by the adjoining warp yarns following a similar zigzag path. They are less sheer, but firmer and stronger. They stretch less than filling

Fig. 25

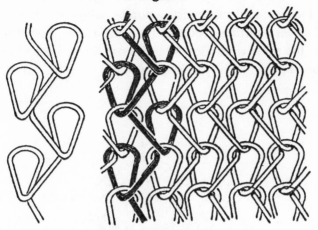

knits. Warp knits are knitted flat. Because they don't run or snag like filling knits, they are used for cloth which can be cut. Some winter coatings are warp knit. (The knitting is visible only on the wrong side if the right side is napped.) Tricot is a silk warp knit.

Like woven fabrics, knitted fabrics are produced in great variety. This is achieved by using different fibers, different yarns, a variety of patterns, a variety of colors, ingenious and intricate methods of interlocking, and combinations of any of these.

Some of the newest and most exciting knits are these variations: an intriguing array of lacy knits, matte jersey in jewel-like colors, silk jersey in delightful prints, laminated fabrics, double knits, and a whole new breed of fake furs.

Double knits. It is easy to understand the current enthusiasm for the new double knits. They have the kind of comfort and fit that is the special delight of all knitted fabrics, yet handle like woven fabric.

The double knits are made on a rib knitting machine. This has two sets of needles producing the same stitches on both sides. In appearance it is as if two layers of similar fabric were knitted together. Unlike most other knits which are tubular, the double knits are flat.

Fake furs are made by an interesting process known as *sliver knitting*. This is a knit-pile construction as velvet is a woven-pile construction. Sliver knitting produces both the plain jersey backing and the pile at the same time. Bunches of loose fibers are locked in place by the looping action of the backing yarn over the knitting needle (Fig. 26).

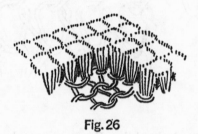

Fig. 26

The straight of goods in knit fabrics. In knitted fabrics the vertical straight of goods is a vertical wale. Factory pressing almost never produces a crease along the wale or vertical grain of tubular jersey. Therefore the crosswise ridges or horizontal grain are seldom right at the cut edge. Before cutting knitted fabric, establish both vertical and horizontal grains (page 383).

FABRIC DECORATION

From earliest times to the present man has felt the need to decorate his surroundings, the objects he uses daily, and himself. Why this is so has been the subject of many interesting studies. Even before he created clothing man decorated his body by painting, staining, tattooed designs, or scar patterns. This same urge for color and design as body adornment is still present today, but we use fabrics instead, to satisfy this continuing need.

Color

Primitive man dyed himself or his cloth with the juice of berries, fruits, barks, and roots. In some areas of the world these dyes are still used. The modern textile industry dyes fabrics chemically.

The fiber, the type of dye and the method of applying it determine the color and the degree of color fastness. Dyes are applied in any of the following ways:

stock-dyed—the fibers are dyed before they are made into yarn

yarn-dyed—the yarns are dyed before they are made into cloth

piece-dyed—the dye is applied after the cloth has been woven or knitted

spun-dyed—dye is added to the solution from which man-made fibers are spun; sometimes this is called "solution dyed" or "color locked"

cross-dyed—different colors are produced at the same time by the same dye on blended fabrics. (Various fibers take dyes differently so that blended fabrics emerge as two dissimilar colors.)

Dye penetrates fiber or yarn better than woven cloth. Colors are more permanent in stock-dyed, yarn-dyed, or spun-dyed than in piece-dyed fabrics.

Printing is much like dyeing. Instead of applying the dye to the whole cloth, it is applied only in certain planned areas which produce a design. The same dyes are used for dyeing and printing except that dye baths use dye in liquid form while printing techniques use it in a paste.

Methods of printing cloth have been many and varied in the world's history. Many of these methods are still being used in nonindustrialized areas where handicrafts flourish. Both ancient and modern methods alike produce beautiful fabrics. Today most printed fabrics are produced by the roller-printing method; a smaller proportion by the screen-printing method.

The roller-printing method. In every fabric there is a place where the motif of the design starts all over again. This is known as a re-peat. The artist's design is transferred to a roller which has a circum-ference of 14" to 36", the size of the repeat. This is a lengthy, intri-cate, and costly process. Each roller prints one repeat of the design in one color. A separate roller is used for each color. As the roller strikes the fabric it prints the repeat over and over again without interrupting the continuity of the design. If there are several colors in the design the cloth passes between several rollers, each of which prints its colors so that the cloth comes out a completed print at the end. The machines are able to get perfect register. Some can print as many as sixteen colors at the rate of 200 yards a minute.

After the colors have been printed the cloth passes through a steam-heated machine which sets the color and washes away any excess compounds.

Sometimes, if the design is not accurately lined up with the warp or filling yarns or if the cloth slips from a true position, it is printed off-grain. This does not happen often since it is carefully checked. When it does, some yardage is imperfect. This rejected material finds its way to mill-end stores and bargain counters. It is a problem to cut such material. If one follows the design motifs the garment will be cut off-grain. If one follows the grain the design can't be matched. Which to do? There is little choice but to match the design and hope for the best from the grain. The wisest thing to do is to examine fabrics carefully before purchasing.

Screen printing is a hand-printing operation calling for great skill in register and application. Production is by carefully trained teams. The screen which is used for printing is of silk, nylon, or fine metal thread attached to a frame. The artist's design is transferred to the screen by a photo-chemical process. A lacquer coating is applied to the areas where the design will not appear. The fabric is laid on a long padded table. Thirty yards of fabric is the smallest amount it is profitable to do at one laying. The screen is then placed over the cloth. A squeegee or hand roller is pushed back and forth across the screen, forcing the dye through the unlacquered surface onto the material. The screen is moved along to do a section of the fabric at a time. Each color is printed through a different screen. The finished printed cloth is lifted from the table to drying racks overhead. When dry it is passed through a steam-heated machine to remove excess dyes and to set the color.

While roller printing is limited by the size of the roller and the number of colors used, in screen printing there is no limit. The size of the repeat, its spacing, and the number of colors are limited only by the desired effect or the use of the fabric.

Roller printing is not profitable except on a huge scale. Screen printing can be done in much smaller yardages, giving the fabric more exclusiveness. Screen printing is often used on a custom-design basis. For all of these reasons hand-screened fabrics are more expensive than roller-printed fabrics.

Design

The design of a woven or knitted fabric depends on what the loom or knitting machine is able to produce. Today's machines are capable of producing a tremendous variety of designs. Printing designs on woven or knitted fabrics offers even greater variety.

Repetition of the design unit: The over-all effect of a design is the result of the repetition of a design unit called a *repeat*. These repeats are arranged in a planned, formal, regular pattern. This is just as true for weaving or knitting as it is for printing. Printing gives more leeway in the design unit and its repetition. The size and complexity of the repeat is limited by the method of its reproduction and the width of the fabric.

When an artist designs a motif for a fabric he must also devise some way in which the unit will repeat itself. There are a number of general layouts within which this may be done.

Exact repeat: In this repeat, the design unit may be repeated in a row, one row parallel to the next (Fig. 27a). The layout structure may be a square, a rectangle, a diamond, a circle, an ellipse, an octagon, or a hexagon (Fig. 27b).

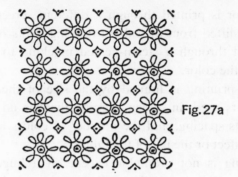

Fig. 27a

Fig. 27b

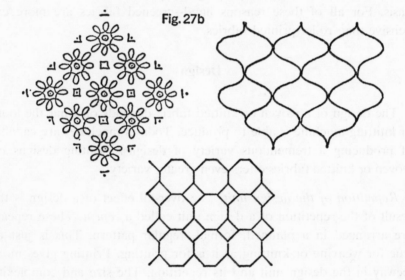

When this layout is used the design may also be repeated in such manner that the units are reversed—turned right to left (Fig. 28a) or top to bottom (Fig. 28b) or turned in any other direction or combination of directions (Fig. 28c).

The position of the design motif may be changed on alternate rows (Fig. 29a). The hue or color values may also be alternated (Fig. 29b).

Fig. 28

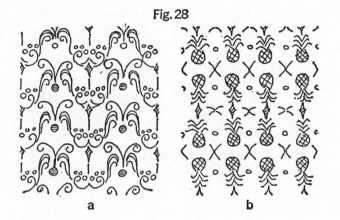

a   b

c

a   Fig. 29   b

Half-drop repeat: Rectangles or squares may shift their placement either horizontally (Fig. 30a) or vertically (Fig. 30b) so that the rows are staggered.

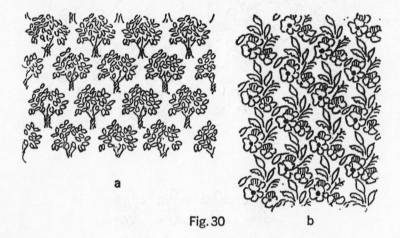

a   Fig. 30   b

Fig. 30a is more commonly called a stagger repeat or brickwork repeat. Fig. 30b is what is most commonly thought of as a half-drop repeat.

Step repeat: Drop repeats may also be in any other fraction of the square or rectangle—⅓ drop, ¼ drop, ⅛ drop, etc. In this type of repeat the movement of the design is more gradual. It takes three rows for a ⅓ drop to return to its original position, four rows for a ¼ drop, etc. These drops, too, may be varied by flopping the design, turning it, alternating it, changing the color or value, or any one of dozens of ingenious ways devised by the designer.

Each motif must be so designed that the top edge of one can be joined to the bottom edge of an adjoining one; the right side of one unit must be joinable to the left side of an adjacent unit. This makes the design flow easily from one motif to another without breaking the continuity. Sometimes to make this easy joining, the motif may extend into the adjoining unit so the design interlocks.

Designers strive to disguise the joining device so that the mechanical structure or layout of the design is indiscernible. This makes it sometimes difficult to determine the repeat. The size of the repeat and the number of pattern pieces which need matching determine how much fabric will be necessary for the garment.

Some fabric surfaces are so designed that there is complete coverage and the repetition of the design is a mystery, at any rate inconspicuous. It is not necessary to match the repeats in such fabrics unless a serious disruption to the continuity would occur because of your style. Watch for the movement of the fabric design. If it flows in one direction, all the pattern pieces must be placed so they go in one direction, too. This takes more yardage. Nondirectional fabrics are more economical since the pattern pieces can be used in any direction.

WHAT'S FOR YOU?

Out of the welter of new styles in any season, how can you really know what is for you? This is a problem which occupies much of every fashion-conscious woman's thought. What is there to guide you? Experience, Experiment, and Education.

Experience—Something to Learn from

Do you recall fondly that blue silk dress that made everyone comment on the blue of your eyes? Do you remember that little horror you kept constantly clutching at the neckline? Do you recall that matte jersey that made you look slim and graceful? Or that little print number which made your friends tactfully suggest a new wonder diet? Your past successes and failures can be an excellent guide if you will permit yourself to learn from them.

Learning requires discipline. Better not use that looped fabric if it makes you look like a Teddy bear. Avoid black if it drains your face of all color. Don't succumb to a dirndl skirt if it makes you look dumpy. This may be the hardest thing in the world to do when you are overwhelmed with desire for a shaggy, black dirndl. Learn to say, "No," if it's not for you.

While it is neither possible nor desirable to duplicate exactly those flattering things you wore once upon a time, your experience can help you decide what of the new is for you.

Experiment

Fortunately, there is enough diversity within any given general silhouette to find that which is best for you. You may have to do a little experimenting though. The sewer is at an advantage here. If the experiment is a failure, she can alter the garment or recut the style to make it more flattering. Or, failing that, pack it up, label it "Mistake," and save the fabric for an inspiration.

You may not like the new style when you first see yourself in it. We are all a little suspicious of the strange. Don't make a quick judgment. Give your eye a chance to grow accustomed to it. Experiment with variations which will suit you. And do remember that it is often more interesting to look chic rather than just pretty.

Education

The people who create fashion are artists. An artist strives to make each thing he produces a work of art in itself.

The dress, *the* suit, or *the* coat is only part of the fashion picture. The complete picture includes the hairdo, the make-up, the hat, the bag, the shoes, the jewelry, the accessories that are worn with each creation. This the designer seldom does himself. Others take up where he leaves off. So that there are a host of associated designers. There are designers of coiffeurs, of make-up, of millinery, bags, shoes, accessories, etc.

Assembling all these items so that the total effect is harmonious and beautiful is also a work of art. This is where you come in. You must select those parts of your costume which will complete the "look" while preserving its beauty. In this sense you are partners with all the designers who created all the individual parts of the costume.

The artist or designer is guided by a set of well-defined principles of art. In choosing and assembling the various parts of a costume to create the total picture, it would be helpful if you, too, were guided by these same principles. Too often, important choices are left to whim, impulse, accident, persuasive salesladies, or compelling advertising copy.

WHAT EVERY SEWER SHOULD KNOW ABOUT DESIGN

The home sewer has an additional need for becoming acquainted with these art principles. Even when she buys the original pattern of a great designer, she still has a long way to go. She must decide whether its lines, shape, and proportion suit her face and figure without the benefit of trying on the garment in advance. She must interpret the design in color and appropriate texture. In addition, she, too, must complete the picture with the right accessories. This is the difficulty, the challenge, and the fun of making your own clothes. And, since fashion is constantly changing, this prolongs the fun— and also the difficulties and the challenges.

Following is a brief discussion of those elements of design with which a designer works. If your sewing is to be a creative experience, they also should be familiar to you.

Line

As the painter uses color, the musician the notes of a scale, the writer words, so the designer uses *line* to express his ideas. Just as some painters delight us because they are great colorists, so some designers delight because they are masters in the use of line. Balenciaga and Givenchy are two such great French masters; Norel and Tassell are two such American greats.

When you consider there are only two kinds of lines with which one can work—straight and curved—you marvel at the ingenuity which provides such a great range of expression. But—lines can be used on the vertical, the horizontal, the oblique. Straight lines can be long, short, or in between. Curved lines can be subtle, slight, or fully curved.

Straight vertical lines suggest height, simplicity, dignity, stateliness (Fig. 31a). Straight horizontal lines suggest width, calmness, repose

(Fig. 31b). Oblique lines suggest drama, movement. They lead the eye on. You expect them to go somewhere (Fig. 31e). Downward curves give a sad feeling (Fig. 31c); upward curves give a lift (Fig. 31d). Subtle curves or combinations of curves are generally more interesting and more rhythmic (Fig. 31f).

Fig. 31

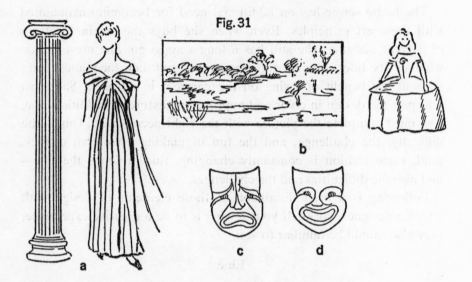

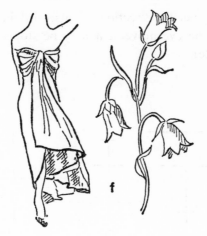

The eye always follows the direction of the line. Effects may be achieved by inviting the eye to continue indefinitely (Fig. 32a); or

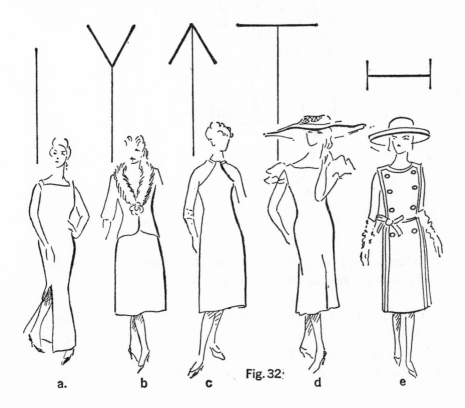

a.   b.   c.   Fig. 32.   d.   e.

to continue in a specific direction—downward in Fig. 32b, upward in Fig. 32c—or the eye movement may be stopped by setting limits (Fig. 32d and 32e).

Fig. 33

When several lines appear as they do in most costumes, the eye will follow the most dominant one (Fig. 33).

Contradictory lines cause confusion (Fig. 34a). Many lines make each vie for attention; this makes the design too busy (Fig. 34b). Lines in opposing directions play tug of war (Fig. 34c). Too many of the same kind of lines tend to become monotonous (Fig. 34d).

Fig. 34

In good design, every line contributes to a central theme, with no distractions or inconsistencies. In Fig. 35a, note how each line "works" with every other line. In Fig. 35b, note that the neckline

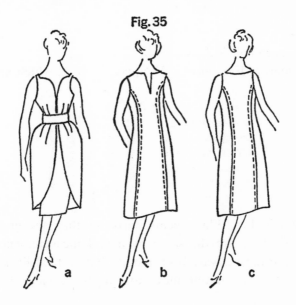

Fig. 35

opening, which is a straight line, is inconsistent with the curved lines of the rest of the design. The design would be improved by the elimination of the opening (Fig. 35c).

The lines of any design can literally point the way to your good and bad features. Is there a moral in this?

Space and Shape

A combination of lines produces shape. The most obvious and therefore the most important shape is the silhouette. Any style lines within it create other shapes. Too many other shapes detract from the over-all effect and make the costume appear crowded (Fig. 34a, 34b, and 34c). It is important that the shapes within the silhouette contribute to and are in harmony with the general design.

The eye plays tricks with shapes as it does with lines. In the following illustration, Fig. 36, which of each pair looks bigger?

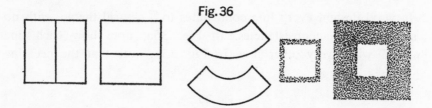

Fig. 36

Actually, each pair is the same size.

Which group of lines in Fig. 37 appears wider, which narrower?

Fig. 37

a   b

The group in Fig. 37a appears narrower than the group in Fig. 37b, although they are the same by actual measurement. Are you surprised? You have always been taught that vertical lines make you look slimmer and horizontal lines make you look wider. In groups of lines, it is not only the direction of the lines but the spaces between the lines which tell the eye how to move. When the eye moves easily without being stopped as in Fig. 37a, the group seems narrower. Where the eye movement is stopped as in Fig. 37b, the group seems wider.

A shape within a shape is contained in Figs. 38a and 38b. Which of these appears narrower?

Fig. 38

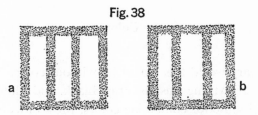

a   b

In Fig. 38a the eye moves upward between the central lines; in Fig. 38b the eye moves from side to side. The first panel makes the square seem taller and narrower. The second panel makes the square appear wider.

Note the effect of these optical illusions in these designs (Fig. 39).

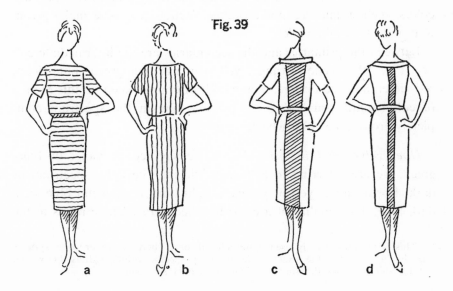

Fig. 39

a   b   c   d

Fig. 39a The horizontal grouping of stripes makes this dress appear slimmer.

Fig. 39b The vertical grouping of stripes makes this dress appear wider.

Fig. 39c The wide panel makes this dress seem wider.

Fig. 39d The narrow panel of the closing makes this dress seem slimmer.

Color

What a dreary world this would be without color. Imagine an existence where everything was just gray, black, and white! Some people have a natural sense for combining colors. Most of us have to work at it. A little information helps.

*Triadic color theory** consists of three primary colors—yellow, red, and blue. They are primary because they cannot be obtained by mixing any colors (Fig. 40a). By combining any two of them we can make new colors.

The secondary colors (Fig. 40b) are made by mixing two primary colors. Yellow and red make orange. Yellow and blue make green. Red and blue make violet.

Between the primaries and the secondaries are the intermediate colors (Fig. 40c): yellow-orange, yellow-green, blue-green, blue-violet, red-violet, and red-orange. You could, of course, keep up this mixing of colors until you had every possible hue in the spectrum completely around the color wheel.

Hue, value, and intensity. When we say red or violet or blue-green, we are referring to a *hue*. A hue may be light, spectrum, or dark. For instance, you may have a light blue, a spectrum blue, or a dark blue. This quality of a color is called *value*. Value refers to the

---

* This is the most widely used basic color theory. There are other color systems used in industry for the exact designation of specific colors (Munsell-Oswald). But for our purposes the simpler triadic system is sufficient.

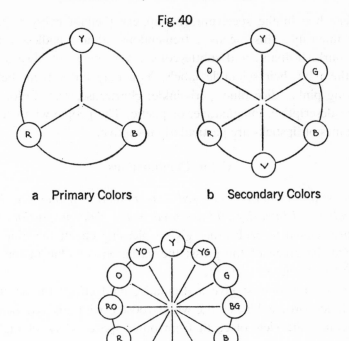

Fig. 40

a   Primary Colors   b   Secondary Colors

c   Intermediate Colors

lightness or darkness of a color. Values range from white to black. Whatever the value, the color is still recognizable as the hue (except, of course, the white and black).

Colors also have a quality of brightness or dullness. This is called *intensity* or chroma. The strength or brilliance of a hue can be tempered or subdued by adding the color directly opposite to it on the color wheel, its complementary color.

Red may be grayed by adding a green, its complement. Yellow may be grayed by adding a violet, its complement. Blue may be grayed by adding an orange, its complement, and so on. Theoretically, the proper proportion of each pair of complementary colors produces gray. The addition of black to a color not only darkens it, it also grays it. Black or any form of gray tends to neutralize.

Every hue in the spectrum can appear then in every value and every intensity. This means a tremendous, almost endless range of light, dark, brilliant, and subtle colors. You may not always recognize them by their scientific labels. You may know them better as shocking pink, Alice blue, periwinkle, chartreuse, rust. Color names can be descriptive, imaginative, or poetic. The people who dream up the names of lipsticks are particularly inventive.

Color Combinations

Almost any colors can be used in combination if they are the correct value and intensity and are used in the right proportion. Colors that are related to each other give a pleasing effect; the blue of the sky and the green of the grass; the variations of blue in sea water, the violet tonality of twilight.

Colors that contrast give a dramatic, bold effect: the spotting of Somali leopard, a black and white rooster with his red beak and cockscomb, the view of earth from outer space—dark of night and light of day.

We do not ever see colors in isolation. We see them in relationship to other colors. How a particular color appears to us is very much affected by its hue, value, intensity, and amount in relationship to the hue, value, intensity, and amount of the surrounding colors. There is always an interaction between the two. Take a simple bowl of fruit. A few peaches surrounded by mounds of green grapes give a different color effect than these same peaches in a bowl of purple grapes. One peach in a bowl of grapes will present an entirely different color effect than a dozen peaches with a few green grapes. Neither the peaches nor the grapes have changed. Their relationship has.

A new color tonality is created when colors are used side by side. A tweed fabric woven of red and blue yarns produces a color effect which is neither red nor blue but a new color with a violet tonality. A color can be darkened by an adjacent color. A cloth woven of red and black yarns gives the appearance of dark red. A color can be grayed by an adjacent color. A fabric woven of gray and pink yarns looks like a warm gray.

A new color is produced when a transparent fabric of one color is used over another. A sky-blue dress has its skirt greened by a top layer of yellow chiffon.

Two contrasting colors make each other more intense. A white coat worn over a black sheath dress makes the white appear whiter and the black appear blacker.

Complementary colors intensify each other. Christmas holly with its red berries and green leaves makes both red and green brighter.

A full intensity color seems even more brilliant when placed next to any neutralized tones. A blue blouse looks very blue when worn with a neutralized orange (brown).

When assembling a costume it is not only the color of the suit or coat or dress which must be considered. This will be worn with accessories which also have color. The color effect of the outfit will depend on all the colors used and their relationship to each other.

Advancing and receding colors. The golden orange of the sun, the red of fire—these are colors we associate with warmth. The dark blue of night, the green-blue of water—these are colors we associate with coolness. The yellows, oranges, reds, and red-violets are the warm colors. The blues, greens, and blue-violets are the cool colors.

Warm colors have a greater luminosity. Your eye seeks them first. We call them advancing colors. Everyone will literally see you coming in a bright-red dress. The cool colors are just the opposite. They retire to the background. They are receding colors. If you want to lose yourself in a crowd, wear blue-violet.

We hasten to add that *normally* warm colors are advancing colors and cool colors are receding ones. This is not always so. The legend is that Gainsborough painted his famous "Blue Boy" to refute the theory that blue is always a receding color. In his painting, blue is an advancing color.

Light values of a color will also make the color advance, while dark values make a color recede. People can spot you more easily in a pink tweed suit than in a deep-garnet one. Here again, we must say this is normally so.

Picture a girl in a black bathing suit walking along a sandy beach.

By all the rules the sand which is light should be the advancing color and the black bathing suit which is dark should be the receding color. Just the opposite happens. The black color stands out (advances) against the sand-color receding background.

A color advances or recedes in relation to the surrounding colors. This is why you may look heavy in a white dress while everyone comments on how slim you look in your black one.

Light colors reflect light; dark colors absorb it. We wear light colors in the summertime. They not only look cooler, they really do keep us cooler because they reflect the light (the warm rays of the sun). We wear dark clothes in the wintertime. They not only look warmer, they actually keep us warmer because they absorb light. Because light colors reflect light they are flattering when worn close to the face. You've undoubtedly had this experience with a white collar or a white necklace. Because dark colors absorb light they rob the face of color. Black worn close to the face requires more make-up to compensate for the loss of color.

The body responds physically to color. For instance, red, which has a strong impact on the visual center, is used as a danger signal. Because of the effect of color on the emotions (Fig. 41), we find it purposefully used in homes, hospitals, factories, schools, etc.

Emotional Color Wheel*

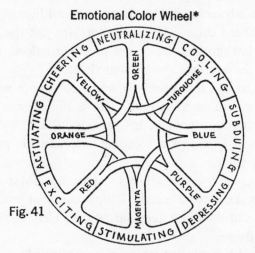

Fig. 41

* Emotional Color Wheel, American Fabrics, Fall–Winter 1960, P. 69.

We use colors as symbols. White, which is "uncorrupted" light, is used as the color of purity. Black, which absorbs all color, which is the "burial" of light, is the color of mourning. We speak of being "in the pink" when we are feeling good. We say we are "blue" when we are depressed.

It's easy enough to expound a great body of rules in regard to color. Then along comes a great creative artist who breaks them all and creates a thing of beauty. One is almost tempted to say there are no rules.

Many of us have been taught to think in terms of "color schemes" which become clichés. We are afraid to depart from combinations of colors which we are accustomed to see together. A creative use of color provides the surprise of unexpected color combinations. These must always be in proper relationship to each other in hue, value, intensity, and the amount used. It is the relationship which is important.

Texture

Texture is the structural quality of a fabric. It refers to whether a fabric is shiny or dull, heavy or gauzy, clinging or stiff, patterned or plain. The texture of a fabric very often dictates the design. The design may call for a particular texture to best realize its beauty. Perhaps you have had the experience of using the same pattern with two fabrics of different textures. You then know how very different the resulting garment can be—successful in one perhaps, unsuccessful in the other.

These textures appear to increase the size of the figure: shiny, stiff, heavy, clinging, fuzzy, shaggy, looped, some prints. These textures appear to decrease the size of the figure: light- or medium-weight fabric, solid colors, some prints, dull textures.

The feel of a fabric, its texture, gives as much joy to the sewer as its color.

Proportion

Your favorite recipe will tell you to use so many eggs to so much flour, or so large a roast for so many people. This is a matter of proportion. In design, proportion is the relationship of one part of a design to another. It may be the amount of bodice to length of skirt, the amount of light to dark, or the amount of one color to another.

In your costume, proportion is the size of your hat or bag in relationship to the rest of your costume. It may be the length of your jacket in relationship to the slimness or fullness of your skirt. It may be the amount of turquoise you are planning to wear with your black dress. The designer works for pleasing proportions in his design. The wearer must consider the rightness of the design to her own proportions. For she has proportions, too: her height to her width, her length from neckline to waist, from waist to toes, her width of shoulders, of bust, of waist, of hips, etc.

In design, an equal division of space or color tends to become monotonous (Fig. 42a). An unequal division of space lends interest (Fig. 42b).

Fig. 42

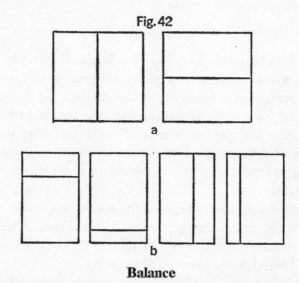

a

b

Balance

We find a kind of anxious enjoyment in watching a tight-rope walker. We hold our breath as he slowly and very carefully makes his way to the opposite side. Should he even momentarily sway, we gasp with fear. When he reaches his little platform on the other side, we applaud vigorously as much with sheer relief as with admiration.

The truth of the matter is, we are always made uncomfortable by unbalance.

Too many little boys sitting on the limb of a tree can send us into a state of alarm. An inexperienced little girl stepping gayly into the prow of a canoe makes us cry out in fright. Unbalance unnerves us. We expect disaster. This is as true in design as in life.

Jack and Jill are twins. They are the same height and the same weight. They like to do the same things. Here they are playing on a seesaw (Fig. 43a). The game is fun for they are evenly matched. This is a balance of equals.

Fig. 43

a

b

Here is a drawing of an enlarged snowflake (Fig. 43b). The same design unit is repeated around its center. This is a balance of equal parts.

A balance is achieved by the exact duplication on either side of a central axis (real or imaginary) or the repetition of an exact unit around a point. This is called formal or symmetrical balance.

Formal or symmetrical balance is the type most frequently used in clothing design (Fig. 44a).

Fig. 44

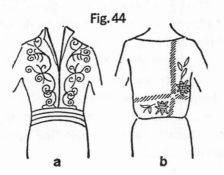

a   b

Do you remember the story of the maiden who was worth her weight in gold? She sat on one side of the scale while the gold was heaped on the other. Now a maiden is not gold. A maiden even takes up more room on her side of the scale than the gold. However, their weights are evenly matched. This is a balance of two unlikes, a balance of equivalents. The gold is the equivalent of the maiden though it is unlike her.

In Fig. 44b a balance exists between the right and left sides though the two are quite different. This is an example of a balance of equivalents.

There is a lovely dogwood tree in blossom in my garden. I look at it from my window. I walk around it on the terrace. From whatever spot I gaze, I see the masses of leaves and pink blossoms. Though always the same in beauty, their growth is different on every side. Yet the tree appears balanced (Fig. 45a). It is a balance of uneven parts, a "felt" balance, the type most seen in Nature. This is called an informal or asymmetrical balance.

Fig. 45

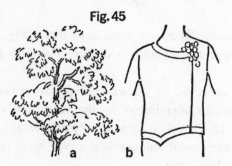

a   b

This suit (Fig. 45b) is a beautiful example of asymmetric balance. This is a difficult type of balance to handle in design. It is so easy to push it to a point that can make us uneasy.

The designer tries to compose his space so that it is divided into interesting shapes and spaces that balance each other. He balances the lines of his design. He uses colors, values, and intensities which balance. He chooses textures which balance. In any good design all the elements with which he works are in fine balance whether it be symmetrical or asymmetrical.

Unity and Variety

In addition to all of the other qualities mentioned, good design must also have unity and variety. Do they sound contradictory? Both are as necessary for art as they are for life. We are all enough alike to make communication and understanding possible. Yet, mentally, physically and emotionally, we are all quite different. This makes life interesting. Unity and variety make design interesting, too.

Unity is a oneness, a belongingness whether it refers to international relations or only to this spring's costume. To achieve it there must be:

1. *A common or specific point of interest.*
If you have decided that your new outfit is to be blue, then every part of your ensemble must contribute to the look of blue. This doesn't mean that everything must be blue; that would be monotonous. Any other color which is used must heighten or intensify the blue.

2. *Every detail of the ensemble must co-operate with every other one.*
The type and size and color of your hat must not be at war with the color and texture and lines of your coat, while your bag and shoes are slugging it out on their own. They are all members of the same team and each must take its proper place and perform THE action required of it.

3. *Each part of the costume must be consistent with the rest.*
You wouldn't think of wearing a pair of soiled sneakers with a pink peau de soie evening dress. This is an exaggerated example of inconsistency. You must be alert to the more subtle ones.

4. *There can be a unity of unlike but related parts.*
Your new fall suit is a handsome plaid. With it you wear alligator shoes. Tweed and alligator are unlike in texture but they are related in character and function.

5. *There can be a unity of opposites.*
An evening dress of black organza embroidered with rows of glittering jet beads makes a memorable gown. The shininess of the beads and the dull matte surface of the organza are opposite in texture. Yet their use together produces harmony.

6. *There can be a unity of diversified elements.*
A sleeveless, flounced sundress has shoestring straps and a parade of buttons down the front, each of a different color. A diversity of elements, yes. But everything about the dress contributes to the theme of playfulness.

Relate—Don't Duplicate

Many women hope to achieve unity by making everything match —dress, coat, hat, shoes, bag. There is the ubiquitous pin-and-earrings set or matching necklace and earrings. This is an obvious kind of unity. It is true that unity comes with the repetition of color, line, shape, or texture. However, too much repetition can become monotonous.

A surprise touch, an off-beat color combination, a combination of textures, a print-and-plain—these can all lend interest to an ensemble. This departure from sameness is variety. You remember the old saying, "Variety is the spice of life." So it is in your costume. Add a dash of color to spice it or a "smidgen" of texture to season it.

But you should be aware that if too much sameness can make for dullness, too much variety can make for chaos. What is needed is a happy balance of the two.

And Here Is a Final Pair to Consider—Emphasis and Restraint

Emphasis is one element of design which is dramatized—color, line, texture. In a costume, emphasis means dramatizing *a* hat *or* dress *or* jewelry. If every part of the costume is shouting for attention it is impossible to really see any part of it. No matter how fine each individual detail may be, it loses something when it is thrust in competition with every other. "Too much of a muchness" is distracting.

Restraint is the other side of the coin. Emphasis of one element implies subordination of the rest. Restraint requires the removal of any element or detail which detracts from the center of interest or the main theme. There is always another time to make another statement. Understatement is a prominent ingredient of elegance.

The pattern, the fabric and you—each could be the subject of long and absorbing study. Restraint, however, is as important for an author as for a designer, especially one who is giving advice on the subject. So perhaps, this is an appropriate place at which to end this discussion. The foregoing discussion should give you a glimpse of some of the problems and considerations which confront you as well as the designer in creating a look of beauty.

CHAPTER III

Fit to Flatter

Given some ability to use one's hands and some ability to interpret printed directions, most everyone can learn to sew. In fact, many become quite accomplished seamstresses. Making clothes fit—that's another matter! More homemade clothing looks that way because of poor fit rather than because of poor workmanship. More home sewers are discouraged by their inability to fit than by their inability to master the techniques of dressmaking or tailoring. They are not alone. Many professional dressmakers suffer from the same failing. You've heard women say, "I've just discovered a wonderful dressmaker. Her work is beautiful. The only trouble is she can't make clothes that fit well." Or, "My husband's tailor is a wonder but he simply refuses to make me a suit. He says, 'Fitting women is too much of a problem.'"

Like sewing, fitting is a technique which can be learned, too. There is no great mystery about it. It follows certain definite rules. If you know how and where the garment should fit, that's half the battle. If you know what to do to correct any fault, that is the other half. This is one big reason why a knowledge of pattern making is of such help to sewers even if they never actually make any patterns.

Fine fit is composed of many things: the right style in the right size; care in layout, cutting, and sewing; proper interfacing or underlining; pressing and shaping; also, a good foundation garment helps. But, to begin with, fine fit depends on adjusting a standard-size pattern to conform to your figure.

A standard-size pattern is made from a table of standard measurements to fit a standard figure (page 12). The standard figure is a myth. Practically no figure conforms to all the standard measurements. There is always some variance. Figures are no more alike than thumbprints. Those who claim they are perfect sizes are either not being honest with themselves or are willing to settle for less than meticulous fit.

The woman who buys her clothes has no choice but to accept the size available or have it altered, frequently an expensive operation. The woman who sews has the advantage of being able to cut and fit her clothes to her figure. It is this flawless fit which is in great part the lure of custom-made tailoring.

WHERE AND HOW THE GARMENT SHOULD FIT

Before beginning any alterations to the pattern perhaps it would be well to know where and how the garment should fit.

Fitting for Ease

The ease we spoke of in Chapter I was a general amount necessary for comfort. Because suits and coats are worn over other garments they must have additional ease. Fig. 46a shows the pattern for a slim dress, ease included. The changes in ease necessary for a suit appear in Fig. 46b, for a coat in Fig. 46c. The broken lines indicate the original dress pattern.

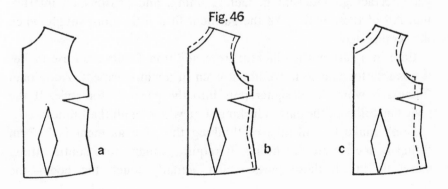

Fig. 46

Note that in both the suit and coat basic patterns, the neckline has been lowered, the shoulders widened, the armhole dropped, and width has been added across the chest and at the side seam. The amount of change is naturally more for a coat than a suit. Corresponding changes are made in a suit or coat sleeve (Fig. 47).

Fig. 47

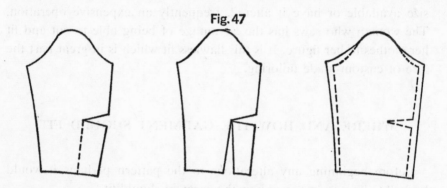

Notice that the sleeve cap has been flattened and widened to fit the extended shoulder and the deepened armhole. The underarm seam has been widened and lengthened and the wrist has been widened to provide easier movement.

In fitting a suit, try the jacket on over a blouse or sweater. In fitting a coat, try it on over the garment to be worn with it—dress, suit, blouse, or sweater. This will give a more accurate idea of the necessary ease.

In early fittings, be mindful of the fact that the garment is yet to get interfacing, underlining, facing, lining, and possibly an interlining. All of these will make the garment fit a little more snugly when it is completed.

Ease in a garment is different from additional fullness. Ease makes it possible for you to move about even in a slim garment. Additional fullness is what the designer puts into the garment for style. If the style has fullness, the ease is lurking somewhere in all the fullness.

Don't make the mistake of thinking that if a garment isn't form fitting it doesn't require fitting. It requires much more subtle fitting. Carefully fit all those parts which actually touch the body—the shoulder seam, the neckline, the waist, or hips. When properly fitted, even an unfitted look seems right.

Don't overfit. Suits and coats which look as if they were just about to pop their buttons make you look like a Bulging Betsy. Your garment should *look* as well as *be* comfortable.

Fitting for Grain

We have spoken at length of the grain and its importance for the true hang of the garment (page 56). This is how the grain should appear in your garment:

The center-front and center-back grain (vertical grain, generally) hang straight at right angles to the floor (Fig. 48a). This places the horizontal grain at right angles to the center-front and center-back grain. Properly placed, it is parallel to the floor. Any crosswise or lengthwise yarn which is prominent will help locate the grain. Any stripe, check, or plaid will serve the same way. If you do not trust your eye, place a line of hand- or machine-guide basting to mark the position of the grain. When hand-guide basting is used it is done so that long floats appear on the right side (Fig. 48e). The horizontal grain can be checked for correct position across the chest, across the bust, across the shoulder blades, and across the hips—both front and back (Fig. 48a).

Fig. 48

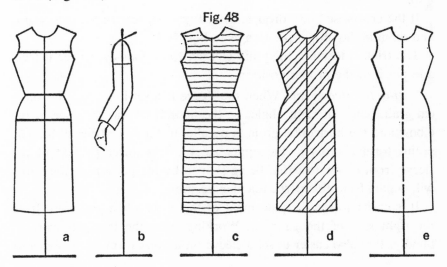

a   b   c   d   e

In a garment which is cut on the horizontal grain or the bias, the center-front and center-back *markings* hang in these positions, too (Fig. 48c and 48d). It is easier, quicker, and more accurate to use hand-guide basting on bias-cut garments.

Wherever the grain departs from the correct position, either unpin or release the seam and reset in the proper position.

Fig. 49

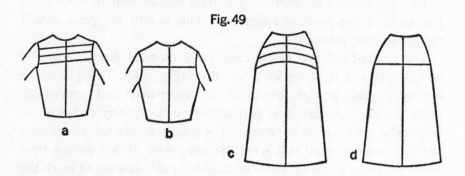

a   b   c   d

For instance:

If the crosswise grain slants out of its horizontal position as in Fig. 49a, release the shoulder seams and repin correctly, as in Fig. 49b.

If the crosswise grain droops, as in Fig. 49c, release the side seams and repin in the proper position as in Fig. 49d.

The trick is to mark the grain clearly, train your eye to see it true, and pin it in the proper position.

Setting the sleeve cap. When the sleeve is a set-in sleeve, the vertical grain hangs at right angles to the floor from the shoulder to the elbow and the horizontal grain is parallel to the floor (Fig. 48b). The grains form a cross in the upper sleeve. The lower portion of the sleeve from elbow to wrist, being shaped by the pattern or the darts, will depart from this perpendicular position.

It is easier to see the placement of the grain when you work from the right side of the garment. Working from the inside is working blindly. It is also easier to set a sleeve on a dress form or on someone else. If you must do this for yourself, you may have to try it several times.

Procedure for setting the sleeve cap from the right side:

1. Shirr the sleeve cap (page 274).

2. Shrink out the fullness (page 274).

3. Turn under the seam allowance.

4. Pin the sleeve at the shoulder seam with the grain in the proper position. One pin will do to set the position.

5. Remove the garment.

6. Mark the shoulder setting on the sleeve cap with thread.

7. Unpin.

8. Set only the sleeve cap from the inside matching the shoulder seam of the garment to the shoulder marking of the sleeve cap. The underarm of the sleeve can be set when the correct position of the cap is determined.

9. Try on the garment. Check the vertical and horizontal grains.

For instance:

If the lengthwise grain is too far forward as in Fig. 50a, the sleeve cap is moved back until the sleeve hangs with the proper grain (Fig. 50b).

If the vertical grain is too far back, as in Fig. 50c, the sleeve cap is moved forward until the sleeve hangs in the proper position (Fig. 50b).

Turn the sleeve cap like a dial until the vertical and horizontal grains are set in the proper position.

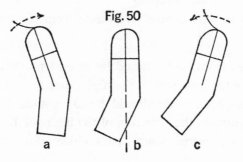

Fig. 50

a | b   c

Fitting for Shape

A few reminders to serve as a review of principles developed in Chapter II.

The control darts and the control seams shape the garment. In order that the shaping is just right for you, this control must be the right amount in the right place.

The dart control is the difference between a large measurement and a smaller one. The larger the amount of stitched dart control, the greater the resulting bulge in the garment. The smaller the amount of stitched dart control, the less the resulting bulge.

Flat figures, whether heavy or slight, need less dart control because there is less difference between the measurements of adjoining areas.

Shapely figures, whether heavy or slight, need more dart control because there is more difference between the measurements of adjoining areas.

You may add or subtract dart control in any darts or seams.

Too much dart control in any one area throws the grain off. It is better to divide the control into two darts.

For more gradual or subtler shaping use divided dart control or multiple darts.

Curved darts or control seams shape more to the body than straight darts or seams.

For large-bosomed figures, dart control in several positions not only controls the grain of the fabric, it gives better fit. The more control darts or control seams, the more opportunity for fitting.

Darts can and must be relocated to the positions where they belong in order to do any shaping.

All changes in dart control are made from the high point of any area:

The bodice-front darts should be at bust-point height and width or heading in the direction of the high point.

The bodice-back darts should be at shoulder-blade height and width or heading in the direction of the high point.

Bodice-front-control seams pass either directly over the bust point or slightly toward the center or side seam; if they are more than 1″ off this line, accommodation for the dart control must be made in the pattern construction.

Bodice-back-control seams pass either directly over the shoulder blades or slightly toward the center or side seam; if they are more than 1″ off this line, accommodation for the dart control must be made in the pattern construction.

The skirt-front darts must be at front-hip depth and width or heading in the direction of the high point of the hip.

The skirt-back darts must be at buttock depth and width or heading in the direction of the high point of the buttock.

Skirt-control seams pass over the high points of hips and buttocks. If they are more than 1″ off this line either toward the center or side seams, accommodation for the dart control must be made in the pattern construction.

The elbow dart should be at the elbow when the arm is bent.

Whenever only one dart is used, it heads toward the high point. When two darts are used they are placed one either side of the high point. When three darts are used, the center one is in the dart-point position, the other two on either side.

Here is an easy way to relocate a dart:

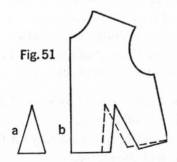

Fig. 51

1. Trace the dart on another piece of paper. Cut it out (Fig. 51a).

2. Place the cut-out dart on your pattern in the position you wish it to be and trace (Fig. 51b). (The broken line shows the position of the original dart.)

NOTE: The dart can be moved to another place *on the same seam line only.*

You *cannot* take a waistline dart and place it on the underarm seam. This would make both waistline and side seams incorrect in length.

Here is an easy way to make multiple darts:

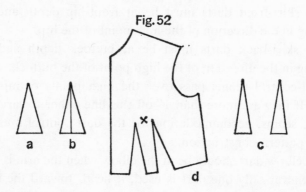

Fig. 52

1. Trace the dart on another piece of paper. Cut it out (Fig. 52a).

2. Divide the dart into the desired number of darts (Fig. 52b). Cut them out.

3. Make the dart legs equal in length (Fig. 52c). (You will find one shorter than the other as the sections are cut.)

4. Place the new dart sections into position on either side of the bust point (X) and about 1″ apart at the seam (Fig. 52d).

5. Trace the darts in their new positions.

NOTE: This method can be used *only* for darts on the *same seam line.* It will not work any other way.

Darts may be relocated in the same way on the bodice back, skirt front and skirt back, and the sleeve.

Darts are meant for you, so don't be afraid to alter the amount and the position of the control darts and the control seams. They are there to shape the garment to conform to your figure.

All pattern changes in dart control are made from the high points of the darts. In dressmaking or tailoring, however, darts are seldom worn stitched to these high points. That would be asking too much of most figures. The darts are shortened for a softer effect.

The darts which extend to the high points are called *designer's darts*. They are used in *making a pattern*. Only in small or youthful figures and only in very fitted garments are darts stitched to these high points.

The more general shortened darts used in dressmaking and tailoring are called *dressmaker's darts*. These darts are used in the *making of a garment*. All darts on commercial patterns are shortened darts.

Here is a guide for shortening the designer's darts to convert them into dressmaker's darts (take into consideration your figure, the type of garment, and your personal preference in fit):

Bodice
Front-waistline dart is shortened ½″ from bust-point height.
Back-waistline dart is shortened 1″ from shoulder-blade height.
Underarm dart is shortened two or more inches from the bust point (this dart always ends at bust-point height). Heavy-bosomed figures may bring this dart closer to the bust point if the garment fits better so.
French underarm dart (an exception) is stitched to the bust point, except in larger figures when it is shortened ½″ to 1″.
Front shoulder dart is shortened 2″ or more from the bust point.
Back shoulder dart is usually stitched to 3″ finished length in Size 14.

Sleeve
Elbow dart is usually stitched to 2½″ finished length in Size 14.

Skirt
Front-skirt dart is shortened 2″ from the high point of the front hipbone.
Back-skirt dart is shortened 1″ from the high point of the buttock.
Frequently skirt darts fit better when unshortened so that the dart releases the greatest amount of material where the figure is fullest. Use your judgment as to the best length for you.

Fitting the Silhouette Seams

Neckline seam. The neckline is a matter of personal preference and fashion. A high neckline is as high as you find comfortable. A low neckline is as low as makes you happy. Or what the style is! It is a little odd to see a heavy winter coat with a dropped neckline and cropped sleeves but when has fashion ever been practical?

If the neckline is too high for you, drop it (Fig. 53a). If it is too low, build it up (Fig. 53b); the broken line shows the original neckline. Changes in the neckline require corresponding changes in collars, facings, interfacings, lining, underlinings, and interlinings.

Fig. 53

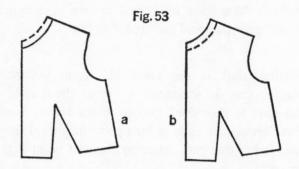

In a standard basic pattern, the neckline of a dress is around the base of the neck starting from the hollow between the collarbones at center front and extending to the prominent bone at the back of the neck at which the head bends (Fig. 54a). A close-fitting string or necklace will help locate this line for a round-neck dress or blouse.

A high-necked-suit neckline drops ⅛″ below this line (Fig. 54b). A high-necked-coat neckline drops ¼″ below this line (Fig. 54c). The neckline of a suit or coat will therefore have a little more ease than a dress.

Fig. 54

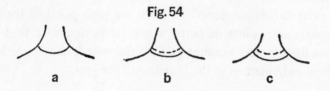

Many current styles are designed with necklines which drop considerably below these basic necklines.

The shoulder seams fit along the top of the shoulder slightly forward of the crest of the trapezius muscle from the hollow at the base of the neck (neckline) to the shoulder point, that prominent bone at which the arm is hinged. This brings the shoulder seam just a *little* forward, making the seam visible from the front (Fig. 55). (Caution—don't bring it so far forward that it looks like a yoke.)

Fig. 55

The armhole seam in a dress curves over the top of the shoulder, continues in a slightly curved line, deeper in front, shallower in back, to the crease where arm and body join. One-quarter-inch ease is added here across the chest. Front and back notches are generally placed at this point (Fig. 56a). Below this, the armhole swings into the underarm curve to about 1″ to 1½″ below the armpit. The armhole and shoulder seams meet just at or a little beyond the shoulder point (Fig. 56b). Shoulder widths vary with style. When a narrow-shouldered look is in vogue, the armhole starts at this point. When a broad-shouldered look is in style, the shoulder seam is extended beyond the shoulder point. When shoulder pads are used, the shoulder seam is raised and extended both front and back to accommodate the pad (Fig. 56c). This amount is equal to the thickness of the pad.

The armhole seam in a suit or coat. The shoulder seam is extended ½″ in both suit and coat. All adjustments are made both front and back.

The shoulder seam is raised and extended the thickness of any shoulder pad used.

Fig. 56

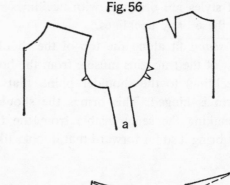

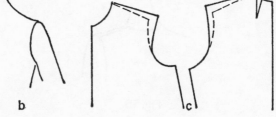

One-half-inch ease is added across the chest.

The suit armhole drops ½″ at the underarm, the coat, 1″.

All ease suggested here is minimum. The armhole drop may be more. The style and the desired fit will determine both.

Side seams start at the underarm about ½″ back of the middle of the armhole (Fig. 57a). They continue in a straight line to the floor (Fig. 57b).

This placement of the side seam makes the front armhole a deeper curve than the back armhole. It also makes the skirt front larger than the skirt back despite any notions you may have to the contrary.

In normal figures, when the arms hang naturally at the sides, the middle fingers touch the side seams.

If the side seam of the skirt swings forward (Fig. 58a) or backward (Fig. 58b), release the side seam. Establish the proper grain line at the hips (Fig. 58c); check the dart control. Fit the skirt above the hips. Allow the rest of the skirt to hang naturally from the hips. Repin the side seams, in the proper position. It may be necessary to

Fig. 57

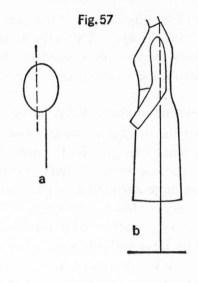

a

b

Fig. 58

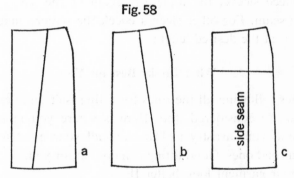

a   b   side seam   c

take off or add to either front or back in order to bring the side seam into position.

The waistline seam is marked the same way in bodice and skirt. Mark each separately. If they are to be joined, they will join at these markings. The waistband joins the skirt at these markings, too.

Here is an easy way to determine your waistline. Pin a tape measure snugly around the waist. Push it so that the bottom of the tape rests at your natural waistline or in the position you would like it to be. Mark the bottom line of the tape measure with pins or tailor's chalk. The width of the tape measure provides ease in length for the bodice. Run a line of basting to replace the pins when the skirt or bodice are removed from the figure. This is the waistline seam.

In normal waistlines the front dips about ½" below the back. In sway-backed individuals, the reverse is true. The waistline dips in the back.

A properly set waistline eliminates wrinkling or pulling.

The hemline is set the number of inches from the floor currently fashionable. (Never mind your promise to yourself not to shorten or lengthen your skirt because you just don't like the current length. You will attract a lot more attention if you are out of fashion than if you expose one inch more or less of your legs.)

Use a skirt marker or yardstick. Wear the shoes to be worn with the outfit or ones of the same heel height.

The sleeve seam. The shoulder notch matches the shoulder seams. In a one-piece sleeve, the underarm seam of the sleeve meets the bodice side seam. For other sleeves check the pattern markings. The sleeve hem is at the desired length.

What Looks Best on You

Sometimes following all the rules for fitting isn't quite enough. The "look" must be considered, too. Here is where you must use your judgment and your artistry to bring out all your good features and hide all your bad ones. Good fitting can do that for you.

Would your garment look better IF:

> the shoulders were a little wider or a little narrower than the rule stated?
>
> the shoulder seams were moved forward or moved backward?
>
> there were a little more ease across the chest, across the back, across the bust?
>
> the waistline and the hipline were not quite so loose or so tight?
>
> the sleeves were wider—or narrower?
>
> there was more dart control—or less dart control?
>
> the darts were moved a bit—or divided?
>
> the waistline were raised or lowered?
>
> the side seams were moved forward—or backward?

Sometimes following the rules may be positively wrong for you. If you are round-shouldered and follow the rule for the placement of the shoulder seam this may emphasize the curve of your back. By all means, ignore the rule—move your shoulder seam back. If you have a heavy posterior and follow the rule for the placement of the side seam you may end up with a rather startling result (Fig. 59a). Ignore the rule for the placement of the side seam. Make your skirt front wider at the hips as well as the waistline in a pleasing proportion. Gently curve the side seam from waistline to hips, then continue straight to the floor (Fig. 59b). This will divide the space from center front to center back so as to minimize the bulk in back.

Fig. 59

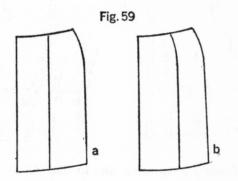

WHAT PATTERN CHANGES ARE NECESSARY

It is to be hoped that the preceding discussion of how and where the garment should fit will make you impatient with anything but perfection. To achieve this you will have to give the subject of pattern changes a little more time and study.

Your previous experience with patterns has taught you that certain changes make the garment fit better. You can handle the simple ones. There may be others indicated which you just don't know how to cope with. Armed with your tape measure, your personal measurements (page 10), the pattern, and some information, you should be able to solve your problems.

Now Measure the Pattern

(You have your measurements in the Personal-Measurement Chart, page 10.)

1. Assemble all the parts which make each unit.

2. Measure that part of the pattern which will appear on the surface of the finished garment. Do not measure anything which will end up in some seam or dart.

For instance:

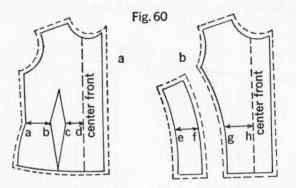

Fig. 60

Fig. 60a. Measure from seam line to dart (a to b), from dart to center front (c to d).

Fig. 60b. Measure from seam line to seam line (e to f), from seam line to center front (g to h). Measurements go only to the line on which the garment will close. The front extension will lap over a part of the garment already measured.

The bust measurement is across the fullest part of the pattern *both front and back*. The hip measurement is across the fullest part of the skirt pattern *both front and back*.

Measure the height and width of the dart points. Remember these are shortened darts in the pattern, unshortened in your measurements.

When the garment has a dropped neckline, it is hard to check the length of center front and center back. Let your past experience guide you. If you generally have to shorten or lengthen the bodice, do so now. You will get a much better idea of whether you need to and how much in the trial muslin.

Measure the dart-point height and width or approximately where they would occur on a control seam.

Keep in mind that:

1. *Your* width measurements are *whole measurements*. The *pattern* generally represents only *half the width measurements*. You will need to halve your width measurements to correspond to those of the pattern.

2. You must add the necessary ease to your measurements. The pattern contains all the necessary ease.

Compare Measurements

Note the difference between your measurements (plus ease) with those of the pattern (Figs. 61 and 62). Mark the necessary changes

Fig. 61

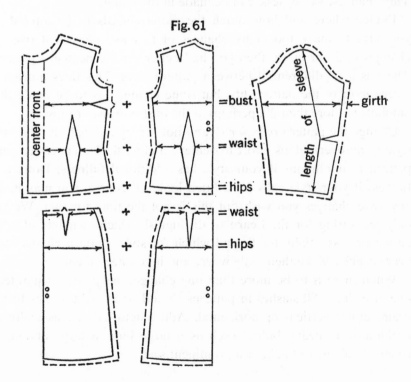

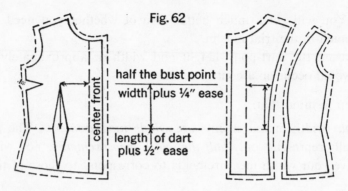

Fig. 62

center front

half the bust point
width plus ¼" ease

length of dart
plus ½" ease

and the amount right on the pattern. You may have to do a little arithmetic at this point but don't get involved in higher mathematics. Tiny changes, ¼" or less, can be made in the seams.

Decide where and how much the pattern needs to be altered. If you have to make too many changes or to make consistent over-all changes of 2" or more, then you had better get the next-size pattern. There is a 2" differential between pattern sizes. This does not apply where *most* of the pattern fits, but some change has to be made that amounts to more than 2", perhaps at the bust or waist or hips.

Change the pattern *only for fit* and not for style. Don't mutilate the style in an overzealous effort to achieve a close fit. Don't reduce your pattern to minimums if your style has additional fullness. Don't add fullness if your style calls for a fitted look. Of course, you may make any style changes you wish but this is not the time for that. We are only measuring for fit. Learn to distinguish which elements of your design are essentially for fit and which for style. Pattern changes are very specific. Make them only where and if you need them.

When there is to be more than one change, make each separately, one at a time. All slashes in patterns should be at right angles to the grain, either vertical or horizontal. Add length as well as width to accommodate heavy bulges such as a large bust, a large abdomen, round shoulders or back, or a prominent seat.

Slash and Spread

Changes within the pattern are made on the principle of slash and spread or its reverse, slash and overlap or tuck.

Patterns may be made larger or smaller in one of two ways. When the change is *equal* across the entire length or width, it is called a *balanced change* (Fig. 63a). When the *change is in one place only* —it is called a change for *circularity* (Fig. 63b).

Fig. 63

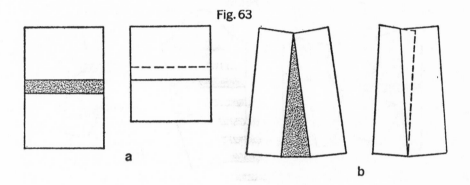

a   b

To make a pattern larger:

1. Draw a slash line at right angles to the grain where the change is to be made.

2. Slash and spread to the desired amount; equally for a balanced change, in one place only for circularity.

3. Insert lightweight paper or tissue paper in the spread area. (Old patterns are fine for this purpose). Fasten with pins or Scotch Tape.

To make a pattern smaller:

1. Draw a line at right angles to the grain where the change is to be made.

2. Slash and overlap or tuck to the desired amount; equally for a balanced change, in one place only for circularity.

3. Pin or Scotch-Tape to position.

Correct any jagged or broken lines which result from slashing, spreading, tucking, or overlapping.

Over-all (balanced) changes in length. This is how the principle of slash and spread or slash and overlap or tuck is applied to the pattern.

Fig. 64

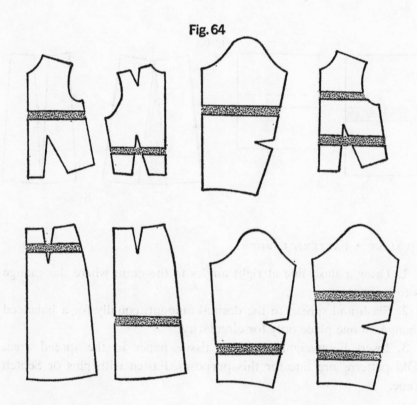

Changes may be made above or below the bust point, above or below the shoulder blades, above or below the hips, above or below the elbows or in both places (Fig. 64).

If the bottom of the pattern contains no style details, a pattern may be lengthened or shortened here, too (Fig. 65a).

In Fig. 65b the amount of fullness would be changed in addition to the change in length. In Fig. 65c the style detail would be destroyed by shortening at the bottom. In each case it would be better to make the change elsewhere on the pattern (broken lines).

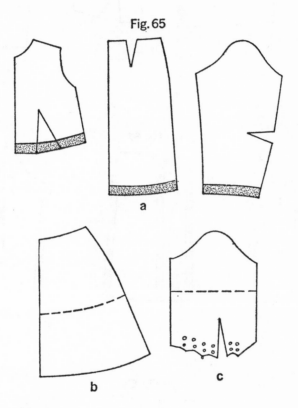

Fig. 65

Over-all (balanced) changes in width. Small changes may be made at center front, center back, side seams, or through the center of any pattern piece (Fig. 66).

Changes of ⅝″ or more distort the neckline and the armhole. When changes of ⅝″ or more are necessary divide the amount be-

Fig. 66

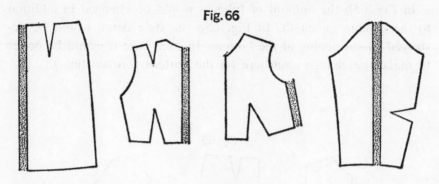

Fig. 67

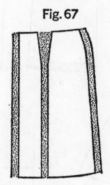
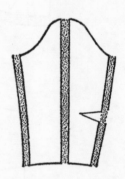

Fig. 68

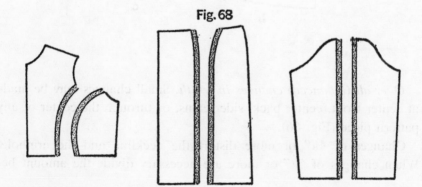

tween front, side, and center (Fig. 67). This changes the pattern piece proportionately while preserving the style line.

Width may also be added in the control seams (Fig. 68).

Changes in one place only (*circularity*). This principle may be applied anywhere on the pattern—the bodice, the skirt, the sleeve, at the neckline, the shoulder, or the armhole—just about any place in the pattern where this type of change is required.

A correction must be made at the center front or the center back. Each must be extended in a straight line for a new center front or back (Fig. 69a). An amount added or subtracted must be balanced by a similar amount added or subtracted at the other side of the

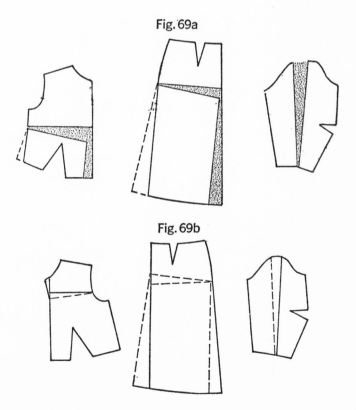

Fig. 69a

Fig. 69b

pattern (broken lines in Fig. 69a). Jagged lines which result from overlapping or tucking must be corrected (Fig. 69b).

Where length as well as width is needed as in a full bust, a heavy arm, abdomen, or seat:

Fig. 70

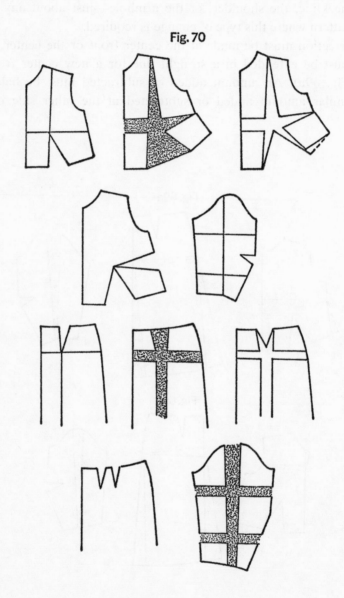

1. Draw a vertical as well as horizontal slash line.

2. Slash and spread in both directions.

3. Relocate the dart when necessary. If there is too much dart control for one dart, divide the control into two darts.

This type of additional fullness may be balanced, circular, or both. *When more ease is desired:*

Fig. 71

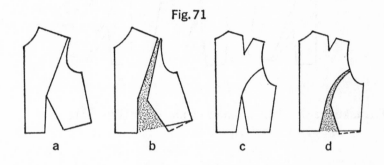

a   b   c   d

1. Draw a slash line from the shoulder point or the armhole (Fig. 71a or c).

2. Slash and spread to the amount of desired ease at the dart point (Fig. 71b or 71d).

3. Relocate the dart in the center of the spread. Correct the dart legs so they are the same length.

Use a slash line from the shoulder when more ease is desired across the chest as well as across the bust. Use the slash line from the armhole when you wish to preserve the fit across the chest and need the fullness only across the bust.

Ease may be added in similar fashion to the back.

Pattern changes at neck, shoulder, and armhole area are difficult to fit. It is also difficult to foretell the necessary pattern alterations because style is such an important element in this area. It is usually better to wait until the muslin fitting to determine what alterations need to be made. If you are fairly sure of the changes, they can be made by the same slash-and-spread or slash-and-overlap method, as shown in the illustrations that follow.

To make the neck larger or smaller (Fig. 72).

Fig. 72

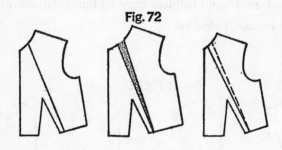

To make the shoulder broader or narrower (Fig. 73).

Fig. 73

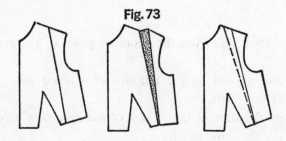

To raise the shoulder or lower it at the armhole (Fig. 74).

Fig. 74

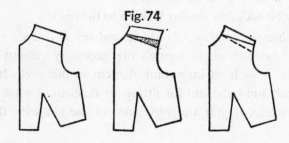

To raise or lower the shoulder at the neckline (Fig. 75).

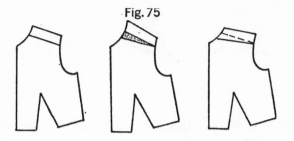

Fig. 75

When the shoulder is raised or lowered, a corresponding change must be made at the underarm or the sleeve will not fit the new armhole (Fig. 76). If the new armhole is right for you, then alter the sleeve to fit it.

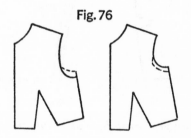

Fig. 76

To make the pattern broader or narrower across the chest as well as the shoulder (Fig. 77).

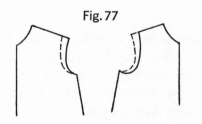

Fig. 77

To make the sleeve cap longer or shorter (Fig. 78).

Fig. 78

To make the sleeve cap broader and flatter and the sleeve longer and wider (Fig. 79).

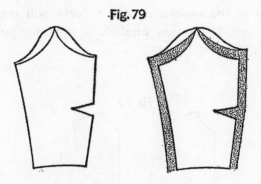

Fig. 79

Corresponding changes must be made on any part of the pattern which joins an altered piece—facings, collar, cuffs, sleeves, side seams, waistline, and so on.

THE TRIAL MUSLIN

No garment of any beauty or value "springs full grown from the brow of Minerva." Much thought, much study, much preparation, much experimentation, much work, and considerable time and money goes into each creation. When you buy a beautiful dress or suit or coat, all of this has been done for you.

The designer, the stylist, the pattern maker, the fabric expert, the dressmaker or tailor—just about everyone concerned with the production of the finished garment—provide the time and talent to achieve that certain perfection. All you have to do is try it on, examine yourself in a mirror, look at the price tag, and decide whether it is for you.

When you sew for yourself, you have to go through this entire procedure yourself since you are designer, sample maker, fabric expert, dressmaker, tailor, and eventual consumer. You alone must make all the judgments. You must visualize that fabric in that style for that use on you. This is not always easy to do. A muslin trial run is an invaluable help in determining how the garment will shape up on you (literally).

Ten Reasons Why You Should Make a Trial Muslin

1. You can see very quickly whether the style is for you.

2. You will have a clearer idea of how the shaping and style details will co-ordinate with the fabric.

3. You can decide what pattern alterations are necessary.

4. You can familiarize yourself with the construction details of the garment.

5. You can determine the most effective placement of the surface design of your fabric; where to place a motif, a plaid, a check, a stripe.

6. Knowing which pattern pieces go together saves possible errors in layout and cutting.

7. You will be able to observe how the grain falls in sleeves, collars, yokes, pockets, etc. You will get a good idea of what to expect in the direction of weave, stripes, checks, plaids.

8. You can decide how and where to interface or underline the garment to sustain the line of the design.

9. If you make your trial muslin before you purchase your fabric, you will have a truer idea of how much fabric you will need.

10. A coat or suit represents a major investment. Muslin is cheap.

Doesn't it make sense to do your experimenting in inexpensive muslin rather than in your expensive, usually limited yardage? Once you've cut into your fine fabric, your opportunities for change are very limited.

Do it always? Use your judgment. If you are sure of a particular style and certain of its fit, then don't bother with the trial muslin. But if you have any uncertainty about it or if it is a very special garment of very expensive fabric, then by all means, play it safe. Make a trial muslin.

Approximate Your Muslin in Yardage and Weight

Use muslin in a weight closest to the weight of your fabric, that is, light, medium, or heavy. While it is true that the garment fabric will hang somewhat differently from the muslin, you still do get a very good idea of the style effect. If your fabric is soft, use a light-weight muslin; if it is medium weight, use a medium-weight muslin; if it is heavy, use a heavy or firm muslin. (Sheer fabrics and draped designs can be tested in voile or batiste.)

Muslin generally comes in a 35" width. Most fabrics are wider than this. The yardage suggested on your pattern envelope will most likely not do for the muslin. Estimate the amount you will need for your suit or coat. In general 3½ to 4 yards will be sufficient for a suit and 4 to 5 yards for a coat.

Roughly Simulate the Surface Design of the Fabric

Stripes, plaids, unusual checks, design motifs may be roughly simulated with colored pencil on the muslin. Don't spend the day duplicating your fabric. Do just enough quick sketching to locate and indicate the essential lines or shapes. If you do this, you can readily observe any directional flow of the design, the interruption to the continuity of the fabric design when stitched in darts and seams, and the seams which require matching. This is an invaluable aid in the placement of the pattern on the fabric.

A Few Preliminaries

Treat the muslin as if it were $150-a-yard vicuña or some rare brocade. Before you cut into this "precious" fabric, a little preliminary study is necessary.

1. Examine the layout chart. Even if you can't follow the chart for the trial muslin you will get an idea of the placement and the relative position of the pattern pieces.

2. Examine the pattern pieces. Select those pieces which are necessary for the trial muslin. You will not need facings, pockets, or trimming details unless they are essential for the completion of a pattern unit. Use the under collar only. Pattern companies have slightly different pattern symbols. Make sure you understand those on your pattern.

3. Read through the instruction sheet. More than the picture on the envelope, the instructions reveal what the designer had in mind and how he hoped to get his effect. This bird's-eye view is important to your understanding of what's involved in the construction. If you merely follow the directions one step at a time you are working blindly without a full realization of your goal.

Prepare the Pattern

1. Press out the wrinkles in the pattern with a warm iron.

2. Extend the grain lines on the pattern to the entire length of the pattern. On most patterns this marking is too short for accurate pinning.

3. Make the necessary pattern alterations.

4. Decide how you will lay out the pattern on the muslin. Plan your own layout chart. Start with the largest pieces and fit in the smaller ones. Observe the grain lines.

Prepare the Muslin

1. Establish the horizontal grain by tearing the muslin at the top and bottom of the fabric.

2. Make a lengthwise or crosswise fold. Pin the torn edges together and the selvages together.

3. Dampen and press into a perfect rectangle.

4. Line up the selvages with the straight edge of the cutting surface.

Lay Out the Pattern* on the Muslin

1. Follow your own layout chart. Since muslin is inexpensive, you don't have to save every inch of it. Make the layout easy for yourself. Save your energy for the more important operations.

2. Lay out the pattern with the grain lines parallel to the selvage.

3. Pin the pattern between the seam line and the cutting line about 2″ apart.

4. Mark generous seam allowances in any area where you suspect further changes may need to be made.

Cut Out the Muslin

1. Cut out the muslin using sharp shears or scissors.

2. Don't bother to cut out the notches beyond the cutting line. This takes too much time.

Mark the Muslin

Transfer *all* the pattern markings to the right side of the muslin, using dressmaker's carbon paper and a tracing wheel. Use a ruler for the straight lines. Trace the curved lines freehand following the pattern. Mark the stitching lines, the placement of buttonholes and pockets, all △s, □s, and ○s. Be sure to mark the center front and center back. Cut the notches. You may number them as they are numbered on the pattern if that will help you to put the pieces together. Take every bit of help which the designer and patternmaker put there for your use. The markings indicate how this puzzle which is a pattern should go together easily.

* See Chapter IV for complete instructions.

Put the Muslin Together

In our trial muslin we are trying to test the effect of the finished garment. This will take a little doing since we are not going to stitch the muslin together. Pinning is much simpler, gives us the information we want and leaves us free to make any alterations quickly.

We will assume that all major changes have been made in the pattern and only minor adjustments need to be made in the muslin to refine the fit.

Regard the side with the pattern markings as the right side of the muslin. All markings should be clearly visible as you work with the right side outside. Lapping the darts and seams will give a more exact picture of the appearance when finished than pinning the darts and seams together as if for stitching. It also makes it easy to make any adjustments.

Lap the darts by slashing one dart leg and lapping over the other. Pin along the stitching line. If by any chance the darts should need relocation, the slash can be repaired with Scotch Tape.

Lap the seams and pin the stitching lines. Ease where necessary. Clip all curved seams.

Lap and pin the under collar over the neckline matching the seam lines. Start at the front and work toward the center back. Lap the center back seams.

Lap the sleeves. In a set-in sleeve, put two rows of running stitches across the cap. Pull the cap into shape. Lap the cap seam over the armhole seam and pin.

Tentatively pin up all the hems.

It is not necessary to use the facings or the upper collar, to apply any trimmings, to make the pockets unless they are an unusual and essential part of the design.

The Muslin Fitting

By this time you've learned a great deal about this newest addition to your wardrobe. And, you haven't even tried it on yet. You've discovered what it will really look like. That sketch on the pattern envelope may not have done it justice. Or, that glamorized photograph in the fashion book may have been deceiving. You did actually put all those pieces together as the instruction sheet directed you. You got a preview of the intricacies of construction. Any tendency to botch has been inflicted on the muslin. You have a very good idea of how your fabric design will locate on the garment. You've observed where the grain falls on the fronts, backs, sleeves, collar, and all the extras. It has been a good test of your power to visualize and your ability to follow the instruction sheet.

Now let us see how it fits!

Suggested Sequence for Fittings

All fitting is done from the right side. Center front and center back must be clearly marked. All openings must be pinned closed. No changes are made at center-front openings. The front extensions, the collar, the lapels, the facings are all involved in pattern changes too difficult for a nonprofessional.

Bodice or jacket

1. Pin the center front closed. Match the neckline and the top button.

2. Pin the shoulder and side seams tentatively. Fit with the appropriate shoulder pads if they are to be used in the finished garment.

3. Check the vertical and horizontal grains.

4. Check the ease.

5. Check the dart control.

6. Correct the shoulder and side seams.

7. Check the neckline.

8. Mark the waistline if necessary.

9. Set the approximate length of the jacket.

Sleeves

1. Set the sleeve cap starting at the shoulder.

2. Check the grain.

3. Pin in the underarm seam where it falls on the bodice.

4. Check the elbow dart for position and amount.

5. Set the approximate length of the sleeve.

6. When the garment is removed mark the armhole seam on bodice and sleeve. Mark the shoulder, front, and back notches.

Skirt

1. Pin the center front and center back in place at the waistline.

2. Pin the hips at the side seams checking the grain.

3. Fit the area between the hips and the waist; check the dart control.

4. Pin the side seams.

5. Determine the waistline and mark it.

6. Set the approximate length.

The hemline of skirt, jacket, and sleeve are set finally when the rest of the garment is completed.

What to Look for in the Muslin Fitting

Is the style right? When you slip your muslin on, your first impression and your first concern is for style. Make allowance for the difference between the muslin and the fabric. But you can tell pretty quickly whether the style is a good one for you. Should you decide it isn't, it is just as well to know it now before expending any more time, effort, and valuable fabric; get a new pattern. If it could be good with some changes, muslin is a fine fabric to experiment with. If all it needs is some minor alterations, these can be easily made. If it is just plain beautiful—lucky you!

Study the muslin for line, proportion, fullness; shoulders, neckline, collar; set of sleeves. Decide whether you will keep all the style details or eliminate some of them. Even if the style does carry a big-name designer label, some changes may be indicated to make it right for you. Monsieur Y and Madame Z would undoubtedly have made some slight changes (consistent with the design) to suit you if you were a private client. You do not have to accept every last little detail in the pattern envelope.

Tied up closely with style is the question of size. Is there too much fullness for you or too little? Is this a question of style or of size? Perhaps a smaller or larger pattern in the same style would be better. Perhaps only a little more or a little less ease will do the trick.

Check the vertical and horizontal grain as directed earlier in this chapter. Check the shaping and the silhouette seams, too.

Don't overfit. Make allowances for the thickness and the texture of your fabric. This is a trial fitting. Later fittings can be more precise.

How to Deal with a Few of the Most Common Problems in Fitting

If the garment keeps *sliding back,* the back neckline is too short and there is not enough length over the shoulders. To correct this, add ½″ to ¾″ to the entire back shoulder seam. This will add length to the back neckline and length over the upper shoulder blades. This added length should bring the shoulder seam into the proper position.

If the skirt *bulges at the dart point,* there is too much dart control. Make smaller darts or eliminate them entirely. Shape the skirt at the side seam.

Wrinkles that appear in either the skirt or the bodice indicate one of several things: the grain is not right, more dart control is needed, or a nearby seam is not in the right place.

For wrinkles, excess or drooping fabric: Check the grain first and adjust as directed. Release the seam involved, smooth out the wrinkles. Push the excess fabric into a seam; the right seam will preserve the position of the grain.

If the grain is correct and wrinkles still persist: More dart control is necessary. (A wrinkle is an uncontrolled dart.) Smooth or push the excess material into any existing dart or make a new dart where it seems necessary.

Smooth out the fabric while adjusting the grain and repin the seam in the proper position.

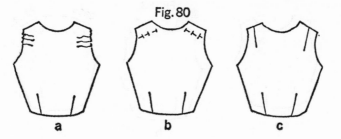

Fig. 80

Correction for wrinkles appearing in the upper armhole (Fig. 80a) —push into the shoulder seam (Fig. 80b) or make shoulder darts (Fig. 80c).

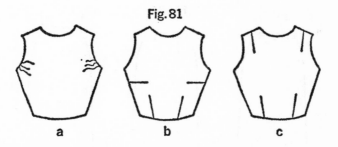

Fig. 81

Correction for wrinkles appearing in lower armhole (81a)—push into an underarm dart (Fig. 81b) or a shoulder dart (Fig. 81c).

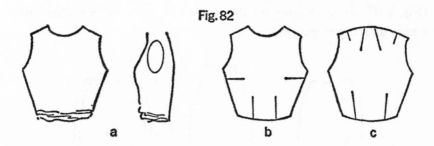

Fig. 82

Correction for wrinkling or "hiking" up at waistline (Fig. 82a)— make a larger waistline dart and/or create an underarm dart (Fig. 82b) in front. Make a larger waistline dart and/or create a neckline dart in back (Fig. 82c).

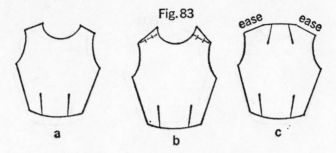

Fig. 83

Correction for a neckline which stands away from the neck (particularly the back) (Fig. 83a)—adjust the shoulder seam at the neckline (83b) or make a neckline dart (83c).

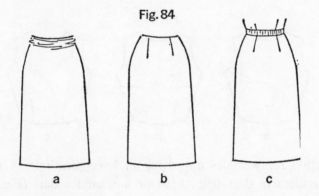

Fig. 84

Correction for wrinkling at the waistline (Fig. 84a)—more darts (Fig. 84b) more shaping on the side seam, reset the waistline using a tape measure (Fig. 84c).

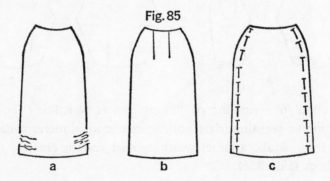

Fig. 85

Correction for wrinkling in the lower part of the skirt (Fig. 85a)
—more dart control (Fig. 85b) or reset side seam (Fig. 85c).

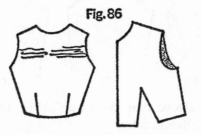

Fig. 86

Correction for pulling, drawing, binding across the chest or across
the back—add more ease in armhole (Fig. 86).

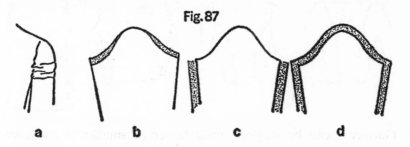

Fig. 87

a   b   c   d

Correction for sleeve cap that strains or wrinkles (Fig. 87a)—add
more width at cap (Fig. 87b) or side seam (Fig. 87c) or both (Fig.
87d).

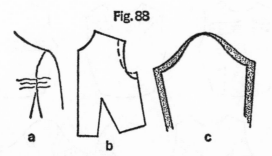

Fig. 88

a   b   c

Correction for tight armhole and strain across the sleeve (Fig. 88a)
—drop the armhole, add width at the bodice armhole (Fig. 88b),
add width to sleeve cap, add width to sleeve seam (Fig. 88c).

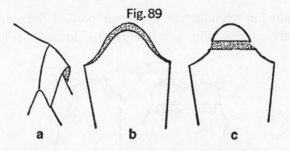

Fig. 89

a   b   c

Correction for sleeve that "hikes up" (Fig. 89a)—add length to sleeve cap (Figs. 89b and 89c).

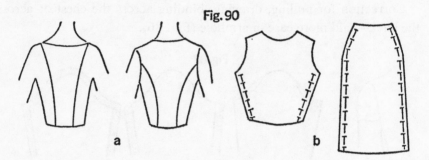

Fig. 90

a   b

Garments can be shaped, made larger or smaller in the control seams (Fig. 90a). Garments can be taken in or let out on side seams (Fig. 90b).

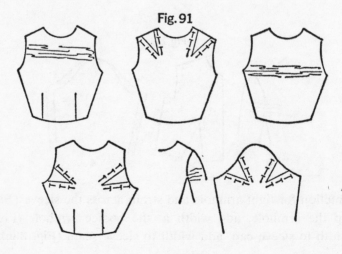

Fig. 91

Correction for pulling, drawing, or binding—slash the muslin, spread to the necessary amount, and pin in an insert of muslin (Fig. 91).

Seams May Be Repositioned

While the placement may be shifted, the over-all length or width remains the same. What is taken off one place is added to the other. For instance:

Fig. 92

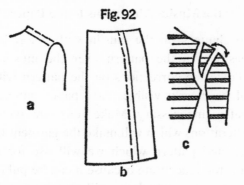

When the shoulder seam is moved forward, the front is shortened while the back is lengthened (Fig. 92a).

When the side seam of a skirt is adjusted, what is taken off the front may be added to the back and vice versa (Fig. 92b).

When the armhole seam is moved in to narrow the shoulder, the sleeve cap must be lengthened a corresponding amount in order to preserve the proper placement of the grain (Fig. 92c).

Displacement is not discarding. In pattern making there is a kind of law of compensation. You just do not discard little parts of the pattern. You put them in another place to compensate for the change.

Fit or Fake

Keep a balanced look where it will show. Fit those deviations from the standard where they won't show.

No one stands like a little tin soldier all the time. No one sits rigidly forever like an Egyptian statue. Your varying positions and movements produce an informal body balance disguising its asymmetry. So, in some respects, it doesn't really matter if both sides are not identical. For instance, shoulders may be fitted for slope. In doing so they appear symmetrical though in reality they are not. Not to do so would make them appear different. On the other hand, shoulders must be made the same width even if they are not, to present a balanced look. To make each the width it may actually be would make you look lopsided or unsymmetrical.

Fit where you can. Fake where necessary.

Transfer the Muslin Alterations to the Paper Pattern

Mark all the changes on the muslin with colored pencil so they can be seen easily. Pin the pattern over the muslin matching the center fronts. Trace the corrections on the pattern with colored pencil so they will be clearly visible. Add paper patches if necessary. Trim away what is unnecessary. Make your new pattern a complete record of any alterations which will make the garment fit you.

It is the corrected pattern which we will use for the layout and cutting. Muslin is too inaccurate because it can be pulled out of shape. It is the corrected pattern which we will also use for the interfacings, underlinings, interlinings, and linings.

When it comes to fitting, most sewers are hampered by fear. Like Chicken-Little and her friends in the old children's story, they expect the sky to fall on their heads should they have the temerity to move a dart or seam. Fitting is like sculpturing. It creates a three-dimensional form. Just as you can push clay around until you get what you want, so you can manipulate your fabric until you get the fit you want. Don't be grim. This is not a matter of life or death. The worst that can happen is that you may spoil a length of fabric. There are always tempting new fabrics. It is more important to overcome your fear. Only then will you be released to do your best work.

CHAPTER IV

Tailoring Tips

There are those (we've all heard of them) who boast of being able to whip up a garment in the morning and wear it to a luncheon the same day. Hm-mm-mmm.

The truth of the matter is that hastily put together garments look it. Beginners often work this way because they don't know any better. Haven't you noticed that the longer you sew, the longer it takes you to make a garment that satisfies you? Experience makes one more demanding. One wouldn't want to dispense with the "instant" altogether. When I am in a great rush I use the "instant" foods in the freezer and on the pantry shelf. They work. However, my "instant" meals are certainly not comparable to my gourmet meals which take time, and thought, and work.

So it is with sewing. Of course there are blouses and skirts and simple dresses which can be put together quickly. These are hardly the clothes you wear when you want to make an impression (which should be just about every time someone looks at you). And while it is conceivable that you might get away with speed sewing in some simple item, this kind of workmanship would never do in a good coat or suit or ensemble. Home sewers have a tendency to make too much, too quickly. (The temptations are very great—just a few yards of material and a few hours at the sewing machine.) The quality and character of their sewing would be greatly improved if they could be persuaded to make fewer things but make each important. Making clothes this way takes time, and thought, and work.

PREPARING THE FABRIC FOR CUTTING

Grain Is All

You will recall in our discussion of how cloth is woven (Chapter II) that: the lengthwise and crosswise yarns are woven at right angles to each other, making the cloth rectangular in shape; the cloth hangs with the grain; it will hang with the grain regardless of the way it is cut.

The designer utilizes this natural "hang" of the fabric in his design. The patternmaker who provides the plan for construction designates on each pattern piece the position of the grain which will achieve the designer's intent. You must observe these pattern markings religiously if your finished garment is to look as it was intended.

Sometimes in the finishing process cloth is pulled "off-grain," that is, it is pulled out of its rectangular form. To complicate matters, most sales people cut fabric in what they are sure is a straight line. It may well be so but the fabric itself is off-grain.

Fabric tears with the grain. Some fabrics tear easily without damage. If the fabric can be torn, ask the sales person to tear it. If it can't be torn, supervise the cutting on-grain. This will not endear you to the one behind the counter for it does take more time and care. It may even mean losing some inches of the fabric. But if everyone were to insist on correct cutting none would be lost. Once the grain is established in a bolt of cloth all subsequent cutting can be accurate.

How to Establish the Proper Grain of the Fabric

To assure the correct cutting, stitching, and fitting of your garment, you must make certain that the vertical and horizontal grains are in a rectangular position. When possible, tear the fabric horizontally, if the sales person has not already done this for you. This will give the horizontal grain. When the fabric does not tear easily or if tearing will harm it in any way, pull a crosswise thread and cut along this drawn thread (Fig. 93).

Fig. 93

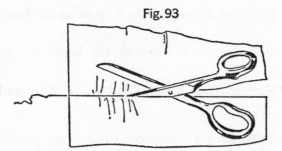

Don't try to do the whole width of the fabric with one pull. Pull a short distance and cut; pull a little more and cut. Work in small sections until you are all the way across. When you can pull a crosswise yarn clear across the width of your fabric you have established the crosswise grain. Both ends of the fabric must be straightened. You can see how it is possible to lose some inches of the material simply by straightening the grain.

Fabrics which have a prominent yarn, rib, or line whether woven or printed are easy to handle. Cut along the line across the width of the fabric.

The selvages are the vertical grain of the fabric. Do *not* cut these away. They are useful in determining the proper placement of the pattern on the cloth. Sometimes they may be used as finished edges which indeed they are. If they should be so tight as to make the material pucker, clip them every so often to release the strain but do not cut them away.

Fig. 94

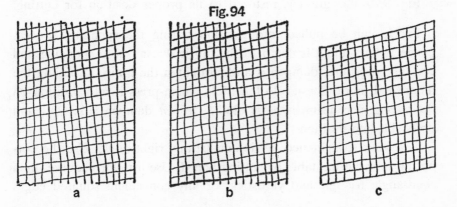

a   b   c

Fig. 94a Fabric as it is cut. It looks rectangular but actually it is off-grain.

Fig. 94b Pull threads to establish the horizontal grain at both ends.

Fig. 94c Now the grain is accurate but the fabric no longer looks rectangular.

Sometimes after the grain has been straightened, the fabric appears at an angle. Perhaps it seems a little strange to start with a perfectly good rectangle and end up with this oddity. As long as you have the true horizontal grains at either end and the selvages, all is well. The fabric just needs a little coaxing into the proper position.

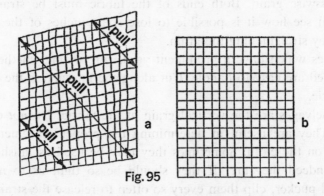

Fig. 95

Fig. 95a Pull in the opposite direction. This is a bias pull.

Fig. 95b The grain is restored to its proper position for cutting.

Fabric can be pulled into position during the sponging process (page 135) while it is damp. If the fabric doesn't need sponging and can take moisture, dampen it and straighten the grain. If pulling the dampened fabric doesn't do the trick, steam-press it into position on the wrong side, using a press cloth. Do *not* dampen silk. Pull and press silk into position.

Test your straightened fabric against any right angle. Use the corner of your cutting table or cutting board. Use a tailor's square, or a right-angle triangle and yardstick, or any convenient squared edges to make sure you have re-established the grain in its original rectangular position.

Everything that goes into the making of a garment must be cut on-grain. The grain must also be established in interfacings, underlingings, interlinings, and linings.

How to Sponge Woolen Fabric

Fabrics marked "ready-to-sew," "sponged," "ready-for-the-needle," "London sponged," "London shrunk," or in some similar way, do not need to be sponged. This has already been done at the factory. All other woolen fabrics should be sponged.

Sponging is only *partial* shrinking of the fabric—just enough to prevent disaster when pressed or dry-cleaned. Guard against excessive shrinking which destroys the beauty and finish of the wool.

Steam-pressing is *not sufficient* for sponging wool. The easiest way to sponge wool is to let a tailor do it for you. However, a very good job can be done at home if you follow these directions:

1. Straighten the grain.

2. Fold the fabric in half lengthwise with the right sides together. Pin or baste together both torn edges and both selvages.

3. Make a preshrinking cloth at least 40″ wide to accommodate the width of the folded fabric and long enough to cover all the fabric. An old sheet will do or two old sheets sewn together or a length of washable cotton bought just for this purpose.

4. Wet the sheet and wring out the excess moisture. It should be damp but not dripping wet.

5. Place the fabric on the sheet in a squared position. Smooth out any wrinkles so that the material is absolutely flat (Fig. 96a).

6. Roll the wool and preshrinking cloth into a cylinder (Fig. 96b). Rolling over a covered cardboard cylinder avoids creasing. Or, fold the fabric carefully into sections from both ends to meet at the center (Fig. 96c). These folds should be loose to avoid sharp creases.

7. Cover the roll or the folds completely with a Turkish towel, brown paper, or a plastic bag (the kind that comes from the cleaner does very well). This prevents the outer layers from drying while the

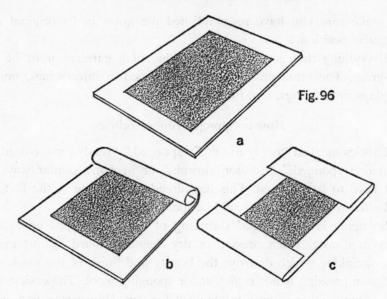

Fig. 96

inner layers remain damp, making for an uneven absorption of moisture.

8. Let stand for several hours. Most tailoring experts say three to four hours are sufficient. The Wool Bureau, Inc., recommends six to eight hours for light woolens, longer for heavier ones. Perhaps the tailoring experts are afraid that amateurs may overshrink or mat the fabric. It might be wise to peep every so often to see how the wool is coming along.

9. When the moisture has been absorbed, unroll the wool. Lay it out flat to dry. Smooth out any wrinkles. Make certain the grain is correct. If you don't have a large enough flat surface for drying, hang the wool over a door or shower rod which has been well padded with Turkish towels. Turn the wool once during the drying process as if you were drying a sweater. Wool should dry naturally. Pressing fabric dry may make it stiff or push the grain out of the position we've taken such pains to set right.

10. If it is necessary to remove any wrinkling after the wool is dry, press it on the wrong side, using a press cloth. Press with the grain. Press to within 1″ of the center fold. Do not press the fold.

Open the fabric and press the center section. See Chapter VII, Pressing Problems, for the correct way to press your fabric. If correct pressing flattens or dulls the surface of the fabric leaving press marks which show, this may unfortunately be the nature of the fabric. Sad as it may be, perhaps it would be better to remove the finish now before cutting and sewing, since it is bound to happen later.

Preshrink Everything That Goes Inside

Everything that goes into the inside of the garment with the exception of the silk lining should also be preshrunk. Establish the horizontal grain first.

Interfacings unless otherwise noted should be preshrunk. Roll in a damp preshrinking cloth and let stand for several hours until the moisture is absorbed. Allow to dry naturally. Press when dry. Most interfacings become very stiff if pressed wet.

Interlinings of lamb's wool are treated the same as wool.

Cotton fabric used as *underlining* or *interfacing* should be washed and pressed.

Caution—do *not* wet or wash silk linings.

Cotton tape—immerse in water. Let it stand until it has thoroughly absorbed the moisture. Allow it to dry.

Shrinking Cotton or Linen to Be Used for the Garment

Shrinkage-resistant finishes added to cottons and linens reduce shrinking to a minimum. However, even the slight shrinkage which occurs may affect the fit, particularly if it is a close one. Since these fabrics will need frequent washing or dry-cleaning, it would be wise to preshrink them before cutting. Use lukewarm water for white or light-colored fabrics, cold water for the dark ones. The use of a fabric softener in the water helps preserve the finish and makes them easier to iron.

1. Establish the grain.
2. Run the fabric through an automatic washer or allow it to soak thoroughly for several hours.

3. Spin-dry or squeeze out the excess moisture. Wringing or twisting produces wrinkles and creases.

4. Hang over a line or rod which has been well padded with Turkish towels. Smooth out all wrinkles.

5. Make sure the horizontal and vertical grains are in the right position.

6. Allow the fabric to drip dry.

7. Iron when almost dry. (See Chapter VII for pressing directions.)

PREPARE THE PATTERN FOR CUTTING

Start with the corrected pattern whether the corrections were arrived at by tracing from the trial muslin or your basic pattern or simply by measurement.

Select all the pattern pieces necessary for cutting the garment. Fold the unnecessary pieces and replace them in the envelope. Group the pattern pieces—those needed for the coat, jacket, or dress, those for the lining, those for the interlining, those for the interfacings. Use each group as you have need for it.

If the pattern is wrinkled, press it flat with a warm iron.

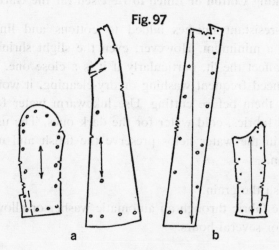

Fig. 97

a   b

Cut off all the unnecessary margins. It is easier to cut beside the paper pattern than through it, particularly heavy woolens. (Sheer fabrics are an exception.)

Extend the grain lines to the entire length of the pattern piece (Fig. 97b). Theoretically, measuring in two places should establish the vertical grain of the pattern parallel to the selvage of the fabric. However, fabrics have been known to slide out of position on the cutting board. Long pattern pieces, coats for instance, need the added precaution of long grain lines for accurate pinning.

The grain line on most commercial patterns is inadequate (Fig. 97a). An extended grain line (Fig. 97b) assures accuracy.

When a pattern piece needs to be used more than once or reversed, it is helpful to trace and cut out an extra one. This is a great advantage in a difficult layout (plaids or diagonal weaves), a tight layout (just making it by a hair'sbreadth), and when a difference in the length or width of your fabric means departing from the suggested layout.

Seam-Roll Allowance

Whenever there are two thicknesses of cloth, an upper and a lower, the seam which joins them is hidden on the under surface. To accomplish this an extra amount is added to the seam allowance of the upper thickness to permit the seam to roll under. This seam roll appears in collars, lapels, cuffs, welts, flaps, pockets, and facings.

Add to the length and the width of the upper thickness. Do *not* change the pattern where it joins the garment. For instance, add to the outer edges (style line) of the collar but not at the neck edge (Fig. 98a); around the outer edge of the cuff but not where it joins the sleeve (Fig. 98b).

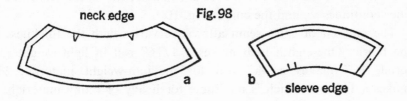

neck edge   Fig. 98

a   b   sleeve edge

For a facing which becomes a lapel, add to the entire outer edge. Use the extra allowance on the upper lapel to the collar break. From the break down the seam roll changes direction. It is now the front edge of the garment which needs the extra seam allowance for the seam roll.

Fig. 99a How the finished garment will look with no joining seams visible from the right side.

Fig. 99b Lapel flipped up showing the seam roll on the under surface of the lapel—no visible seam below the break. The garment buttons at the break.

Fig. 99c The facing which becomes the lapel. No seam shows on the lapel above the break—the seam roll is visible on the under surface below the break.

Fig. 99

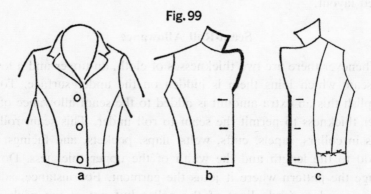

a   b   c

If the lower edge of the jacket is rounded, this extra seam allowance continues around the curve (Fig. 100).

The amount of extra seam allowance varies with the thickness of the fabric. One-eighth inch makes a 1/16″ roll in light-weight material, ¼″ makes a ⅛″ roll for medium-weight material, ½″ makes a ¼″ roll which is advisable for heavy or bulky materials.

This principle and these allowances work wherever in the garment there is an upper and under thickness of fabric.

Fig. 100

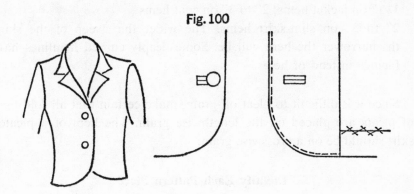

Seams and Hems

Add ½″ extra seam allowance from waistline to the length of the placket opening on that skirt seam where a zipper will be placed (Fig. 101).

Fig. 101

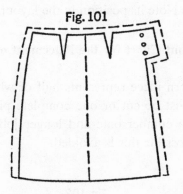

Seam allowances are generally ½″ or ⅝″ on medium-weight fabrics. Sheer fabrics need less since they are usually trimmed close to the stitching line. Heavier fabrics may need more, particularly if they have a tendency to ravel.

Patterns generally allow hems of:

1½″ on jacket sleeves, 2″ on coat sleeves
1½″ on jacket hems, 2″ to 3″ on coat hems
2″ to 3″ on slim-skirt hems. The wider the sweep of the skirt, the narrower the hem will be. Some deeply curved hemlines have facings instead of hems.

Since it is difficult to pleat off-grain, make certain that all fold lines of pleats are placed on the lengthwise grain. The hem of a pleated skirt should be on a crosswise grain.

Identify Each Pattern Piece

All pattern pieces are identified in some way. Since each pattern company uses different markings, different identifications, different pattern symbols, it is well to study the chart which accompanies the pattern. Sometimes the pattern pieces are labelled by letter—A, B, C, D, E, F, etc.—sometimes by the sequence in which they are used—1, 2, 3, 4, 5, etc.—sometimes by name—front, back, side front, etc. Identify each piece. Note its position in the layout.

Examine the Layout Chart for the Placement of the Pattern Pieces

Usually the pattern piece represents half of what is needed. Therefore, two halves must be cut or one complete piece on a fold of the fabric. It is a more cumbersome and longer job to cut one piece at a time. Wherever possible this is avoided.

Fig. 102   fold

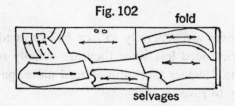

selvages

When cutting by twos or on a fold, it makes no difference whether the printed side of the pattern is up or down (Fig. 102). Some pattern companies use shaded areas to indicate that the pattern is placed face down.

Your clue to the placement of the pattern on the fabric is the shape of the piece and the position of the notches. Note the position of the notches to indicate when the pattern is reversed (Fig. 103).

Fig. 103

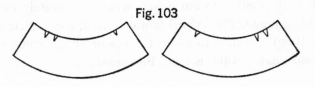

Dotted lines mean that the piece is either used on a fold or used a second time (Fig. 104).

Fig. 104

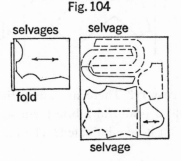

When the pattern piece is shown extending beyond the edge of the fabric on a folded edge, this means to cut one in this amount of space after the other pieces have been cut and the folded piece of cloth is opened out. Be careful that you note the grain line on the cloth before the surrounding pieces are cut away or you will have the trouble of re-establishing the grain in this piece (Fig. 105).

Fig. 105

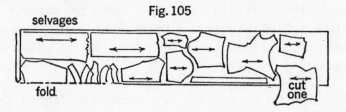

Often the layout is easier if you use a whole pattern rather than a half. Trace the other half and Scotch-Tape it to the original piece (Fig. 106a). Use the entire pattern when cutting on the bias (Fig. 106b). It is impossible to cut a bias section accurately on a fold of fabric. When diagonally striped fabric is used, a complete under collar (Fig. 106c) will help to avoid the mismatching which results frequently when half a collar is used (Fig. 106d).

Fig. 106

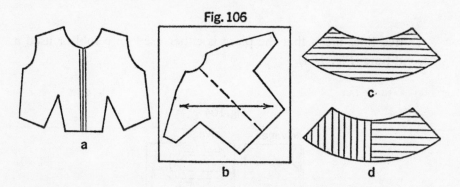

Are all seams necessary? There are many times when one would prefer not to cut into a beautiful fabric for a seam which has no apparent advantage. Can it be eliminated? The answer is "Yes, in some cases."

Two adjacent pattern pieces may be joined as one, thereby eliminating the seam IF:

1. the edges are on straight grain
2. it is not a shaping seam
3. the fabric is wide enough and long enough to accommodate the newly created pattern piece
4. there is sufficient material for the necessary new layout

Fig. 107

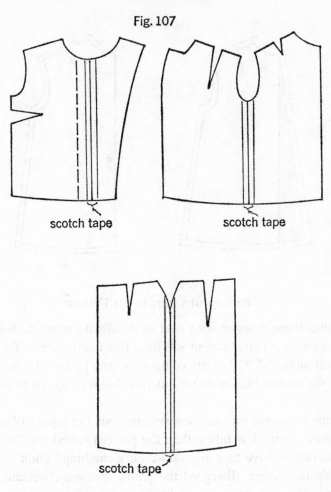

scotch tape   scotch tape

scotch tape

To join two adjacent pattern pieces:

Lap the seam lines. Pin or Scotch-Tape together (Fig. 107).

To alter a flared pattern so that the center may be placed on a fold:

1. Cut off the pattern at the center line eliminating the flare (Fig. 108a).

2. Use the center line as a fold of fabric (Fig. 108b).

Fig. 108

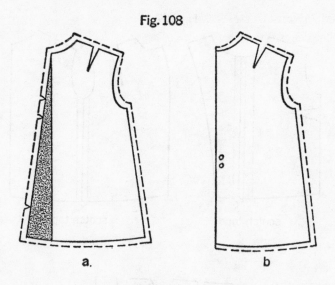

a.   b

The Layout Chart in the Pattern

Breathes there a sewer with soul so dead who never to herself has said, "I can do a better layout job than this chart shows. This wastes too much material"? Pattern companies are guilty of some of the charges we sewers hurl at them but this doesn't happen to be one of them.

Perhaps you have on occasion sweated out the layout of a pattern on a remnant with less fabric than the pattern called for. But confess now, didn't you have to compromise on something? Didn't you have to modify the design, disregard the grain, shorten, eliminate, or supplement with some other material?

The layout chart presents the best arrangement of the pattern on a particular width of fabric with strict respect for how the garment is intended to hang from smallest to largest piece. Considerable experimenting was done before deciding on this particular layout. It will save a lot of figuring if you accept the pattern company's suggestions.

Of course variations are possible. After all, yours is a custom-made job. Your fabric may be wider, your figure requirements less. The garment may have been shortened. Perhaps you are using a contrasting collar and cuffs or facing. You may get away with less fabric in a modified layout. But even so, use the layout chart as a model for placing the pieces and possible dovetailing.

Devising Your Own Layout Chart

Should you wish to work out your own layouts, it is a good idea to keep on hand several lengths of wrapping paper cut to standard widths of fabric—35″, 39″, 44″, 54″. Have them long enough to test the entire length necessary for the design. Mark the selvages. Use any fold of the paper—lengthwise or crosswise—which will provide the width for your pattern pieces. Cut two at a time wherever possible. Place the largest pieces first. Fit in the smaller pieces around the larger ones and in the spaces left along the fold and along the selvages. Fit shapes against each other, locking them wherever possible.

If the fabric you are planning to use has nap, pile, or a directional weave or print, arrange all the pattern pieces so they go in the same direction—neck to hem. The repeat of design units on prints, weaves, plaids, or stripes must match.

When you are satisfied with the layout, make a little working chart so you can duplicate this experimental layout on the fabric. This is also a good way to estimate the yardage for a particular design.

Using the Layout Chart in the Pattern

When you are using the layout chart in the pattern, select the one for the view of the style you are making, your size, and the correct width of fabric with or without nap.

Circle the chart with colored pencil so that your eye will light on it easily (Fig. 109).

Fig. 109

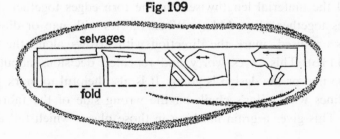

GETTING THE FABRIC IN POSITION FOR CUTTING

To facilitate your work, material may be folded in one of a number of ways. The right side of the fabric is folded inside to protect it and to make marking it easier.

Lengthwise fold (Fig. 110).

Fig. 110

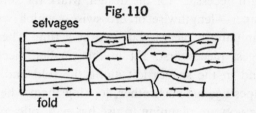

selvages

fold

Fig. 111

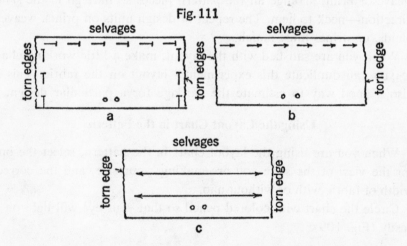

Fold the material lengthwise. Pin the torn edges together. Pin the selvages together (Fig. 111a). When fabrics with nap or directional designs are used, mark the direction with arrows along the selvage (Fig. 111b). This saves worry and repeated decisions about which way the nap or the design is going. It is also helpful to mark parallel grain lines with tailor's chalk on the wrong side of the fabric (Fig. 111c). This gives a grain marking in those places which fall away in cutting. If this is not done, the grain has to be re-established in these cut-away pieces.

Crosswise fold without nap.

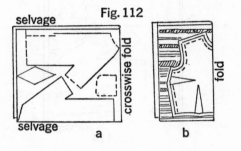

Fig. 112

This fold is used when the pattern pieces are too wide to fit half the width of the fabric. Kimono-sleeved garments, flared designs, circle skirts are laid out this way on the pattern (Fig. 112a). Striped fabric may be used on the crosswise grain for special design effects (Fig. 112b).

Fold the fabric with the full width across (Fig. 113). With right sides inside, pin the torn edges together. Pin the selvages together. Obviously this fold is not for naps, piles, or one-way weaves or prints which would end upside down on part of the garment.

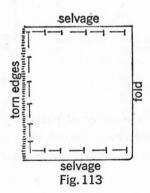

Fig. 113

Open double (two thicknesses of full-width fabric) for naps, piles, and one-way designs (Fig. 114).

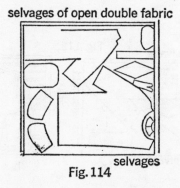

selvages of open double fabric

selvages
Fig. 114

Mark the direction of the nap along the selvages on the wrong side. Measure the required length of the material. Cut along this line (Fig. 115a). Place the right sides together with the nap going in the same direction (Fig. 115b). Pin.

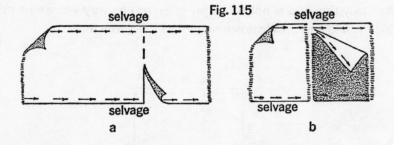

Fig. 115

selvage

selvage

selvage

selvage

a   b

Double fold: When a number of pattern pieces all need to be cut on a fold the fabric may be arranged on a double fold (Fig. 116a). Or the layout may call for a single width of fabric and a partial fold (Fig. 116b).

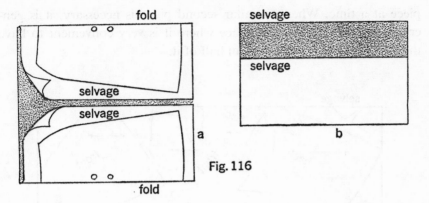

Fig. 116

Measure the required depth from the selvage to the fold line in a number of places. This makes the fold line parallel to the selvage. Mark the fold line in chalk, pins or basting. Fold on the fold line. Pin in place.

Fig. 117

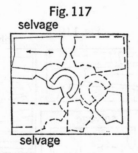

Full width: Sometimes a most economical use of the fabric requires each piece be cut individually on the full width of the fabric (Fig. 117). Asymmetric designs or patterns cut on the bias also call for fabric opened to the full width (Fig. 118). Line up the squared edges of the cloth with a corner of the cutting surface. Pin or weight the material in place. The fabric and the pattern are used right side up. Place the pattern as it will appear in the finished garment. Cut one piece at a time. When a similar second piece is necessary, it is generally reversed. This is one place where it is very convenient to have the complete pattern rather than half of it.

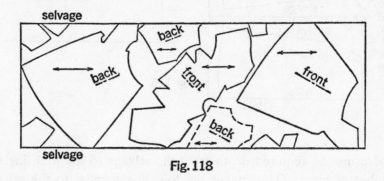

Fig. 118

Combinations: Frequently pattern layouts use a combination of folds. Part of the garment may be cut on one type, the rest on another. Here are a few examples (Fig. 119):

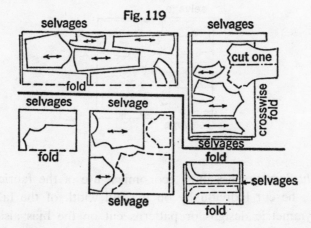

Fig. 119

For this type of layout, place, pin, and cut out the fabric on the lengthwise fold first. Then fold the fabric for the new layout, place, pin, and cut.

TRIAL LAYOUT OF THE CORRECTED PATTERN

Have you ever had the experience of starting your cutting at one end, proceeding merrily for most of the length of the fabric only to find, as you near the end, that there is not quite enough material to finish? A trial layout would have prevented this disaster.

Place the fabric on a flat surface. Line up the straight edges of the fabric with the straight edges of the cutting surface. Place the pattern in the position indicated on the layout chart.

Place the grain of the pattern parallel to the selvage of the material. Theoretically, pinning the straight of goods parallel to the selvage in two places should make it parallel throughout. If your fabric is fastened down to the board this will work. Most of the time pinning in just two places is no guarantee that the remaining straight of goods is still parallel to the selvage. Fabrics have been known to slide out of place. Measure a sufficient number of times to ensure that the grain is parallel throughout the length of the pattern piece.

When a pattern piece needs to be used again or reversed or opened to its full width, it is easier to do this with a second pattern piece traced from the original. This gives a complete layout. When only one pattern piece is used, measure the area of cloth involved and pass over it to the next placement of the pattern.

Start at one end of the fabric. Support the weight of the rest of the cloth at the other end of the table, on an ironing board, or on a chair. This prevents a pull on the cloth by its own weight. When the pattern has been temporarily pinned to the material, fold the finished end to make room on the flat surface for the new part.

Place the pattern pieces close to each other. Spaces between add up and may result in a shortage of as much as five or six inches. This could mean the difference between being able to get the pattern out of the length of cloth or not.

Arrange the pattern pieces so that if any fabric is left it will be in one usable piece at the end. Or, if the pattern is placed from both ends, the extra fabric will be left in one piece in the middle. You may find use for a larger piece—a hat, shoes, bag, scarf, trimming. Otherwise you may accumulate pounds of unusable scraps.

Since this is only a trial, use as few pins as will give you the information you want. If changes need to be made, it won't take hours to unpin.

If the trial layout reveals that there is not enough material:

1. Make smaller seam allowances and a narrower hem.

2. Piece the material. (The "piece" is on the same grain. It is as if you were adding another piece to make it wider or longer. Piece in some place where the joining seam will be least conspicuous.)

3. Face or trim in another color or fabric. Velvet is a fine trimming for suits and coats.

4. Combine with another fabric—suede, leather, knitted sections.

5. If possible, change the lengthwise grain of some of the sections to a crosswise grain.

6. Eliminate the waistband of the skirt. Use matching grosgrain ribbon for a waistband or finish the waistline with an inside band.

7. Eliminate or change some detail. For instance, patch pockets could become bound pockets or welt pockets, neither of which take as much fabric.

8. If you are too short of fabric, get another pattern with fewer pattern pieces and less detail.

SPECIAL LAYOUTS

Fabric designers are smart ones. They have a way of luring us with the beauty of their designs while skillfully hiding all the intricacies which are lurking there to entrap us. Sometimes in our innocence we do step in "where angels fear to tread." Sometimes even knowing better, we permit ourselves to be beguiled by the handsomeness of the fabric. In either case, we have a problem on our hands.

Naps, piles, and one-way weaves or printed designs require special layouts. Plaids, stripes, and diagonal weaves or prints do, too. It is almost impossible to give an accurate estimate of the yardage when fabrics of this kind are used. One can only say "Buy more." How much more will depend on:

the number of pattern pieces which need to be placed going in one direction
the number of pieces which need matching
the size and spacing of the design motifs
the placement of the fabric design on the figure for most interest and most flattery
the size of plaids, stripes, checks
whether the plaids or stripes are balanced or unbalanced, vertical or horizontal

Short-Nap or Pile Fabrics

The short-nap or pile fabrics are velvet, velveteen, and corduroy. Pile reflects light. Pile fabric is one color when the nap runs down and another when the nap runs up. This makes it imperative that all pattern pieces be placed in the same direction—neck to hem. *Pile* fabrics are cut with the *nap* running *up* because the color is richer in this direction (Fig. 120). Panne velvet is an exception. The nap has been pressed flat. It is cut with the nap going down.

Fig. 120

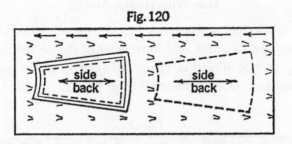

To determine the direction of the nap, place your fingers lightly on the surface of the material. Move them gently back and forth. Where there is resistance, there is nap. When the surface feels smooth, the nap is running down. When the surface is rough, the nap is running up. Mark the direction in which the nap moves (Fig. 120).

If you discover in cutting that the nap is running the wrong way, stick with it. It is better to be consistent and cut the nap in the wrong direction than to switch in mid-cutting and have two different colors or a patchwork of colors in the garment.

Long-Nap Fabric or Furry Fabric

The long-napped fabrics such as fleece, brushed wool, camel's hair, broadcloth, or any of the new shaggy cloths are cut with the nap going down as if they were fur. Just remember the way in which you would stroke a pet. You start at the head and stroke down. If you were to start at the tail and stroke up, you would be "rubbing it the wrong way." Pattern pieces in long-nap fabrics all go in one direction—neck to hem.

Long-Float Fabric

Like pile fabrics, long-float fabrics catch the light, producing a sheen and color which varies with the direction of the light. Satin, sateen, polished cotton, brocades must be treated like napped fabrics. All pattern pieces must be placed in the same direction lengthwise.

Fabrics with pile, short or long nap, or sheen should not be cut on the crosswise grain.

One-Way Design Motifs

When a fabric has a repeat of a design motif, whether woven or printed, study the direction and movement of the design units. If they are moving in one direction (Fig. 121a), a one-way placement of pattern pieces must also be observed (Fig. 121b).

Fig. 121

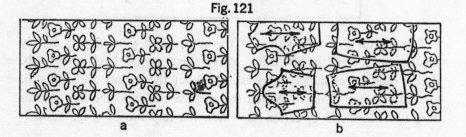

a   b

Placement of Design Units

A real consideration in the use of your fabric is a judicious placement of its design units. Drape the fabric over yourself and study the effect in a mirror.

Fig. 122

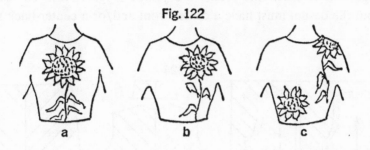

a   b   c

Centering the unit makes for formal balance (Fig. 122a). The unit placed to one side results in an asymmetric balance (Fig. 122b). An unusual or unexpected placement produces a dramatic effect (Fig. 122c).

Diagonal Weaves or Prints

These are the real "problem children" in the fabric family. There are very few patterns designed for diagonal fabrics because they are so difficult to handle. Many patterns are marked specifically, "diagonal fabrics not suitable." It is well to heed this advice.

One of the real difficulties with diagonal fabrics is the mismatching of the stripes or ribs at the seam lines (Fig. 123) when the usual pattern layouts are used.

Fig. 123

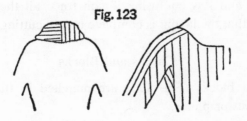

If the fabric is reversible, that is, if it has no right or wrong side this can be overcome by using the following layout:

Place the pattern on a single thickness of the fabric. Cut two identical pieces, using the same pattern piece going in the same direction (Fig. 124a). Use the reverse side of one as the right side. A chevron design results when the seams are joined (Fig. 124b). To use this layout the design must have a center front and/or a center-back seam.

Fig. 124

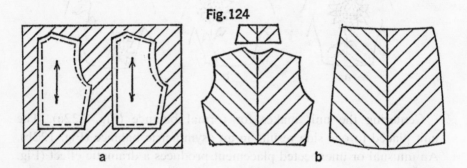

a   b

If the fabric does have a right and a wrong side, whether it is woven or printed, then find a pattern that will present the least difficulties. Avoid kimono sleeves and shawl collars.

In working with any diagonal material, choose a pattern that has simple lines and few pattern pieces, straight seams rather than curved or bias seams, slim skirt rather than a gored or flared one, set-in sleeves rather than kimono sleeves. A collarless design is preferable to a collared one which presents difficulties in cutting. When a design has been created specifically for a diagonal material, the pattern will include a special cutting chart.

It is easier and less confusing if you trace all the necessary pattern pieces so that the layout is complete before cutting.

Checks and Blocks

Checks and blocks (Fig. 125) are matched in the same way as balanced stripes or plaids.

Fig. 125

Stripes and Plaids

Despite the stongest resolutions to stick to solid colors, there is something about stripes and plaids that stirs us. Memory? Nostalgia? Flags floating in the breeze, peppermint sticks, first days at school, a parade of plaid-clad figures and the enchanting sound of bagpipes?

Whatever it is, the charm of stripes and plaids appears everlasting. Every season we are presented with a host of old and new ones with their constant challenge in design and construction.

The choice of pattern is important for the most interesting use of stripes and plaids. The style lines must be consistent with the straight lines of the fabric. So should the control dart and control seams. Many patterns state flatly they are not meant to be used for stripes and plaids.

Stripes and plaids are designed with an even (balanced) or uneven (unbalanced) placement of lines, bars, and colors. Before you can decide how to use them you must determine which type they are.

Does the fabric have an up-and-down effect? Find the center or dominant horizontal line or bar or color. "Read" the lines above and below this. If they are the same (Fig. 126a), the plaid or stripe is balanced or even. If they are different (Fig. 126b), the plaid or stripe is unbalanced or uneven.

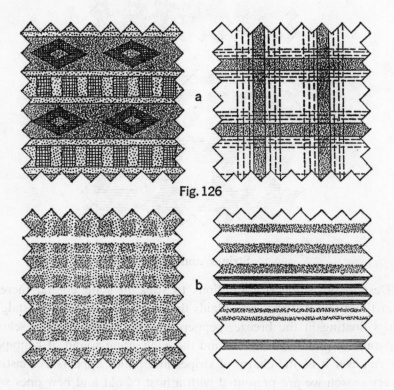

Fig. 126

Does the fabric have a right-and-left effect? Find the dominant vertical line or bar or color. Read the lines, bars, or colors to the right and left of this. If they are the same on both sides, the stripe is balanced or even (Fig. 127). If they are different, the plaid or stripe is unbalanced or uneven (Fig. 128).

The combinations and permutations are infinite. It is very possible to get fabrics where the lines, bars, or colors are even in one direction and uneven in another; even in both directions; uneven in both directions. And, designers being the devilish fellows they are often

Fig. 127

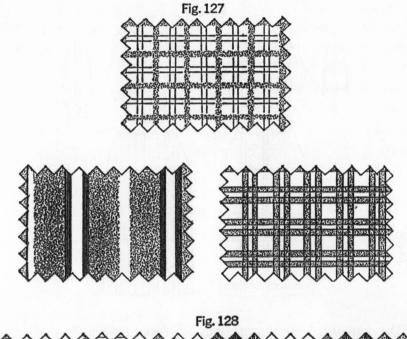

Fig. 128

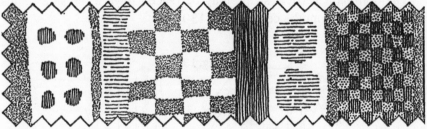

complicate matters by using a lovely, diagonal twill weave along with stripes or bars or colors.

The placement of stripes and plaids on the figure. Before deciding on this, it would be well to review the optical illusions created by lines, groups of lines and spaces in Chapter II.

The dominant vertical stripe, bar, or color may be placed at the center front and center back with the stripes or plaids evenly balanced on either side (Fig. 129). A similar stripe, bar, or color is placed at the center of the sleeve.

Fig. 129

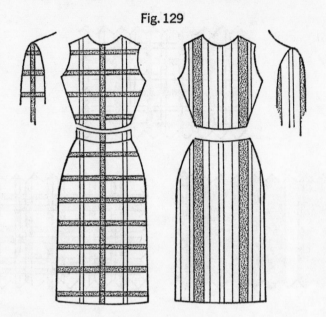

The dominant vertical stripe may be placed toward the side seams equally placed from the center (Fig. 130).

Fig. 130

The dominant crosswise line is placed just below the shoulders and in a corresponding position on the sleeve. The dominant crosswise line in the skirt is placed at the waistline or just below it and at the lower finished edge (Fig. 131). The weight or heaviness of the dominant stripe seems an appropriate finish to the garment.

Fig. 131

For design interest, often the dominant lines are used vertically in one part of the garment and horizontally or on the bias in another (Fig. 132).

Fig. 132

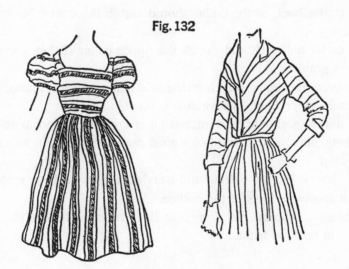

Even a check which appears to have an all-over look (Fig. 133a) has a dominant stripe—the dark one. The darker bar of a simple stripe (Fig. 133b) is the dominant one. So these, too, need to be considered for placement.

Fig. 133

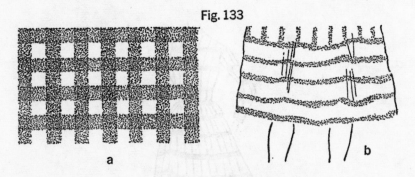

a   b

Stripes, plaids, and checks need meticulous matching if the garment is to look well made. Matching takes time, forethought, care, and extra material. It is difficult and tedious labor.

The garment should close with the crosswise dominating lines matching. Stripes and plaids are closed over each other so that a complete plaid or stripe or group of stripes is directly on center.

The dominant vertical lines of the bodice should be carried down into the skirt.

The center back of the collar should match the center back of the bodice.

The under collar should match the upper collar if they are cut on the same grain.

Crosswise lines must match at the side seams, control seams, center front and center back, sleeve seam, lapel, and facing.

The dart legs should be centered on straight lines and match.

Pockets, belts, and buttonholes must match the area in which they are located.

The sleeves are set so that the heaviest crosswise lines match the heaviest crosswise lines of the bodice.

In kimono sleeves, the dominant lines must match at the seams which join back to front.

In a suit, all dominant lines must be so placed that the finished look is one of continuous stripes, plaids, or checks with no break between jacket and skirt.

In other words, every part of a garment which joins another part or overlaps another part must match. This takes some doing!

Much of the difficulty lies in the inability to foretell with any certainty the exact position of all of the lines which need matching. For instance, the shoulder seams may need adjustment in the final fitting before setting the sleeves. Even this minor adjustment would be enough to throw off the matching of sleeve and bodice were the sleeve already cut out. So it would be with any of the other parts which

Fig. 134

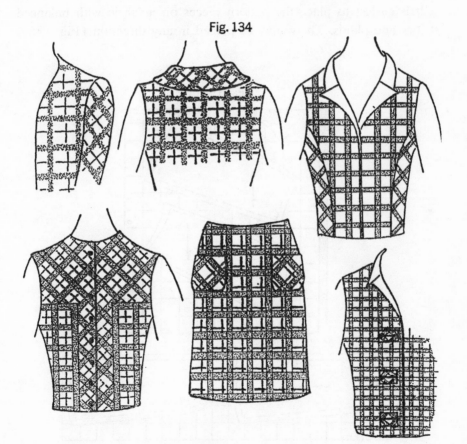

are set or applied after the main pieces have been joined, namely, the collar, the pockets, and the buttonholes.

It is wise in using stripes or plaids to let the pattern, pinned and uncut, rest in the area in which it is likely to be located. Leave sufficient room for minor changes. Do *not* cut out the pattern until a final fitting assures you of the correct placement.

A good design way to eliminate some of these troublesome problems is to cut some of the garment sections on the bias (Fig. 134) —sleeves, yokes, bands, collars, side sections, buttonholes, pockets, etc.

The placement of the pattern pieces on the fabric:

It is easiest to place the pattern pieces on a fabric with balanced stripes and plaids. These may be placed in any direction (Fig. 135).

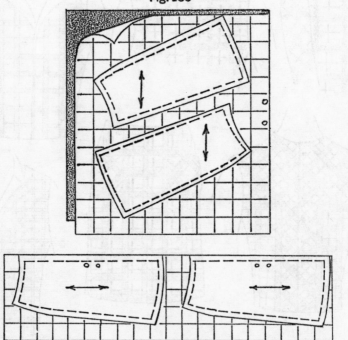

Fig. 135

When the center front or back is on a fold of fabric, the fold should be on the center of the stripe or plaid (Fig. 136a). Where a seam is necessary the seam line should be at the center so that the full stripe or plaid will result when the seam is stitched and opened out (Fig. 136b). Allow sufficient room for the seam allowance.

Fig. 136

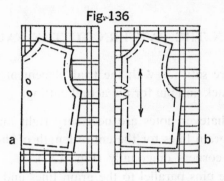

If the stripes or plaids are unbalanced lengthwise, they must all be treated like a one-way design. All the pattern pieces must be placed going in the same direction.

A crosswise unbalance can only be balanced by cutting and matching from the right and wrong side of the fabric as was suggested for diagonal stripes. This can only be done when the fabric is reversible and where there will be a center-front or center-back seam.

Line up! To ensure the under layer of the double thickness of fabric is on exactly the same stripe as the upper layer, pin or baste the matching lines or colors across the entire width of the fabric as frequently as it is necessary to keep it in place.

Place the pattern pieces so that the matching notches are on the same line, color, or bar.

Remember that it is the seam line which needs matching, not the cutting line.

Set the position of your key pattern piece. Roughly trace the main lines of the stripe, plaid, or design units along the seam lines which match. Mark the notches. Place the matching pattern piece over it and trace. Even if the pattern pieces are not laid close to each other you will still have a record of just what must match.

You can see what an engineering project it is to use stripes, plaids, checks, and even design units which must match. Anybody still for making a garment of these problem fabrics? Never mind the firm resolutions. You'll probably be carried away by the next complicated fabric you come across.

PIN THE PATTERN TO THE FABRIC

When you are satisfied with the trial placement of the pattern on the fabric, go back and pin for the actual cutting.

1. Make whatever notes are necessary right on the pattern.

2. Pin the grain lines for the entire length of the pattern piece.

3. Pin the corners diagonally (Fig. 137).

4. Place the pins parallel to the grain lines and at right angles to the cutting edge about two to three inches apart (Fig. 137).

5. Curves take a few more pins than straight edges.

6. Keep the pattern and the fabric flat against the cutting surface.

7. Use one hand as an anchor, the other to pin.

8. Keep smoothing the fabric as you go along.

9. The pins go through the paper pattern and both thicknesses of the cloth.

10. Pin sufficiently to give a true cutting edge but not so many as to make the material pucker.

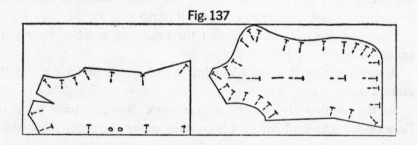

Fig. 137

11. Pin sheer, stretchy, or "creepy" fabrics to paper before placing the pattern.

12. Use weights rather than pins to hold the pattern in place on slippery or heavy fabrics.

13. Fine needles instead of pins are often used on satins and velvets which bruise easily. Place the pins parallel to the grain and use as few as possible. Place the pins close to the cutting line so that bruise marks will land in the seam allowance where they won't be seen.

14. Mark additional allowances with tailor's chalk.

15. If a combination of folds are used, place and cut the lengthwise fold first, then the other.

CUT OUT THE GARMENT

1. Cut along the cutting line of the pattern or your altered cutting line.

2. Cut beside the pattern rather than through it except when cutting sheer materials. Cutting through the paper is an advantage then.

3. Use long, firm strokes of sharp shears for the straight edges, short strokes for the curves.

4. Cut with the middle of the blade. Stop before coming to the point. Slide along.

5. Do not use pinking shears. They do not give an accurate line. It is hard to use them on heavy fabrics. They are rather useless on the inside of a coat or jacket since pinking is meant as an edge finish. All of the edges of a tailored garment will be hidden by the lining.

6. Don't lift the cloth; keep it flat on the table.

7. Cut in the direction of the nap—up for pile fabrics, down for long naps.

8. Do not stop to cut the notches out; they will be marked otherwise.

9. It is difficult to cut accurately through two layers of very heavy or very bulky fabric. It is sometimes necessary after the piece is cut out to place the pattern on the underneath fabric and correct the cutting.

10. As the pieces are cut, lay them flat or hang them on a hanger. If folding is necessary, use as few folds as possible. Keep the pattern side out for easy identification of the pieces and protection of the fabric.

TRANSFER THE MARKINGS FROM THE PATTERN TO THE FABRIC

There appears to be a rather general, deep-rooted belief that things that come easy are not quite honest or right. To accomplish something worth while one must toil and perhaps even suffer a little. Sewers are great ones for this philosophy. It's a matter of principle with many of them to ignore all the markings on a pattern. Somehow it seems more sporting to improvise as they go along. This makes things a little harder, therefore a little nobler. Rest assured that it is no violation of integrity to use all the help you can get on the purely mechanical parts of the work of construction. There will be labor enough to satisfy the noblest soul.

Mark everything! The more time you take to mark now, the less work and guesswork when you come to join the sections of your garment.

Notches

A notch is a tiny V-shaped marking which shows where and which two seams join.

To cut a notch:

1. Fold the fabric where it is indicated on the pattern (Fig. 138a).
2. Snip diagonally across the corner (Fig. 138b).
3. When the fabric is opened the complete notch will appear (Fig. 138c).

The notch should be small. It is meant only for your eyes. Don't cut a big chunk out of the seam allowance. Most pattern directions

Fig. 138

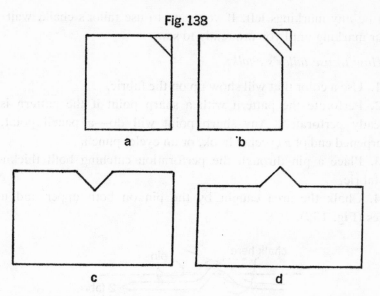

a   b

c   d

advise cutting the notches outward (Fig. 138d). This method of marking keeps the seam allowance intact should it be needed for fitting. However, we have taken so many precautions to ensure correct fit that this should not be necessary. If you are in doubt, however, cut the notches outward. Many patterns have numbered notches. Note the corresponding numbers when matching the notches.

Sometimes a ¼" snip is used instead of a notch but this is harder to see. If the fabric ravels easily, use loops of thread to mark the notch instead of cutting it out.

When notches can be used on a fabric, use them wherever else they will make joining easy.

Markings on the Wrong Side of the Fabric

Most markings are made on the wrong side of the material. This is where they are needed for construction. There are several methods by which the material may be marked.

Tailor's chalk makes the safest and easiest marking. The chalky kind brushes off very easily. It leaves no permanent marks on the material. This virtue is at once an asset and a drawback. You can't mark now and sew later. When you pick up your work there may not be any markings left. If you plan to use tailor's chalk, wait with your marking until you are ready to sew.

How to use tailor's chalk:

1. Use a color that will show up on the fabric.

2. Perforate the pattern with a sharp point if the pattern is not already perforated. Any sharp point will do—a pencil point, the sharpened end of a crochet hook, or an eyelet punch.

3. Place a pin through the perforation catching both thicknesses of fabric.

4. Chalk the area caught by the pin on both upper and under sides (Fig. 139).

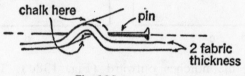

Fig. 139

Dressmaker's carbon paper and a tracing wheel make excellent markings. They give true and clearly visible stitching lines. This marking won't come off—ever. You could mark now and come back to your work months later and it would still be there. These are great advantages.

There are also some drawbacks. It is a permanent marking which even cleaning will not remove. The tracing wheel injures some fabrics. It is difficult to trace on heavy fabrics. It is fairly impossible to see the markings on some wools, while it shines through brightly (and permanently) on light colors and sheer fabrics.

Better test this method on a scrap of fabric to see if it can take it. If it can, this is a wonderfully accurate marking.

How to mark with dressmaker's carbon:

1. Unpin a section of your pattern.

2. Use a contrasting color of carbon paper.

3. Slip the carbon paper between the pattern and the fabric with the carbon side against the fabric. Both sides of the fabric can be marked simultaneously by slipping a second sheet of carbon against the under thickness of the fabric. The fabric is enclosed by carbon paper (Fig. 140).

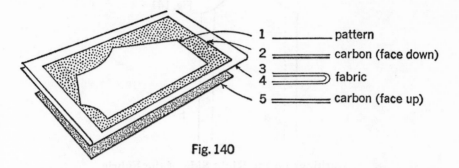

1	———— pattern
2	carbon (face down)
3	
4	fabric
5	carbon (face up)

Fig. 140

4. Repin the pattern with very few pins—just enough to hold in place.

5. Lay a ruler along any straight lines to be marked. Trace along the ruler's edge with the tracing wheel.

6. Curves may be traced freehand following the seam line of the pattern.

7. Remove the carbon. Slide it along to a new section. Repeat the entire marking procedure.

8. In marking heavy fabrics, mark one side at a time. Cardboard between the two layers of the material will provide a firm base.

This method of marking may tear the pattern but it can be repaired with Scotch Tape.

Work on a surface that won't resist the prongs of the tracing wheel. The dining-room table would be perfect if it weren't for those awful little tracks that the tracing wheel leaves. Use wood, cardboard, or a magazine as an under surface. The surface of an aluminum or metal table is not satisfactory.

Mark everything! Even those markings that need to appear on the right side can be transferred later with basting thread. The carbon marking gives a more accurate line than looped thread which pulls out easily. For example, mark the center-front line with carbon paper on the wrong side (Fig. 141a). When the pattern is removed, run a line of basting along the marking. Baste so that a long float of thread will appear on the right side (Fig. 141b).

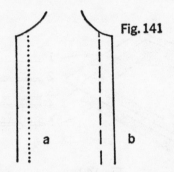

Fig. 141

Markings on the Right Side of the Fabric

Some markings are essential on the right side of the fabric. Basting and tailor's tacks are best. It is true that these are time consuming and tedious work but they are the safest method for marking the right side. They are, incidentally, the oldest method of marking.

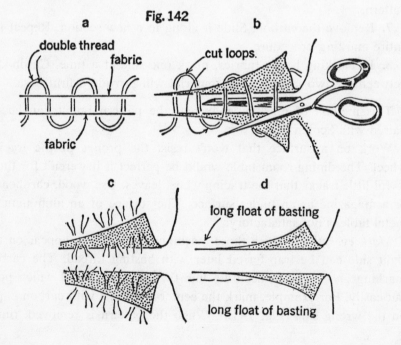

Fig. 142

Guide bastings:

1. Use a double thread.

2. Take a stitch through both layers of fabric leaving loops of thread (Fig. 142a).

3. Cut the loops (Fig. 142b). Remove the pattern.

4. Open the layers of fabric carefully. Cut the threads between the layers (Fig. 142c).

5. Run a line of basting along the tufts before they pull out (Fig. 142d). The long float of the basting thread is on the right side.

How to make tailor's tacks:

1. Use a double thread of contrasting color.

2. Take a stitch which goes through both thicknesses of the fabric. Leave an end about 1″ long.

3. Take another stitch through the fabric, making a loop about ½″ high.

4. Repeat making a double loop. Cut the thread leaving an end 1″ long (Fig. 143a).

5. If the pattern is perforated, remove it. If it is a printed pattern, leave it in place.

6. Separate the two thicknesses of the fabric carefully. A small stitch now appears on the outside of each layer of material which holds the fabric in place (Fig. 143b).

7. Cut the threads between the layers of fabric, leaving small tufts on each piece (Fig. 143c).

Fig. 143

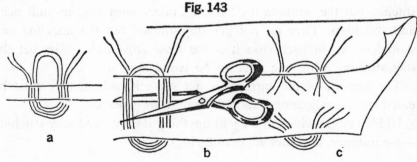

a   b   c

The trick in successful tailor's tacks is *not* to cut the loops until the layers of fabric have been separated. If you cut them before, the tufts will pull out as you separate the two thicknesses.

If the fabric is too thick to make tailor's tacks through both layers, make them through the upper layer first. Push the needle through the center of the first tacks to mark the position of those on the under side. Make the tailor's tacks where indicated on the under surface.

Different colors of basting thread can be used for the various markings. Don't use so many that you will need a legend (like a map) to identify the markings.

A beginning student once asked me where she could buy tailor's tacks. No doubt some of us more experienced sewers would be equally happy to purchase any item that could dispense with the seeming miles of looped thread.

Stay Stitching

Whether it be straight or curved, any edge which departs from the vertical or horizontal grain will stretch. Stay stitching preserves the size and shape of all such edges. It also serves to arrest raveling.

What to stay-stitch. The curved edges of necklines, armholes, and style lines should be stay-stitched, as should straight edges cut on an angle—shoulders, side seams, style lines.

What not to stay-stitch. Edges cut on the true lengthwise or crosswise grain do not need stay stitching (unless the fabric ravels easily) nor any edge that needs to be eased into another. For example, the sleeve cap must be eased into the armhole. It does not get stay-stitched but the armhole itself does. Collars must ease around neck and shoulders. They do not get stay-stitched but the neckline and shoulders do. In each case it is the *fixed edge* which *does* get the stay stitching while the *edge to be eased does not*.

The hemline of the garment is not stay-stitched. It, too, must be eased into the adjoining area without darts or gathers.

Hidden edges which don't join anything do not need stay stitching —for instance, the outer edges of facings.

True bias is never stay-stitched. Its charm is its hang and drape. It should not be restricted with stay stitching.

Stay-stitch each piece of fabric where necessary as soon as the pattern is removed after marking. Stay stitching is done through a single layer of fabric about ½″ in from the cut edge. Use cotton thread of matching color. Save your silk thread for the construction seams. Use a stitch slightly larger than the one to be used for the seams but smaller than a basting stitch. Eight stitches to the inch is a generally good size.

Fig. 144

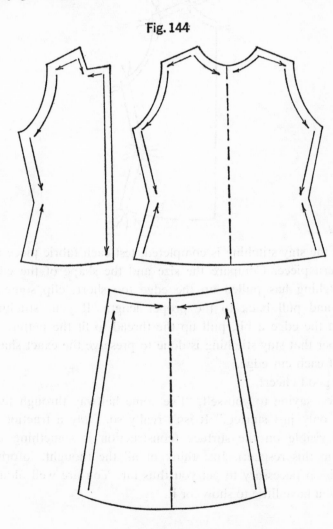

If stay stitching is really to hold the grain in place, it must be directional. Stitch from a high point to a low point or from a wide point to a narrow point (Fig. 144). The rule wide to narrow takes precedence over high to low.

Never use a continuous line of stitching around corners. Break the thread at the end of each row of stitching or wherever the direction changes (Fig. 145).

Fig. 145

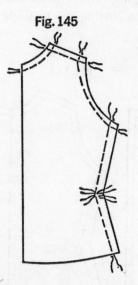

When the stay stitching is completed, test each fabric piece against the pattern piece. Compare the size and the shape of the edges. If your stitching has pulled up the edge too short, clip some of the stitches and pull back to the proper length. If your stitching has stretched the edge a bit, pull up the thread to fit the pattern shape. Remember that stay stitching is done to preserve the exact shape and length of each cut edge.

Be of good cheer!

Are you saying to yourself, "I've come halfway through the book and I'm only just started." It isn't really so. Only a fraction of the work is visible on the surface (construction is something like an iceberg in this respect). Just think of all the thought, information, and decision necessary to get you thus far. You are well along even though you have little to show for it.

CHAPTER V

The Shape of Things to Come

THE BODY BEAUTIFUL
VERSUS THE SHAPE OF FASHION

Ideas of what constitutes beauty have changed through the centuries. What has remained unchanged has been man's stubborn persistence in trying to improve upon Nature by designing clothing which uses the human body merely as a point of departure.

Every age and every culture has had its own ways of demonstrating its dissatisfaction with the shape which Nature provided for us. The poets might sing the praises of the "form divine" but the designers ignored it, exaggerated it, swaddled it, padded it out, pushed it in, distorted it, tortured it, and—when all else failed—concealed it. The history of costume design discloses that clothing practically never has truly followed the contour of the body.

Lacking the human body as support, some other propping became imperative. Fabric, of itself, could seldom hold the line. With great ingenuity we have devised all sorts of contraptions of bone, steel, wire, and wood to support the shape of fashion. There have been steel girdles and whalebone corsets, farthingales and panniers, crinolines and hoopskirts. There have been stays and bustles, inflatable bras and padded posteriors. When it comes to buttressing a shape, anything goes—from chicken wire to foam rubber! By comparison, present styling, while following in the tradition, is heroically restrained. It is no longer dependent on undercover carpentry. Fortunately, too, there is a wide assortment of interfacing and underlining fabrics which can be used as an integral part of the construction of the garment. These assure the subtle shaping of present-day fashion.

More Than Meets the Eye

The old adage has it that you only get out of a dress what you put into it. Undoubtedly a good figure is an invaluable aid. But it is a known fact that even the seductive sequin and satin numbers which adorn many a glamorous movie star have their shape built right into them. What meets the eye is a beautiful girl, plus an assist from unseen underpinnings. All the lady need wear is this little nothing of a dress complete with built-ins.

Foundation garments, taking their cue from fashion's contours, are styled to help sustain the shape. But in the main, it is the garment itself which literally must stand on its own. This calls for interfacing, underlining, lining, padding, and weighting. There is a bewildering array of these materials on the market. Each product makes extravagant claims of effectiveness. And there is plenty of conflicting advice. Pity the poor home sewer!

New styles make new demands of the understructure. Each new garment presents a new problem. Which to choose? There are no hard and fast rules as to which interfacings are for what fabric. Anything is right that will give the desired lines. *Choose that interfacing or underlining which will best maintain the contour of the design.*

An interfacing is a reinforcing or shaping fabric used between the outer fabric and the facing or the lining. It adds strength to all areas of stress—the closing, the neck, across the back, the armscye and the hems. It also builds a permanent shape into the garment at the shoulders, bust, collar, lapels, and often the hips.

Interfacings should be compatible in weight with the fabrics which they interface. In general, light-weight fabrics take light-weight interfacings, medium-weight fabrics take medium-weight interfacings, heavy fabrics take heavy interfacings.

An underlining is a backing fabric used to create a new fabric with the surface appearance of the original fabric but the character of the underlining.

Underlinings may be any weight which will provide the body necessary to realize the design. For example: chiffon backed with crepe creates a new fabric which retains the frosted sheer of the chiffon while adding the body of crepe. This crepe-backed chiffon can now be used for a sheath instead of the more characteristic filmy, floating styles. Wool backed with organza creates a new fabric with just that extra necessary stiffness for a dress with gentle but definite lines. Without the underlining, the wool would be too limp for such a style. A heavy wool coat which, because of its weight, would normally hang in folds can have its slight flare buoyed by a very firm underlining. The use of an underlining provides great latitude in the use of fabric for any silhouette.

Each interfacing and underlining possesses individual qualities. Each is meant to produce a specific effect. The same interfacing may be used on a variety of fabrics. A particular fabric may take any one of a number of interfacings. *The determining factor is the design of the garment.*

Sometimes several different interfacings are used in one garment. For instance: hair canvas may be used to interface the front of a coat, muslin the back, and tailor's linen the collar. A jacket may be underlined with lawn and interfaced with formite. Any combination is possible. Each interfacing and underlining should provide the appropriate support for a particular *part* of the design. Often an entire under-shell is made for the garment of several different interfacings and underlinings.

A word of caution! Don't get so anxious about the understructure that you overload your garment with it. Many fabrics need only the gentlest persuasion to keep them in line. It is a joy to wear something that doesn't feel like a suit of armor or weigh a ton. Strike a happy balance between wearability and fashion.

Shaping and Foundation Fabrics

Almost any fabric can be used as an interfacing, either for itself or for any other. Every sewer has drawers full of odds and ends which can be pressed into service as interfacing or underlining. There are many commercial fabrics designed specifically for this use. Some are woven, some nonwoven.

Woven fabric can be eased, stretched, and blocked to fit the figure. Nonwoven fabrics cannot. For example, wool which is a woven fabric can be molded into a figure-conforming shape while the nonwoven felt cannot. The same holds true for interfacings and underlinings. Those which are woven can be blocked into the same shape as the outer fabric. Nonwoven ones cannot. Shaping is a very important part of the tailoring process. Therefore it is wise to choose woven interfacings and underlinings for this purpose.

Following is a list of shaping fabrics currently available for home sewers. Some are generally used as interfacings, some as underlinings. Most may be used for either purpose.

Woven interfacings and underlinings
These are the most widely used in tailoring

Name	Remarks	Weight	Color	Width	D–Dry Cleaning W–Washable
Hair canvas made by Armo and Hymo	woven of wool or cotton or both plus goat's hair; molds beautifully into shape; adheres to wool; provides springiness for lapels and roll collars; adds firmness	light medium heavy	natural	25"–27" Most economical is the double width, 66"–72"; sometimes fabric stores split this to 33"–36"	D
Armo Finolight	for warm-weather fashions wool, cotton, and goat's hair	very lightweight	sand	25"	D
Wool canvas	similar to hair canvas but made of coarse worsted wool fibers almost like goat's hair	medium	natural	25"	D
Tailor's linen	used for tailored set-on neck-hugging collars; molds well; must be cut on the bias	medium	natural	25"	D

Name	Remarks	Weight	Color	Width	D or W
French collar canvas-Elastique	stiffer than tailor's linen but equally good for the same type of collar; also good for standing collars when cut double on straight grain and firmed with rows of stitching	medium to heavy	brownish natural	25″	D
Melton cloth	used as interfacing and under collar in one; provides the firm, flat collar of men's suits; must be cut on the bias	medium	brown tan gray black navy	sold by the collar	D
Acro	rayon, dacron and goat's hair; used for washable dresses, suits, coats	light	ecru	25″	W

These materials are used as soft backing or padding

Name	Remarks	Weight	Color	Width	D or W
Flannel, cotton	used for backing light wool or heavy silks, satins, brocades; backing for fur	light	natural	72″	D
Felting	can be used the same way as flannel; can also be used as padding	medium	black white	72″	D
Tailor's felt	used as backing or padding	soft firm	natural white gray	72″	D
Cotton wadding	used as padding	light	charcoal white	sheets 36″×31″ 33″×45″	D

This is a group of woven sheer canvases which can be molded in the same way as hair canvas. They are used for the softer styles of dressmaker suits, coats, and ensembles. All of these mold well and add firmness and body.

Name	Remarks	Weight	Color	Width	D or W
Formite	sheer canvas of cotton and viscose	light	black white natural	25″	D and W
Sta-Shape	tailor's canvas	medium	white black natural		D
Wigan	sturdy	light	gray	36″	D
Capri	soft finish for easy molded silhouettes	light	black		D and W
Veriform–soft	noncrushable, crease and shrink resistant	light	black white colors	39″	D and W

Firmer wovens for more crisply defined shapes

Name	Remarks	Weight	Color	Width	D or W
Formite–stiff	a stiffer version of regular formite	medium	black white natural	39″	D and W
Super Siri–firm	makes a firm underlining viscose—resembles cotton	medium-light	black white	45″	D and W
Veriform–crisp	for belled and bouffant silhouettes	light	black white	39″	D and W
Taffeta	either rayon or silk	light	all colors	45″	D

Name	Remarks	Weight	Color	Width	
Capri	crisp finish for belled and bouffant silhouettes	light	black white		D and W
Challis Shape-well	comes in four stiffnesses	medium	black white		D
Everflex	for belled and bouffant silhouettes	medium	black white natural		D and W

These add a stiffer finish to limp or delicate fabrics
They cannot support too much weight

Name	Remarks	Weight	Color	Width	D or W
Marquisette rayon	soft mesh—tendency to shrink	very light	all colors	45"	D and W
nylon	stiff mesh			45"	
Net	soft English cotton	very light	all colors	72"	D
Organdy	crisp, permanent finish	light	all colors	36"	W
Organza	crisp, silky finish	very light	all colors	42"	D

Supple fabrics which add soft body

Name	Remarks	Weight	Color	Width	D or W
Batiste	cotton	light	all colors	36"	W
China silk all silk	a luxury lining or underlining called	light	all colors	36"	D
part silk	sheath lining	light	all colors	40"	D

Name	Remarks	Weight	Color	Width	
acetate	called sheath lining firmer—less expensive	medium	all colors	45"	D
Crepe flat crepe tissue faille	lining or underlining	light medium	all colors	40" 45"	D D
Lawn	cotton	light	white	36"	W
Muslin	soft cotton	light	un-bleached white	39"	W
Super Siri (super-soft)	spun-viscose, resembles cotton	light	black white	45"	D W

These are firmer fabrics which add firmer body

Name	Remarks	Weight	Color	Width	D or W
Muslin	unbleached	medium to heavy	natural	39"	W
Permanent-finish cottons	firm, crisp	light	all colors	35"	W
Silesia	firmly woven, sturdy	medium	black brown tan gray	36"	D
Super Siri (soft)	spun viscose to resemble cotton	light	black white	45"	D and W

The nonwoven interfacings for special effects

Name	Remarks	Weight	Color	Width	D or W
Evershape	thin almost transparent	very light and medium	white black	20"	D and W
Keybak	resembles mesh	light medium heavy	black white	25" 37"	D and W
Interlon	supple to buoyant effects	light regular heavy	black white	25" 37"	D and W
Kyrel	reinforces necklines, sleeve edges, belts, hems, pockets, made of dacron polyester fibers	very light	white	25" or 45"	D and W
Stretch Kyrel	for bias-cut designs, stretches in all directions	light	white	25"	D and W
Pellon bias	stretches in all directions	light medium	charcoal white		D and W
Pellon regular	used as underlining to maintain shape no give in any direction	light medium	black white	25" 36" 54"	D and W

Iron-ons both woven and nonwoven

Name	Remarks	Weight	Color	Width	
Adheron	nonwoven reinforces small areas	very light	white		D and W

Name	Remarks	Weight	Color	Width	
Interlon	nonwoven crisp effects—firm shaping in small areas	medium	white black	18″	D and W
Keybak Hot Iron	nonwoven reinforcement for small areas	medium	white black	20″	D and W
Pellomite Detail	nonwoven reinforcement for small areas	very light	white	18″	D and W
Pellomite Shape retaining	interfacing for larger areas, necklines, front facings, etc.	medium	white	36″	D and W
Pressto	woven, iron-on	medium	white black	19″ 38″	D and W
Stay-flex	"all-purpose"—woven for medium soft, supple body; reinforcement in large or small areas; used on all but multifilament fabrics	medium	black white	18″ and 36″	D and W
Weldex	woven cotton	medium	white black	36″	D and W

Since anything's fair game as an interfacing or underlining, don't overlook the millinery-supply stores. They are wonderful sources for foundation and shaping fabrics. You'll find there the following useful materials. Since washability is no requirement of millinery, it is safe to assume all the following need dry cleaning.

Name	Remarks	Weight	Color	Width
French crepe	looks like a closely woven, springy light mesh; so woven that it won't shrink; can be beautifully blocked	light	white black navy brown moss green	39″
Flaline	a combination of scrim and flannel; can be molded; works well in collars	medium	white	36″
Scrim (crinoline)	stiff; is apt to lose stiffness when washed or dry-cleaned	medium	white	36″
Flexible cloth	sized, which is stiff, can be used for standing collars; unsized—soft	medium soft	black white	39″
Horsehair braid	stiff, loosely woven braid for stiffening hems, edges, trimmings	very light weight	all colors can be dyed any color	¼″–12″

As you can see there is much to choose from—something for every style and fabric! Does this multiply your problem of choice? Let the desired weight, finish, texture, the degree of flexibility, softness, suppleness, firmness, or crispness determine the choice. You are the best judge as to the effect *you* want.

INTERFACINGS

Classic tailoring. Have you ever noticed the soft roll of the lapel of a man's suit? This is due to the great resilience and springiness of the mohair in the hair-canvas interfacing. It is woven specially to assure this. The warp fibers are of cotton or wool; the filler of mohair. The roll of the lapel is horizontal, following the direction of the mohair-filler yarns.

Whenever a soft roll is desirable in a collar as well as lapels, use hair canvas for the interfacing. Cut the pattern pieces on the lengthwise grain to take advantage of the crosswise roll of the mohair fibers.

There are various grades of hair canvas, depending on the kind and quality of the mohair and cotton or wool. A good choice for collars and lapels is one that is pliable, firmly woven, noncrushable and springy. In addition to its traditional use as interfacing, hair canvas may also be used as an underlining. The stiffer types of hair canvas are used for this purpose.

Dressmaker styles call for a lighter weight, softer interfacing. As our list indicates, there are a number of suitable woven interfacings on the market. A good choice is one that is light, firm, noncrushable and that can be blocked or molded.

Semifitted and unfitted styles may call for underlining in place of or in addition to interfacing. Here there is great latitude in your choice for this purpose. If the backing is to act as interfacing too, choose one of the type suggested for dressmaker styles. When underlining is to be used in addition to an interfacing, it should be lighter than the interfacing. Whether you use a firm underlining or a soft one depends on the style and the outer fabric.

Collars. Use that interfacing which will give the desired firmness and the degree of roll of the collar.

Collar style	*Interfacing*
Tailored notched (Fig. 146a)	1. Tailor's linen
	2. French collar canvas
	3. Melton cloth for strictly man-tailored suit
	4. Any of the firm, crisp, moldable sheer canvases
	5. Flaline

Fig. 146

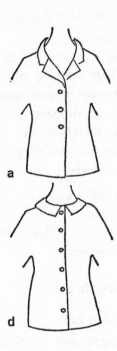
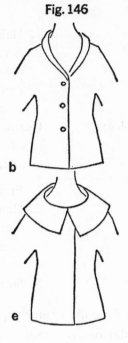

Collar style		Interfacing
Shawl (Fig. 146b)	1.	Continue the interfacing of the body of the garment into the collar
	2.	Cut a separate collar of any of those listed for the tailored notched collar
Soft rolled collar on a	1.	Hair canvas
dropped neckline (Fig. 146c)	2.	Any suitable woven sheer canvas
Flat collar (Fig. 146d)	1.	Hair canvas
(Peter Pan or any version thereof)	2.	Any of the woven sheer canvases

Collar style	*Interfacing*
Cape collars (Fig. 146e)	1. Hair canvas 2. Any other interfacing fabric which will produce the desired degree of roll, drape, softness, or stiffness
Standing collars (Fig. 146f)	Use double thickness with rows of machine stitching for added stiffness 1. French collar canvas 2. Hair canvas 3. Any of the stiffer woven sheer canvases 4. Scrim 5. Sized flexible cloth

Cuffs. The suggestions for collars can be applied to cuffs.

Flaps and welts. Muslin or any other lightweight, soft interfacing is generally sufficient. If a little more stiffness is required, use one of the nonwovens or horsehair braid.

Pockets. Muslin or a similar fabric is sufficient for most. Standaway styles require the use of stiffer interfacing.

Hems. Use a bias strip of muslin or similar fabric ¼" to ½" wider than the depth of the hem. For added firmness or weight, use a double thickness of the interfacing. A silk hem may be folded back against itself two or three times for interfacing. If a soft, padded weighting is desired, use cotton wadding, flannel, or felting.

How to make strips on the true bias:

1. Bring the lengthwise grain to meet the crosswise grain (Fig. 147a).
2. Cut carefully along the bias fold.
3. Rule off strips parallel to the bias edge and cut (Fig. 147b).
4. Join the strips on the straight grain (Fig. 147c).
5. Fig. 147d shows the finished bias strip with joining seam pressed open.

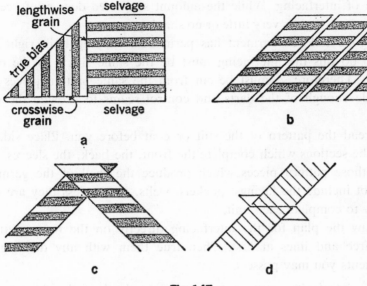

Fig. 147

Waistbands. What interfacing you use for the waistband (or don't use!) depends as much on your personal likes and dislikes as on the style and the fabric. Some women do not like to be constricted around the waist, while others like a very firm band.

These are all satisfactory as interfacings: self fabric, hair canvas, belting, French belting, grosgrain ribbon, or any other firm interfacing.

The "insiders." Any material used on the inside of the garment for whatever reason also helps to give shape and firmness. Considered in this light, any lining, stay, or interlining acts as a shaping and firming agent.

Unless very sheer, these insiders also add weight and warmth. Be mindful of this when you are considering the type and amount of underlining to use in the garment.

Make Your Own Pattern for the Interfacing

One of the big differences between professional and home sewing is the amount of interfacing used in a garment. The pattern, which most home sewers are dependent on, generally provides only a minimum of interfacing. While the amount suggested does reinforce the stress areas, it gives very little or no shaping.

A good tailored garment has permanent shaping built right into it. To do this the interfacing must be the same shape as the outer fabric. Therefore, it must be cut from the same pattern pieces and include enough of the darts and control seams to provide the contours.

Spread the pattern of the suit or coat before you. Place side by side the sections which complete the front, the back, the sleeves. Use only those pattern pieces which produce the shell of the garment. Do not include the facings, pockets, welts, etc., unless they are necessary to complete each unit.

Draw the plan for the interfacing directly on the tissue pattern. Use freehand lines at first. Then true them with any drafting instruments you may possess.

The interfacing pattern for a lined, classic tailored jacket or coat with set-in sleeves and set-on collar. The over-all shape of the interfacing includes the front closing and lapels, the neck, shoulders, and armscyes of both front and back, and enough of the darts and/or control seams to maintain the contour. The interfacing extends the length of the pattern piece. Eventually it will be cut away at the hemline. But you have no way of knowing exactly where this will be at the present time.

The interfacing is ½" wider than the facing itself. If this brings

Fig. 148

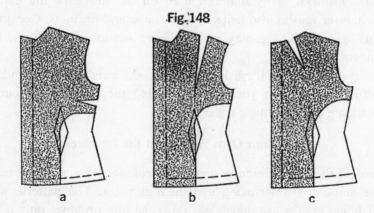

a   b   c

the edge of it close to a dart or seam, bring it all the way over to the center of the dart or to the seam line.

The interfacing comes down about 3½" on the side seam. When there is an underarm dart this is included in the interfacing (Fig. 148a).

Any dart which appears within this area is included since this creates the shaping. Fig. 148b shows the pattern for waistline and shoulder darts; Fig. 148c the pattern for waistline and neck darts. Whatever dart provides the shaping in the pattern *must* be included in the interfacing pattern as well.

The interfacing is cut on the same grain as the garment.

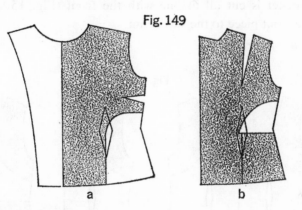

Fig. 149

a   b

When the facing is all in one with the jacket or coat, cut the interfacing only to the fold line (Fig. 149a). It is the garment that gets interfaced, not the facing.

If more firmness or shaping is desired through the hip area, add interfacing from the waist down (Fig. 149b).

When the shaping of the garment is accomplished by seams rather than darts, the pattern for the interfacing must be cut in as many pieces as the outer fabric. The shaping of the garment is lost if the interfacing pattern is made in one piece. Maintain the over-all outline as in Fig. 148a, 148b, or 148c.

Note that in Fig. 150a the entire front section is used and part of the side front.

In Fig. 150b a separate piece is added from the waistline down to assure the contour of the hips.

Fig. 150

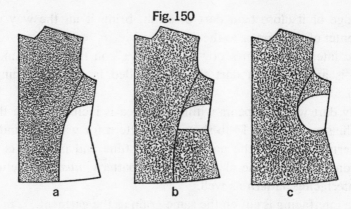

a   b   c

If a pocket is cut all in one with the front (Fig. 150c), interface the entire front piece to the side seam.

The back interfacing:

Fig. 151

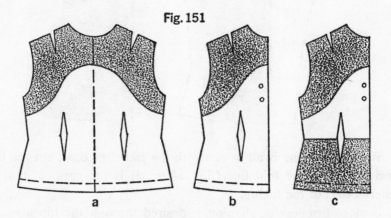

a   b   c

The back interfacing reinforces and shapes the shoulders, the neck, and the armscyes (Fig. 151a). It comes down about 4″ on the center back. It matches the depth of the front interfacing at the side seam. This is a very free compound curve (Fig. 151b).

The movement of the arms and shoulders is forward. This is one place where the garment needs to "give." The curved lower edge of the interfacing which is bias, permits the forward motion. A straight edge would inhibit it. Sometimes the entire back interfacing is actually cut on the bias to provide freedom of movement.

When hair canvas is used for the front interfacing, the back interfacing may be of hair canvas, too. Often, in coats, the back interfacing is a firm muslin.

Fig. 151c shows the interfacing for the hips when used.

If the back shaping is accomplished by seams instead of darts, cut the interfacing of as many pattern pieces as the outer fabric (Fig. 152a). Preserve the same over-all outline of the back interfacing.

If hip interfacing is required, cut this, too, in as many sections as the original pattern (Fig. 152b).

Some styles are cut in such manner that the side front and side back are joined in one piece creating an underarm section (Fig. 152c).

When interfacing is used at the hips, too, very little of the garment is left without interfacing. In many such instances it is just as well

Fig. 152

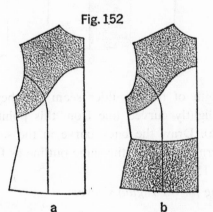

a   b

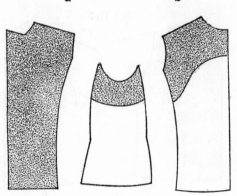

c

to underline the entire jacket. Whether you underline or interface depends on the effect you have in mind and the material.

The interfacing for the kimono sleeve. Unlike the garment with a set-in sleeve, the kimono-sleeved garment has no armscye for a guide as a stopping place for the interfacing. It is therefore necessary to draw one.

Fig. 153

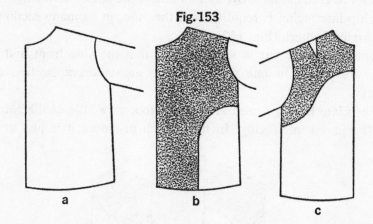

a   b   c

Mark the length of the shoulder seam ½" beyond the shoulder bone. Draw a slightly curved line from this point to the underarm seam (Fig. 153a). Draw the back curve in the same way. Now the interfacing pattern can follow the same outline as for the set-in sleeve (Fig. 153b and 153c).

The interfacing for the raglan sleeve:

Fig. 154

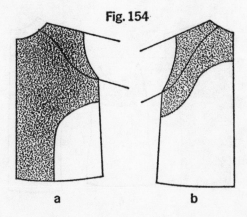

a   b

The interfacing for the raglan-sleeved garment has the same over-all outline as that of the kimono sleeve. However, each front and each back is cut in two pieces (Fig. 154a and 154b).

Yoke designs. If the jacket or coat has a yoke design, interface the entire yoke plus the underarm sections (Fig. 155). The interfacing is made in two sections. Use muslin or any similar soft but firm fabric.

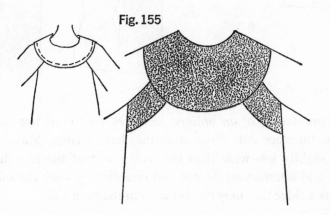

Fig. 155

The shawl-collar suit or coat. The characteristic cut of this design is the collar all in one with the front and joined at a center-back seam (Fig. 156a). The part that is visible as collar is a continuation of the facing.

If the jacket or coat as well as the facing are cut in this way, the interfacing is similarly cut (Fig. 156b).

Sometimes the garment is cut with a separate under collar (Fig. 156c). If this is so, cut the under collar of any of the interfacings recommended for the tailored notched collar.

Collar interfacings for all *other* collars are cut from the under-collar pattern. When the collar requires molding to the shape of the neck, it is cut on the bias. This may be in one piece if you have sufficient fabric. If not, cut two pieces and join them at a center-back seam. Flat collars and standing collars are generally cut on straight grain. Always use the same grain as for the under collar.

Fig. 156

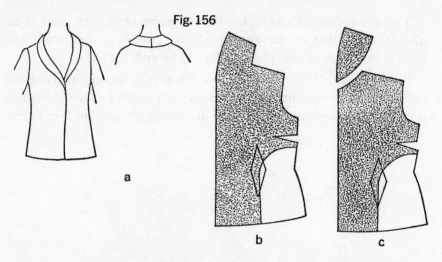

a

b

c

The interfacing of an unlined jacket or coat must not be exposed to view. Interface only those areas that have facings. Make the interfacing slightly less wide than the facing so that the two thicknesses (fabric and interfacing) do not end one directly over the other. This prevents a ridge that may be visible from the right side.

Cut Out the Interfacing Pattern

1. When the interfacing outline has been drawn on the pattern, slide a fresh piece of paper under it. Shelf paper or wrapping paper will do.

2. Trace the interfacing pattern. Be sure to trace *all* the markings including the grain. These are just as essential for the interfacing pattern as for the style pattern.

3. Cut out the interfacing pattern.

4. Determine the yardage necessary.

5. Preshrink or sponge the interfacing material (except silk).

6. Establish the grain of the interfacing material.

7. Lay out and pin the interfacing pattern on the material.

8. Cut out the interfacing.

9. Transfer all the markings. Use dressmaker's carbon paper and tracing wheel for accurate stitching lines.

UNDERLINING—THE INSIDE STORY

The interfacing just described produces all the shaping needed by many suits and coats. Others call for the more complete support offered by an underlining.

Cut the underlining from the same pattern pieces as the outer fabric. (Fig. 157a and 157b).

Fig. 157

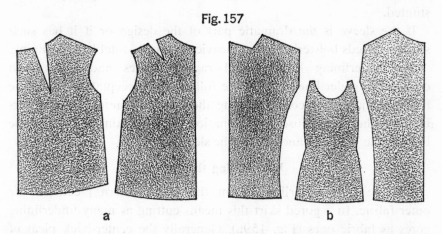

a   b

If the underlining has sufficient body the garment does not need an interfacing, too. When lighter-weight underlinings are used, additional interfacing will be necessary in those areas subject to stress—around the neck and the front opening (Fig. 158a). In this case the interfacing is cut from the same pattern as the facing and ½″ wider.

Fig. 158

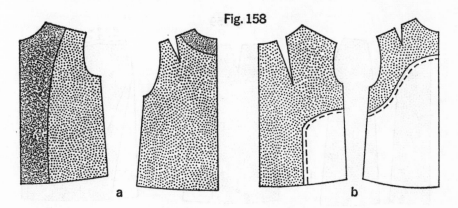

a   b

Another way of handling the interfacing-underlining combination is as follows. Cut a standard interfacing; underline only those portions of the garment not interfaced. Join the two with lapped seams (Fig. 158b).

Other Combinations of Interfacing-Underlining

If the underlining used in the rest of the garment is too heavy for comfort in the sleeves, then a lighter-weight underlining may be substituted.

If the sleeve is *the* dramatic part of the design or if it has such shape as needs bolstering, use a heavier or more suitable underlining.

For underlining kimono and raglan sleeves and styles with dropped shoulder lines, any of the following is acceptable: Underline the entire jacket or coat including the sleeves; eliminate the underlining in the sleeves; use a combination of underlinings—one for the body of the garment, another for the sleeves.

Underlining the Skirt

Cut the skirt underlining from the same pattern pieces as the outer fabric. In a gored skirt this means cutting as many underlining gores as fabric ones (Fig. 159a). Generally the center-back pleat of a straight skirt is not underlined since this would add to the bulk without adding to the design (Fig. 159b).

Either unpressed or pressed pleats in a full skirt may be underlined (Fig. 159c). In this case the underlining helps to define the bouffant or belled shape.

Fig. 159

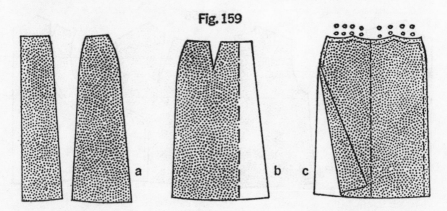

a   b   c

Cut and Mark the Underlining Pattern

1. Determine the amount of yardage necessary for the underlining.

2. Preshrink or sponge all underlining material except silk.

3. Establish the grain in the material.

4. Lay out the pattern on perfect grain. Pin.

5. Cut out the underlining.

6. Transfer all the pattern markings.

What it all adds up to is that any amount of interfacing or underlining is right. Any kind of interfacing or underlining is right. Any combination in any proportion is right. In short, anything is right which builds a foundation capable of sustaining the contour of the design. Use your good judgment and your ingenuity.

LINING AS A STAY

Lining is used in straight skirts as a stay to prevent bagging in the seat. A back lining to mid-thigh length is sufficient to take care of the "bump." But so conscious have we become of fine custom touches that many times the entire skirt is lined even though this is not really necessary. There is no doubt that a complete skirt lining gives a luxury touch.

A Half Lining

Use fabric with little give. When possible cut the lining on a crosswise grain so that the hip width lies on the vertical grain which does not stretch (Fig. 160a).

1. Use the pattern for the skirt back to mid-thigh length. Eliminate any center-back pleat (Fig. 160b).

2. Establish a new grain at right angles to the center back (Fig. 160c). Use a 45-degree triangle or any other square.

3. Place the pattern on the crosswise grain of the fabric with the lower edge on a selvage whenever possible (Fig. 160d). Use this as the finished edge of the stay. If the zipper is to be set in the side seam place the center back on the crosswise fold. If a back zipper is to be used, place the center back on the torn edges.

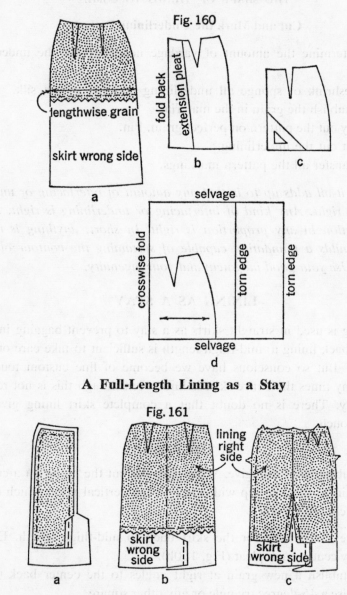

Fig. 160

(a) lengthwise grain / skirt wrong side

(b) fold back / extension pleat

(c)

(d) crosswise fold / selvage / torn edge / torn edge / selvage

A Full-Length Lining as a Stay

Fig. 161

(a)

(b) lining right side / skirt wrong side

(c) skirt wrong side

A full-length back-skirt lining is handled the same way as a half lining. If a pleat occurs only at the bottom of the skirt, cut the lining off at the fold line of the pleat (Fig. 161a), or at the top of the pleat (Fig. 161b), or leave a slit in the lining to permit the same freedom of movement as the pleat gives (Fig. 161c).

Fig. 162

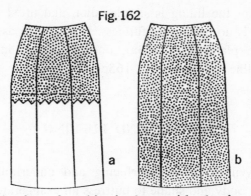

When the shaping of a skirt is done with shaping seams instead of darts, cut as many pattern pieces for the stay as in the original pattern of the skirt (Fig. 162a and 162b).

Any Fullness May Be Stayed

Lining may be used as a stay wherever there is fullness. It preserves the shaping of the unfull part by keeping the fullness where it belongs.

Fig. 163

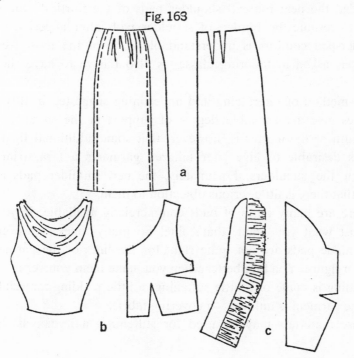

The pattern for the lining is simple, slim, and fitted to the figure by darts. There is no additional fullness. Lining used as a stay holds skirt fullness in place (Fig. 163a), bodice fullness in place (Fig. 163b), sleeve fullness in place (Fig. 163c).

PADDING AND PUFFING

Sometimes even extensive interfacing and underlining does not produce enough body and shape to buttress an exaggerated silhouette. In this event, the most common devices used are padding and puffing.

Padding may be used anywhere in the garment to provide the desired curves or contour—shoulders, sleeves, bust, or hips. The amount of padding varies with the style, the type of garment, and the personal needs of the wearer.

What a great sense of relief many of us experienced when fashion discarded the near-football shoulder pads of the thirties! Our reluctance to resume the burden of shoulder pads after a period of no-shoulder-pad comfort is understandable. One of the most frequent questions asked in tailoring classes is "Do I have to have shoulder pads?"

The method of interfacing and underlining suggested in this chapter does give a reasonable degree of support in the shoulder area. The truth of the matter is, however, that some additional light padding is desirable to give your tailored garments a firm, trim look through the shoulders. Fortunately, the new shoulder pads are so slight that there is little serious objection to them.

There are many types of pads commercially available. If you can find just what you want, that's fine! So many times, however, the ready-made pads are not quite right for the lines of the garment or for your figure. You fare better when you make them yourself.

Padding is made of a little stiffening, a little padding material, and —if the garment is unlined—a covering fabric.

These materials may be used for stiffening: hair canvas or any other canvas, pellon, crinoline, flaline, or any other sufficiently stiff foundation fabric.

The materials used for padding are flannel, felting, cotton wadding, quilting cotton, foam rubber, or any other similar materials you may have in your collection.

The covering fabric may be a light-weight silk or self fabric.

Puffing for sleeves may be made of taffeta, muslin, crepe, or grosgrain ribbon. If the sleeve fabric is sheer use a stiff, sheer material for the puff—starched organdy, organza, horsehair, net, or any similar fabric.

A Pattern for the Pad

Often a garment pattern contains a pattern for the appropriate padding. If it doesn't include a pattern for the pad, it does include some suggestion as to what kind of pad to use for the style.

As with interfacing, the best pads are made from the garment pattern itself. This has the advantage of providing the exact shape envisioned by the designer. Of course this may be modified to suit your own figure needs.

A good shoulder pad to use for a suit or coat with set-in sleeves.

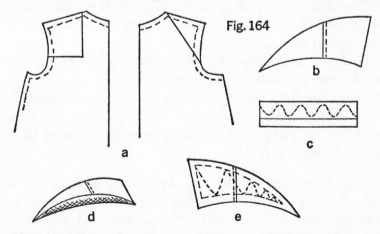

Fig. 164

1. Use the pattern for the garment front and back. If necessary, pin together any pattern pieces which form the shoulder and armhole area.

2. Sketch the shape of the shoulder pad on the front and back patterns (Fig. 164a). The pad comes halfway down the armhole on both front and back. The front shape is squared off; the back is almost triangular. The square front helps to fill out the front hollow at the armhole.

3. Slip a fresh piece of paper under the pattern and trace the pad pattern.

4. Cut it of hair canvas, either single or double.

5. Join the front and back hair canvas by lapping the shoulder seam. Stitch. Trim away the excess seam allowance (Fig. 164b).

6. Make a cap lift of light-weight unbleached muslin and cotton wadding. Cut a strip of bias muslin 9″ long by 2½″ wide. Fold it in half lengthwise and insert one light layer of cotton wadding. Pad-stitch to hold in place (Fig. 164c). Stitch the cap lift to the underside of the hair canvas, extending it about ½″ at the shoulder of the armhole edge and tapering it to nothing at each end (Fig. 164d).

7. Pad the canvas with cotton wadding or foam rubber, the thickest part at the shoulder of the armhole edge and tapering toward the ends. (This is your great chance to get just *the* thickness or thinness of shoulder pad you like.)

8. Trim away the wadding about ½″ in from the inner edge (toward the neckline) of the hair canvas. Bevel this edge by using the scissors held at an angle.

9. *Optional.* Use a layer of pellon or crinoline for further support. Cover this with a thin sheet of the cotton wadding.

10. Quilt the pad with rows of hand stitching to hold all the padding in place (Fig. 164e).

11. Shape the pad over any appropriate press pad using the steam iron (see Chapter VII).

An even lighter pad may be made by substituting a layer of felting or flannelette for the cotton wadding or foam rubber. A very satisfactory pad may be made of the hair canvas and several graded layers of pellon. If a commercial pad is used, you may remove some of the cotton wadding. But do use some shoulder padding for a professional look.

This same method with some modifications may be applied to bust pads and hip pads, too.

A shoulder pad for kimono or raglan sleeves and dropped-shoulder styles. Your chances for getting away without shoulder pads are best in kimono or raglan sleeves and dropped-shoulder styles. The soft, sloping lines are part of the charm of these designs. If padding is used to define the shoulder, it looks best when it is light and when it cups the shoulder. Here is an easy-to-make pattern for this type of pad.

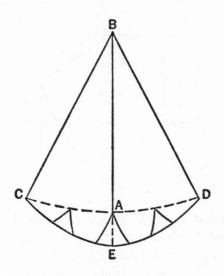

Fig. 165

AB equals the shoulder length
CA equals half the front armhole
DA equals half the back armhole
AE equals the desired depth of the pad over the shoulder

   1. Using this pattern, cut the pad of stiff shaping fabric.
   2. Overlap the darts and pin. Fit it carefully to your shoulder. Curved darts provide a better cupping.
   3. Stitch. Trim away the excess seam allowance.
   4. Pad with cotton wadding or foam rubber to the desired thick-

ness (keep it light). For extra-light padding use a layer of felting instead. If foam rubber is used, cover it with a thin sheet of cotton wadding.

5. Pad-stitch to hold all the thicknesses in place.

6. Stitch around all the outer edges or bind them with seam binding.

7. Block into shape over an appropriate press pad, using the steam iron.

A pattern for bust shaping (medium size) Fig. 166.

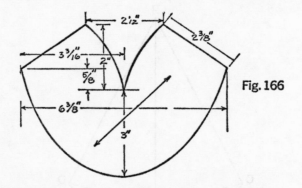

Fig. 166

This type of pad is designed to define and hold the shape of the garment at the bust. It is not a substitute for a brassière. If you have problems in this department, make a pattern from a brassière which fits well and follow its shaping, firming, and stitching. Fig. 166 is a simple pattern for a medium size. It can be made proportionately larger or smaller to fit.

Make the pad of ⅛" foam rubber covered with, or laminated to, light-weight silk, sheeting, or tricot. You can also make the pad of hair canvas lightly padded. Bind the edges with seam binding or tape.

If hair canvas is used, lap the dart legs and stitch. Trim away excess fabric beyond the seam. If foam rubber is used, cut it to the seam line of the dart, leaving no seam allowance. Bring the dart legs together and join with overhand stitches or machine-stitch to a tape stay. (Above techniques are described fully in the next chapter.)

When the style lines of any design do the shaping (Fig. 167a), a fine bust pad may be made using the garment pattern (Fig. 167b). Adapt the method suggested for the set-in-sleeve shoulder pad.

Fig. 167

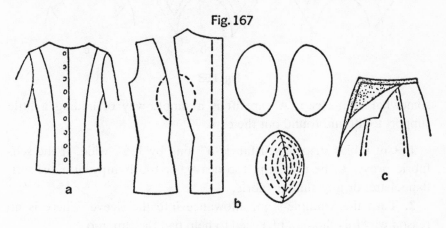

Hip Pads

If hips ever come back into style use the same method as for the set-in-sleeve shoulder pad (Fig. 167c).

Soft Padding at Neckline or Hem

Many of the new styles call for soft padding at the neckline or the hem. Use any of the following cut on the bias or to shape.

1. muslin
2. siri–soft
3. cotton flannel
4. cotton wadding
5. felting

Use as much or as little as will give the effect you want.

Something Up Your Sleeve?

Sleeves have always been a very important part of styling. Whether of the extravagant dimensions of the Gay Nineties or simply a well-set, slim tailored sleeve, some kind of support is necessary at the cap.

A cap lift. Even a perfectly set sleeve has a tendency to collapse

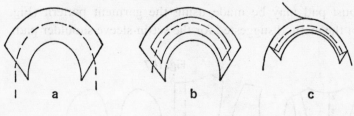

Fig. 168

somewhat at the cap. A cap lift is a simple way of adding a little support to lift and round out the cap.

1. Cut a bias strip of self-fabric 6″ long by 1½″ wide. If the self-fabric proves to be too limp, too heavy, or too bumpy, use siri-soft, flannelette, or any similar fabric.

2. Turn the armhole-seam allowance into the sleeve. There is no reason why this shouldn't be used to help pad the cap, too.

3. Place the strip over the shoulder and cap of the sleeve extending it into the sleeve just a little beyond the seam allowance.

4. Stitch by hand on the seam allowance close to the seam line of the armhole (Fig. 168a).

5. Use either of these methods:

    a. Cut a second bias strip 5″ long by 1″ wide. Place the smaller strip over the first, staggering the layers. Stitch by hand close to the seam line (Fig. 168b).

    b. Simply fold the remainder of the original strip into the sleeve, too (Fig. 168c).

A cap lift may be used in addition to some light padding. The cap lift rounds out the cap while the shoulder pad firms the shoulder line.

Built-in stays and stiffening are required when there is considerable fullness at the sleeve cap. Use an interfacing fabric compatible with the outer fabric—crisp sheers for sheer material; crisp, firm materials for heavier fabric.

For exaggerated silhouettes interface the entire sleeve (Fig. 169a).

If it is just the sleeve cap which needs support, cut a stay from the sleeve pattern (Fig. 169b). The amount of interfacing or stay depends on the style of the sleeve.

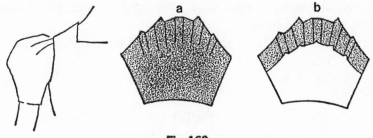

Fig. 169

1. Transfer the pattern markings to the stay rather than the sleeve.

2. Apply the marked interfacing or stay to the underside of the sleeve and baste them together.

3. Pleat or gather across the cap, treating the sleeve and interfacing as if it were one fabric.

4. Baste across the top to hold the pleats or gathers in place.

Sometimes separate pads are stitched in place after the sleeve has been set and stitched into the armhole. Here are two such pads.

Crescent Pad

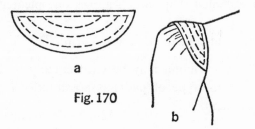

Fig. 170

1. Make a pattern in a crescent shape to the desired length and depth. Leave no seam allowance (Fig. 170a).

2. Using this pattern, cut two of some stiff foundation material.

3. Cut two thicknesses of some light-weight covering fabric, using the same pattern with a ¼"-seam allowance.

4. Stitch the covering fabric together leaving the straight edge open. Trim the seam allowance close to the stitching. Turn to the right side.

5. Insert the stiffening.

6. Make rows of machine stitching for extra stiffening.

7. Close the open straight edge with slip stitching. Or, finish off all edges with seam binding.

8. Tack the straight edge in place at the armhole seam (Fig. 170b).

Strip Pad

Fig. 171

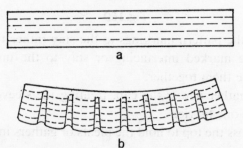

a

b

1. Cut a strip of taffeta to the desired length and twice the depth.

2. Fold lengthwise and insert stiffening in the fold.

3. Make rows of machine stitching across the strip to stiffen it further (Fig. 171a).

4. Pleat the stiffened strip. Stitch across one pleated edge or bind with seam binding (Fig. 171b).

5. Tack the bound edge in place at the armhole.

Any stiff fabric or ribbon may be used equally well to make this type of support. This type of pad has possibilities for use in other places on the garment.

The Shape of Things to Come

The vagaries of fashion being what they are there is no way of foretelling the shaping needs of the uncountable present styles and ones to come. Unfortunately, there is no one ready-made formula. It is the author's hope that this chapter has provided an approach to and a method for solving types of shaping problems.

Use this basic information with ingenuity and freedom. Just remember that if it works to produce the lines you want, it's right. When it comes to shaping—anything goes!

CHAPTER VI

And Sew a Fine Seam

Many sewers regard layout, cutting, and marking as burdensome but necessary preliminaries. When they speak of sewing they refer to the actual construction. Generally, this is even further defined to mean machine sewing. Glossed over are the literally thousands of tiny, invisible hand stitches which ensure the subtle shaping and long life of a good tailored garment.

Machines do everything—or do they? We Americans have implicit faith in the omnipotence of machines. Our attitude is hardly surprising since we absorb this outlook from childhood along with our hot dogs and Cokes. We make machines that do everything. And it appears we are only at the beginning. Automation promises machines that will do even more than everything. Consider the appeal of the latest sewing machine. All we have to do is push a button and all our stitching problems are solved—or so we are told. We merely turn a dial and the garment presumably makes itself.

Then, too, there is the constant example of machine-made clothing before us. This is what many sewers strive for—a finished factory look. This is what most sewing courses teach and what most pattern directions call for. That all important dial on the sewing machine must surely include an M for Murder. Much beautiful material and excellent style are killed by poor machine sewing in an inept attempt to ape mass production. When people say "Homemade," this is largely what they mean. If a strictly machine-made product is what you want, you will do much better to buy one. The operators who spend a lifetime doing one single operation do so much better than you can ever hope to do.

The case for hand sewing in a machine age. Imagine a factory where the workers added their own individual touches as the piece work flew by or who took time out to do some handwork where they thought the effect was prettier! It's not that factory workers lack skills and creativeness but hand details take time. Time costs money.

Tailoring entails a considerable amount of fine handwork (even in factories). The amount of handwork is what gives custom-made clothes their superior look and higher-price tags. By adding these hand techniques you can turn out expensive-looking clothing. After all, the major cost of any garment is the labor.

Both machine and hand sewing are necessary for fine craftsmanship. Despite the disdain which home sewers say they feel for an assembly-line product, we have been known to "spy" on store-bought clothes to see how the machine specialists deal with details that puzzle us. It would be folly to deny their skill. It would be somewhat anachronistic to put a dress together by hand while the dishwasher is chugging away, the clothes dryer is whirring, the television going, the transistor radio in the children's room blaring, and jet planes zooming overhead. Use the sewing machine where it will be effective and where it will shorten the work. Use handwork for all those details that will make the garment look better, fit better, and which are more easily accomplished by hand.

REFRESHERS AND REMINDERS OF BASIC SEWING TECHNIQUES

Tailoring takes straightforward machine stitching without any fancy attachments. Aside from a sewing machine in good working order, successful machine stitching depends on the combination of needle, thread, and fabric best suited to each other. Since silk and mercerized thread come only in one size there is no problem of selection here apart from color. Choose thread that corresponds to the fabric fiber (page 19). The size of the machine needle and the machine stitch is governed by the weight of the fabric.

Guide for the Selection of Machine Needle and Stitch

Type of fabric	Machine needle	Stitch size
Fine		
very sheer – chiffon	finest	16–18 stitches per inch
sheer – organdy	fine	14–16 stitches per inch
Medium		
medium sheer – sheer wool	fine	12 stitches per inch
medium – jersey	medium	10–12 stitches per inch
medium heavy – gabardine tweed	medium coarse	10 stitches per inch
Coarse		
heavy – upholstery fabrics	coarse	8 stitches per inch
very heavy – duck	coarsest	6 stitches per inch

(The size numbers of machine needles vary with the different brands. Translate the general designation above to the size number of your particular brand.)

Some women use the needle that comes with the machine until it breaks and then substitute another one just like it. It is very important to use the correct size of needle for your fabric. If the needle is too fine for your fabric it may break. If the needle is too coarse for your fabric it will make holes in it.

It is a good idea to make a test seam on a scrap of the garment fabric to check the correctness of the machine stitching. It should "ride" smoothly. The tension should be neither too tight nor too loose. Balanced stitches should lock properly on both upper and lower thicknesses. There should be no puckering or creeping of fabric. The pressure should be neither so light as to raise the fabric with the feed nor so heavy as to leave an imprint of the feed on the material. Check the length of the stitch. If any adjustment should be necessary to the upper or lower tensions or to the pressure of the presser bar, consult your sewing-machine manual for directions.

To Baste or Not to Baste

Many a would-be sewer has been discouraged by the prospect of endless and laborious basting before stitching. In most instances, basting is unnecessary, inefficient, and a waste of time. As fabric feeds into the machine, the upper layer has a tendency to stretch. Though never right, the result is particularly serious when matching seams, plaids, stripes, and checks are involved. Even careful basting cannot prevent this stretching, and the matching is thrown off by the machine stitching.

Pins hold fabric in place much better. There is no slipping as the fabric is fed into the machine. There is no danger of stitching over the basting with the subsequent struggle to remove it. Save the basting for those few places where it is absolutely necessary.

Pins Ensure Perfection

Discard the old, bent, rusted, or coarse pins. Use fine dressmaker pins. On very sheer fabrics or those that bruise easily, use fine hand needles or glass-headed toilet pins, both of which slide into the fabric readily.

Pin at the beginning and end of the seam, the notches, and the spaces between. Place the pins at right angles to the seam line to avoid puckering and to make removal easy (Fig. 172a). Some people prefer pins placed lengthwise on the true seam line (Fig. 172b).

Fig. 172

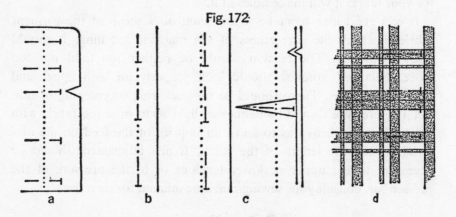

Pin in as few places as will hold the fabric in place—about 3″ apart. Use more pins on curved edges than on straight edges. Pin satin weaves parallel to the floats to avoid snagging. Place them in the seam allowance rather than on the stitching line (Fig. 172c) so that any marks left by the pins will not be seen in the finished garment.

Remove the pins just before the presser foot reaches them. The flexible presser foot is reputed to sew right over the pins but by the law of averages the needle is bound to hit a pin sooner or later. Result: one broken machine needle. (The exception to this advice is when stitching plaids, stripes, checks, and matching seams.)

Stitch slowly. Speed sewing is of no particular value to home sewers. There is not enough time saved on one garment to risk spoiling it with faulty stitching.

To Join Matching Cross Seams, Plaids, Stripes, and Checks

All seams should be pressed open first and trimmed to reduce bulk. Place the two thicknesses of fabric in the proper position, matching seam lines, bars, or checks. Put the point of the pin through the matching lines of both upper and lower thicknesses, slide it along the line of the under surface and bring it up on the matching line of the upper surface. The pin holds the seam line in place (Fig. 172d). Stitch across the pin very slowly and very carefully to run less risk of striking it.

Use safety pins if you must use pins for locating buttons, pockets, and other details on the right side. They will not fall out the way straight pins do with much handling.

SPECIAL STITCHING SITUATIONS

Stitching Seams

Seam stitching is directional just as stay stitching is and for the same reason—to preserve the shape of the piece and the grain of the fabric. Stitch seams from high to low and from wide to narrow (Fig. 173). This means that the shoulder is stitched from neck to armhole, the underarm seam from armhole to waist, the skirt seam from hem to waist, the sleeve seam from underarm down.

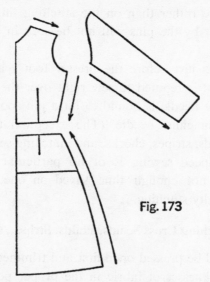

Fig. 173

Stitching long seams. On long seams the feed dog carries along the under layers of cloth faster than the presser foot does. This eases in the under layer while the upper layer has a tendency to creep and stretch. If you are not careful in stitching, you may wind up with lengths of cloth that don't match—the upper being longer than the under layer.

First compare the pattern seam lengths. If one is really meant to be longer than the other, the extra length must be eased in. If the pattern lengths are equal, pin the top and bottom of the seam. Pin in a sufficient number of places between so the two lengths match. To prevent slipping while stitching, place the forefingers either side of the presser foot and pull the fabric slightly horizontally as you feed it into the machine (Fig. 174a). Stitch a little bit at a time, slowly, in this position. The horizontal pull prevents a vertical stretch.

Thick woolens and pile materials are particularly difficult to control on long seams because the pressure of the presser foot pushes the upper layer of fabric along faster than the feed dog can ease it into the seam. Release the pressure by adjusting the presser bar according to the fabric. A walking presser foot is also helpful. This is a two-toed attachment: the right toe holds the fabric in place while the left toe "walks" with the stitching.

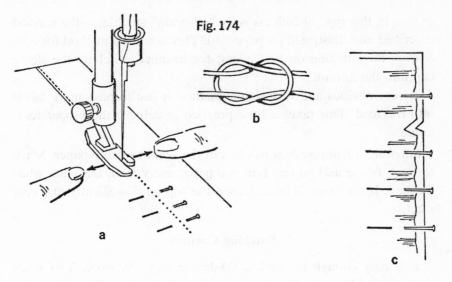

Fig. 174

Secure the stitching at the beginning and the end of the seam by

1. stitching forward and backward on the machine.

2. lock stitching: lift the presser foot slightly above the fabric and take several stitches in place; hold the fabric with one hand to prevent feeding into the machine and the presser bar lifter with the other.

3. pulling the thread through to one side of the fabric and tying in a square knot (Fig. 174b). Loop the thread right over left, knot; then left over right, knot (all former Girl Scouts will recognize this knot).

Easing in fullness. Wool is very obliging. It is easy enough to stretch a shorter length to meet a longer one. This is much simpler and faster than adjusting the longer length to meet the shorter. Pin the ends of the seam with the shorter side up. Stretch the shorter length to meet the longer and pin into position. Stitch with the shorter side up. The tendency of the upper layer is to stretch in stitching anyway. Why not let this work to your advantage?

However, there are some instances when it is advisable to stitch with the fullness toward you. For this type of easing, mark the middle, quarters, and eighths of both edges. Pin at each end, at each of the above markings, and at intervals between (Fig. 174c). Stitch carefully and slowly over the pins controlling the fullness. Another way to ease in this type of fullness is by "off-grain" stitching—the method described and illustrated on page 220. This is a good method for *controlling* the stitching on bias edges; for instance, stitching the sleeve cap into the armhole.

A very obvious and very simple method is just to push more fabric into the feed. This takes a little practice to achieve the proper technique.

Stitching a seam on bias fabric. Pin the seam to tissue paper. Stitch through fabric and paper. Tear the paper away from the seam when finished. If no paper is used, loosen the top tension slightly and ease stitch.

Stitching Corners

It is easy enough to stitch a 90-degree angle in wool. You stitch down one side, turn sharply on your needle and continue along the other side. But getting the corner to look square when turned to the right side is practically impossible. In our frustration we poke at the corner with any handy gadget and end up with a misshapen peninsula of fabric. The paradox is that if you stitch across the corner, it is more apt to look like a rectangle when turned to the right side. In light-weight fabrics, stitch almost up to the point of turning, take one stitch across the point, then stitch the other side (Fig. 175a). In heavier fabrics take three stitches to turn the corner (Fig. 175b). Needless to say, in sewing, as in driving a car, go slowly when rounding a corner.

Fig. 175

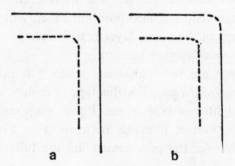

a   b

Stitching Pile Fabrics

To prevent the pile from locking, keep the layers separated until they are fed into the presser foot (Fig. 176a).

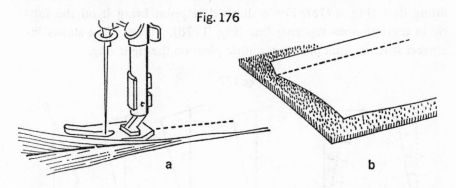

Fig. 176

a   b

If you do not feel confident enough that you can handle a long seam in this way then backstitch both lengths in place before machine stitching.

When joining a pile fabric and a plain fabric, machine-stitch with the plain fabric on top. The right side of the plain fabric is against the pile (Fig. 176b).

Stitching Shaggy Fabrics

When the seam has been stitched, turn to the right side. Using a fine needle, work out the long hairs which have been caught in the seam. When released, these shaggy hairs pretty well cover the seam and make the fabric appear uninterrupted by seaming.

For stitching any other fabrics which require special handling see Chapter X.

Stitching Darts

1. Pin the seam lines together.
2. Stitch the dart from the wide end to the dart point.
3. Lock the stitches by any method you choose at the wide end.
4. Hold the fabric in such a position on the machine that the line of stitching will be at right angles to your body; that is, coming straight

toward you (Fig. 177a). If you hold the fold of the dart straight toward you (Fig. 177b) the stitching line is on an angle and you practically have to sit sidesaddle to do the stitching.

5. Keep the last few stitches almost parallel to the fold for a better fitting dart (Fig. 177c). For a sharp dart point bring it off the fabric in a continuous tapering line (Fig. 177d). Figure 177e shows incorrect stitching that produces a little pleat on the right side.

Fig. 177

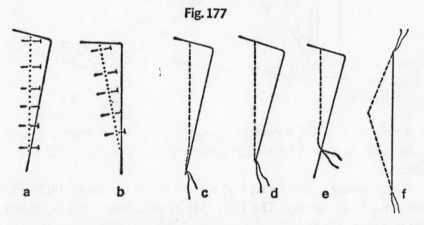

a   b   c   d   e   f

6. Cut the thread. Tie the ends in a square knot. Do not attempt to lock the stitching by reversing it. You almost never can get directly back on the stitching line.

7. A waistline-fitting dart follows the same principles. It may be started at either end (Fig. 177f).

Reinforcing a Line to Be Slashed

When a slash line is indicated on the pattern (gusset, sleeve opening, neck opening, etc.), it should be reinforced with a line of machine stitching. Stitch either side of the marking line, take one stitch across the end to provide the necessary space for cutting (Fig. 178a).

Stitch a Curve

To stitch similarly curved edges where the fullness of one edge must be eased into the other—for example, the curved seam line over the bust (Fig. 178b).

Fig. 178

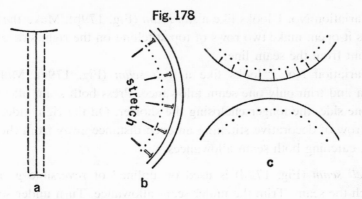

pin at each end of the curve
stretch the shorter side to match the longer
pin and stitch with the shorter side up

To stitch a curved seam when one side is concave and the other convex—for example, a curved welt to the curved opening of a welt pocket (Fig. 178c).

stay-stitch each curve
clip the concave curve (the inside curve) to within an inch of either end
stretch it to match the convex curve
pin and stitch

VARIATIONS ON A SEAM

Here are a group of seams most often used in tailoring. The type of seam used for any particular garment or any special part of it depends on the fabric, the style, and whether or not it will be exposed.

Plain seam (Fig. 179a) is the one most frequently used in tailoring since the seams are generally covered by lining. Simply stitch the seam on the stitching line, trim, and press open.

Plain seam top-stitched is a variation of the plain seam that not only adds strength but decorativeness as well. It is presently a very important trimming detail for skirts, jackets, and coats.

Variation No. 1 looks like a *slot seam* (Fig. 179b). Make the seam, press it open, make two rows of top stitching on the right side equally distant from the seam line.

Variation No. 2 looks like a *welt seam* (Fig. 179c). Make the seam and trim only one seam allowance. Press both seam allowances to one side, the longer enclosing the shorter. On the right side, make one row of decorative stitching an even distance away from the seam line, catching both seam allowances.

Fell seam (Fig. 179d) is used on unlined or reversible garments. Stitch the seam. Trim the under-seam allowance. Turn under some of the upper-seam allowance and top-stitch by machine or by hand. This may be made on either the right or wrong side.

Felled French seam or standing fell (Fig. 179e) is a fine seam for sheer fabrics. Trim the edge to be enclosed. Turn under the edge of the upper-seam allowance and bring the fold to the line of stitching. Stitch closed with a hemming stitch.

Welt seam (Fig. 179f) is used on heavy and very heavy fabrics. It is a strong seam and resembles the fell seam in appearance but has less bulk. Stitch with right sides together. Trim one seam allowance. Press both seam allowances to one side, the longer enclosing the shorter. On the right side make a row of decorative stitching the desired distance from the seam. Do *not* catch the shorter width of the graded seam.

Double-stitched welt seam (Fig. 179g) is made the same way as the welt seam. Add a second row of decorative stitching close to the original seam line.

Lapped seam or overlap seam (Fig. 179h). Turn under the seam allowance of one raw edge; press to position. Lap the turned edge over the other, matching the raw edges. It is easier to match the raw edges from the wrong side. Pin and stitch on the right side an even distance from the fold.

Lapped seam on a curve (Fig. 179i) is frequently used on yokes. Clip the seam allowance on the edge to be turned. Turn under the

Fig. 179

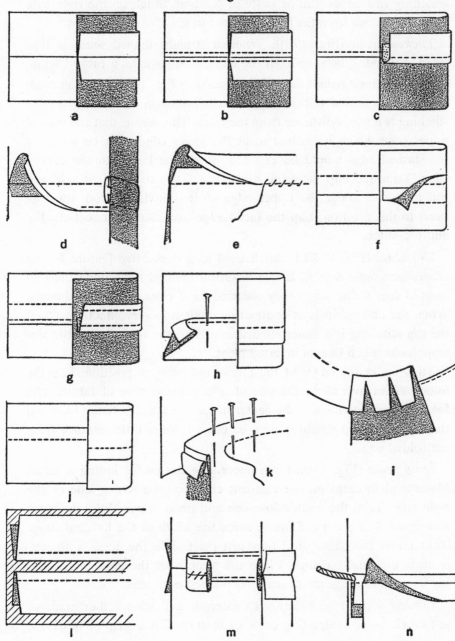

seam allowance and press to position. Lap over the under section matching raw edges. Pin or baste to position. Stitch on the right side an even distance from the fold and close to it.

Tucked seam (Fig. 179j). When a straight lapped seam is top-stitched a wider distance from the edge, it appears as a tucked seam.

Faced, lapped seam (curved-tuck seam) (Fig. 179k). The curved-tuck seam is similar to the straight-tucked seam in that the decorative stitching is a wider distance from the edge. This means that the curved upper edge which is slashed to fit the lower edge must be faced or the slashed edge would be exposed. Stitch the facing to the curved edge. Trim and clip the seam allowance. Turn to the right side and roll the seam under the upper edge so it is invisible from the top. Press to this position. Lap the faced edge over the under section. Pin and top-stitch.

Slot seam (Fig. 179l) is much used as a decorative feature for an otherwise simple design. It is a beautiful method for joining the sections of suede skins when they are used for dresses, jackets, and coats. When the understrip is of contrasting color it is very effective. When the top stitching is a generous distance from the folded edge the slot seam looks much like an inverted pleat.

Turn under the edges of the fabric and press to position. Lap the folded edges over the right side of a lengthwise strip of fabric. The folded edges may meet at the center or leave a space between to reveal the strip. The top stitching may be close to or a little distance from the folded edge.

Strap seam (Fig. 179m) is a decorative device for hiding a seam. Make a plain seam on the garment either on the wrong side or the right side. Trim the seam allowance and press open. Make the strap as follows: Cut a strip of fabric twice the width of the finished strap. Turn under the edges until they just meet. Join the edges with permanent diagonal bastings. Place the strap over the garment matching its seam to the garment seam. Top-stitch each edge.

Corded seam (Fig. 179n) is an interesting finish whether made of self-fabric or of contrasting color or texture. Cut a strip of fabric on the true bias wide enough to cover the cord plus two seam allowances. Fold the strip right side out. Slip the cord into the fold. Backstitch close to the cord with matching thread or machine-stitch using a cording or zipper foot. Baste the corded strip in place on the right side of one thickness of the fabric. Place the second thickness over it right sides together, matching all the seam lines and all the raw edges. Machine-stitch through all the thicknesses using the cording or zipper foot. Grade the seam allowances.

Piped seam is made in the same way as a corded seam except that the cord is omitted.

Top stitching as decoration. While a seam is essentially functional it can be made decorative by top stitching (Fig. 180a). This may be done with a stitch of regulation length and the thread used for the rest of the garment. It is particularly lovely when buttonhole twist is used for the stitching and the machine stitch is lengthened in size.

Buttonhole twist may be used for the bobbin, the upper thread, or both. If used in one place only, the stitch is locked by the regular thread. If used for both bobbin and upper threading, the same top stitching appears on both sides. This is preferable in any style where the fabric reverses itself—for instance the front closing and lapel of a shawl-collar style.

Use a machine needle with a large enough eye or one of the self-threading kind which can take the thicker thread.

If you prefer, the top stitching may be done by hand. Hand-stitching gives a fine custom touch to a garment. Use either buttonhole twist or several strands of embroidery thread.

Glove stitching is composed of small, even stitches ¼″ to ½″ in size on both sides.

Saddle stitching is made with longer stitches on the outside and shorter ones on the inside.

The seed stitch is really a little backstitch. It is one of the basic stitches in smocking. This variation of it looks very attractive on slubbed or rough-surface silks. Use two or three strands of embroidery floss. Make a tiny backstitch. Permit the threads to pull up unevenly making a tiny irregular stitch on top. It looks more like a seed pearl than a seed. Whether by hand or by machine the stitching is uniformly in from the finished edge to the desired depth.

Top stitching serves another purpose. It prevents the under layer of cloth from slipping out and exposing the seam. There are many styles which would be spoiled by top stitching and yet need the same permanent positioning of the under thickness. This can be accomplished by understitching.

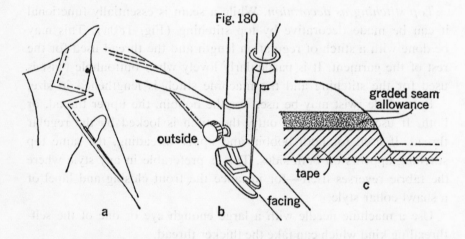

Fig. 180

Understitching. When understitching is done by machine both seam allowances are stitched to the facing very close to the seam line (Fig. 180b). This line of stitching is rolled to the inside so that the seam as well as the stitching does not show. When done by hand on an encased seam (page 248) fasten the wider edge of the graded seam allowance to the tape or the interfacing (Fig. 180c). This automatically encloses the narrower seam allowance. Fasten with either permanent basting or catch stitching.

Seam finishes depend on the characteristics of the fabric and whether or not a lining is used to cover the construction. When a lining is used no special finish is necessary unless the fabric ravels. When a lining is not used choose any one of the following finishes suitable to the fabric.

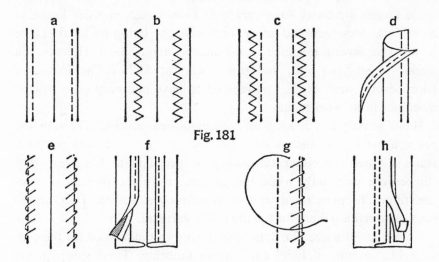

Fig. 181

Fig. 181a a row of machine stitching on each seam allowance

Fig. 181b pinked edges for fabrics that don't fray

Fig. 181c a combination of both stitching and pinking

Fig. 181d for thin fabrics: turn under the edges of the seam allowance and stitch close to the edge; a good finish for unlined garments

Fig. 181e for heavy fabrics that ravel easily or bulky fabrics: overcast the edges; do not pull up too tight or a hard line will appear on the right side; machine zigzagging saves time

Fig. 181f for fabrics that ravel easily: use commercial seam binding or bias strips of lining fabric pressed in half lengthwise; enclose the seam allowance either by hand or by machine; good for unlined garments

Fig. 181g closed seam overcast—both seam allowances are closed and overcast

Fig. 181h for sheer fabrics: stitch the seam; make a second row of stitching about ⅛″ away from the first; trim both seam allowances close to the second row of stitching

HAND STITCHING

Time was when all sewing was hand stitching. Even today in some fine custom shops both here and abroad fine tailored garments are made largely by hand. One very well known custom-order house in New York does each and every stitch save the lining by hand. There is only one sewing machine in the entire establishment. (It takes six weeks to get your suit, and prices start at $625.) The House of Dior, several years back, was reputed to have had only eight sewing machines in its workrooms.

Hand sewing has a long and distinguished history. Through the years, a variety of stitches were devised for every stitching purpose. Hand stitches are either temporary or permanent. The temporary stitches are used only while the garment is in the process of construction. The permanent stitches are *the* construction. They are so sewn as to remain there for the life of the garment.

Crewel needles size No. 8 and No. 10 are recommended for the considerable amount of hand stitching in tailoring. Their sharp points slide into the fabric easily. Their large eyes are easy to thread. Generally it is best to use a single strand of thread. It makes a neater stitch. Double threads may twist, knot, and pull up unevenly leaving a loop. (Use a single strand of thread even for sewing on buttons.) Cut the thread at an angle with sharp scissors. Thread the needle with the end cut from the spool. It is a sharp, clean cut and threads easier. Use a thimble. Have hand scissors and stitch ripper handy.

Temporary Hand Stitches

Basting (Fig. 182a). Despite everything said to the contrary, there are still times when basting may be necessary. Basting is a basic stitch with many variations. It consists of a succession of stitches and spaces either large or small, even or uneven. The size of the stitch varies with the use and the amount of strain exerted on the seam. Where the strain is great—as in fitting—use small basting stitches; where there is no strain, use longer stitches.

Use a single thread of contrasting color to ensure visibility. Use a convenient but not too long thread. Start with a knotted end and finish with several over-and-over stitches. Use silk thread for basting velvets, fine silks, and some woolens. Silk thread is less likely to leave marks. Baste beside the seam line to facilitate removal. To remove, clip the bastings at intervals and remove the threads. Pulling out a long basting thread may mark or cut the fabric. Remove bastings *before* pressing, since pressing will leave the imprint of the basting.

Even basting (Fig. 182a). The stitches and spaces are equal in length on both sides.

Uneven basting (Fig. 182b). The stitches and spaces are unequal in length, the longer float being on top.

Dressmaker's basting (Fig. 182c) consists of one long stitch and two shorter ones.

Running stitch (Fig. 182d). Work from right to left using a double thread (an exception to the general rule). The needle is woven through the material by an up-and-down wrist motion while the fabric is held still. When the needle is full of tiny running stitches the thread is drawn through.

Slip basting or alteration basting (Fig. 182e). This is a very useful stitch in matching stripes and plaids and in transferring alterations made on the right side of the garment to the wrong side.

For matching plaids: Fold under the seam allowance of one side and press. With right sides up, pin the folded edge over the matching stripe or bar of the other section. Join with slip basting.

For transferring alterations to the wrong side: Fit the garment and pin any necessary alterations in place on the right side. Mark with slip basting.

How to do slip basting: Working from the right side, slip the needle along the fold of the upper layer for a distance of about ¼". Bring the needle out of the fold. Point it directly down through the under layer, take a small stitch on the wrong side and bring the needle back to the right side. Repeat, alternating between the fold and the single thickness. This makes a row of basting on the wrong

TEMPORARY HAND STITCHES

Fig. 182

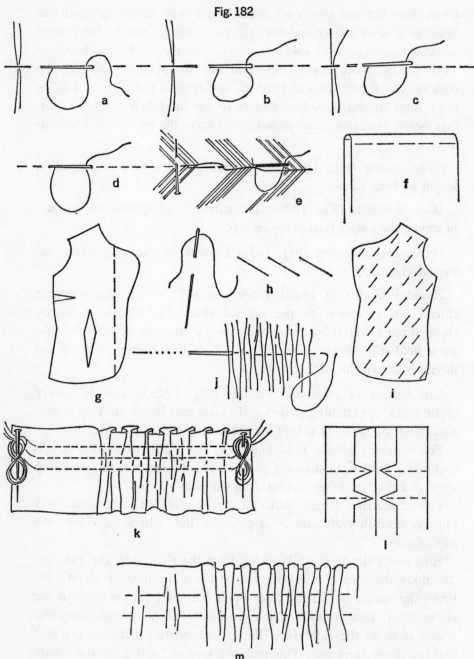

side of the garment which is invisible from the right side. The machine stitching follows the line of basting, using it as a guide.

Edge basting (Fig. 182f). Roll the seam to the underside so that it is invisible from the right side. Run a line of small bastings on the right side close to the finished edge of the garment. Edge basting holds the rolled edge in place so that the seam allowances may be secured by either top stitching or understitching.

Guide basting (Fig. 182g) is used for marking. Make a row of uneven basting with long floats on the right side and short stitches on the underside.

Diagonal basting (Fig. 182h) is used to hold several layers without slipping. It is a basting stitch with a long float on the upper side and a short stitch on the underside. The needle is held perpendicular to the line of stitching as it makes the stitch on the underside of the cloth. As the thread is brought into position to start the next under-stitch, it makes a diagonal stitch on the surface. This should be a "lazy" stitch—not tight.

Tailor basting (Fig. 182i) is long diagonal basting worked from the right side. It is used to join the interfacing or underlining to the fabric while the garment is in construction. Don't pull up the stitches too tight. Tight stitches produce a quilted effect.

Gathering (Fig. 182j) is used to draw up fullness. It may be done by hand or by machine. When done by hand, gathering is made with a running stitch and drawn up to the desired length. Strong thread makes it easier to pull. Use a double thread or buttonhole twist. When done by machine set to the largest stitch. Adjust either the upper or lower tension. Use a tighter tension and heavy-duty thread or buttonhole twist for the thread to be pulled. Whichever method is used, hand or machine, it is easier to distribute the fullness evenly if there are at least two rows of gathering. Three rows are even better.

Shirring (Fig. 180k) is several rows of gathering. The rows are an equal distance apart. The first row is on the seam line, the second slightly above and the third, when used, slightly below the seam line.

If the shirring is used decoratively, most of the rows are below the seam line.

Divide the edge to be shirred into half, quarters, eighths, etc., and mark with pins. Divide the desired length of stay (seam binding or ribbon) or garment section into an equal number of parts and mark with pins. Fasten one end by winding around a pin in a figure eight. Draw up the rows of shirring to the predetermined length and fasten the end around another pin in the figure eight. Match the markings and pin them together with pins at right angles to the seam. Distribute the gathers evenly between the pins. For a fine distribution, use a needle or pin to separate the gathers. To eliminate the bulk in a seam to be gathered, notch as illustrated (Fig. 182l).

Gauging (Fig. 182m) is used when there is a great deal of material which is to be gathered into a small length. The first row is unequal basting—long stitches on the right side, short ones on the wrong side. The stitches of the second row are directly under the first row. When the fullness is drawn up it lies in deep folds.

Permanent Hand Stitches

Backstitch (Fig. 183a) is the hand-stitch substitute for machine stitching. The continuous line of stitches resembles machine stitching. It is the strongest of the hand stitches. Start with a running stitch at the right end. Pull the thread to the right side. Working backward, insert the needle at the start of the first stitch and bring it out a stitch ahead. Repeat. The stitching is worked from right to left.

Over-and-over stitches (Fig. 183b) are two or more backstitches sewn on top of one another. They are used as reinforcement.

Pad stitching (Fig. 183c) permanently joins the interfacing and an under surface of the fabric. It is applied to the lapel, collar, cuff, or any other part of the garment which must maintain a permanent roll. It adds firmness and some stiffness to the area. It is done on an under surface only where it will not show.

The stitch itself is a smaller tailor basting except that the needle picks up only one thread from the underside. Generally the stitches follow the grain of the fabric. They are about ¼″ to ½″ in length, the rows of stitching are usually about ¼" to ½" apart. They can be worked in both directions. These should be "lazy" stitches to prevent a quilted effect. Use a single strand of matching mercerized thread.

Cross-stitch (Fig. 183d). The cross-stitch is used as a finishing detail. It holds in place the center-back pleat and the front-dart fold of the lining. Working from left to right make a row of diagonal bastings. When the row is finished in one direction, the same stitch is worked from right to left completing the stitch.

Catch stitch (Fig. 183e) sometimes called a herringbone stitch, somewhat resembles the cross-stitch, and is used a great deal in tailoring. It appears as a seam finish, a tailor's hem, and as a fastening for facings and seam allowances. It is usually used over raw edges.

The stitch is worked from left to right. Bring the needle out at the lower left. Backstitch on an imaginary upper line a little to the right with the thread below the needle. Pick up only a yarn or two. Backstitch on an imaginary lower line a little to the right with the thread above the needle. The movement is to the right. The stitch should be loose to prevent puckering.

Overcasting (Fig. 183f) is a series of slanting stitches worked over either single or double raw edges. The stitches are evenly spaced and even in depth. This, too, is a loose stitch. A tight stitch forms a hard edge which appears as a ridge on the right side.

Whipping stitch (Fig. 183g) is used in making a rolled or finished edge. Roll a small section of the edge toward you with thumb and forefinger. The stitch is like a small overcasting or overhand stitch which passes over and under the roll but never through it. Both the needle and the stitches are slanted.

Overhand stitch (Fig. 183h) is used whenever a strong, flat seam is desired; for instance, in working with fur or applying lace. The needle is held perpendicular to the edge. The stitches are small and close to the edges. They should not be drawn up tight so that the seam can open flat. A short needle is advisable for this stitch.

Slipstitch (blind stitch) (Fig. 183i) is similar to the slip basting

PERMANENT HAND STITCHES

Fig. 183

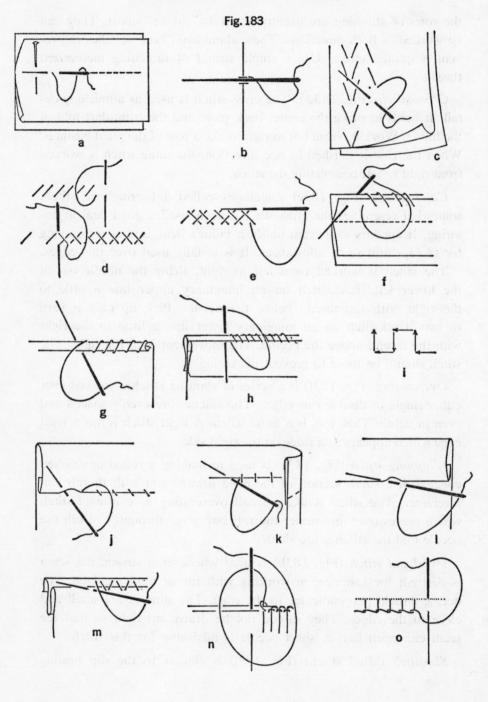

except that it joins two folded edges permanently. It is worked from the right side. Slip the needle through the fold of one edge. Bring the point of the needle down perpendicularly to the second folded edge. At this point, directly under the end of the first stitch, slip the needle through the second folded edge. Bring the point of the needle perpendicularly up to the first fold and repeat the stitch, weaving from one folded edge to the other. When the thread is drawn up a row of close, tiny, permanent basting stitches appears on the wrong side which is invisible from the right side. A diagram of the weaving motion looks like the Walls of Troy design.

Hemming Ways

Hemming stitches are tiny inconspicuous stitches which fasten the folded or stitched edge of a hem to the fabric. For most hemming, only one or two threads of the fabric are caught so that the stitching is invisible from the right side. The exception to this rule is slant hemming.

Slant hemming (Fig. 183j) is the fastest, strongest, but most conspicuous of the hemming stitches. It is best used when it can be concealed. The needle goes through the lower fabric close to the edge of the hem and through the edge of the hem. It is as if you were making small diagonal bastings through both fabric and hem. The needle is slanted, and the stitches are slanted and visible on both the right and wrong sides of the fabric.

Vertical or straight hemming (Fig. 183k) can be made practically invisible. It is the one most used on hems. Take a tiny stitch, catching only one yarn of fabric on the right side parallel to the hem. Bring the needle up on a slant through the edge of the hem. The beginning of the next stitch is directly under the ending of the upper stitch. The stitches on the wrong side are vertical; those on the right side are horizontal.

Blind hemming (Fig. 183l) is really the slip basting applied to hems. Catch a single yarn of the garment fabric. Bring the needle directly up and slide it along the fold of the hem. Bring the needle down perpendicularly and pick up a single yarn again. This stitch should be invisible on both sides (at least inconspicuous).

Running hemming (Fig. 183m) is a series of loose, small, basting stitches that weave back and forth between the hem edge and the garment.

Buttonhole stitch (Fig. 183n). Hand-worked buttonholes are made with the buttonhole stitch. Use mercerized thread, silk thread, or buttonhole twist. Work from right to left. The stitches should be close together and even in depth. Each purl should be on the edge of the slit. The needle is held vertical and goes through a loop of the thread. The loop is formed by placing the thread behind the eye of the needle and under its point.

Blanket stitch (Fig. 183o) has many uses—making the thread loop for a button, French tacks to hold lining in place, etc. It is similar to the buttonhole stitch except that it is worked from left to right and does not form a purl. The needle is vertical and the thread which forms the loop is under its point.

Hem Finishes

Tailor's hem is used for heavy and firmly woven woolens and jerseys. A tailor's hem may be made at the raw edge of a hem (Fig. 184a), a raw edge pinked and edge-stitched (Fig. 184b), a bound edge (Fig. 184c). The advantage of this hem finish is not only its speed, but that it is invisible and lies flat, eliminating the risk of a ridge or press mark on the right side.

For making a quick stitch, fold back the edge of the hem toward the hem; fold back the garment toward the outside. The two folds of hem and garment are now opposite to each other (Fig. 184a). Pick up one yarn of the hem, then one in the garment about ¼" to ½" away. Continue working across the length of hem, alternating between the hem and the garment. Use either a running hemming stitch or a catch stitch. The stitching is loose and drawn up only enough to make the hem lie flat.

French dressmaker's hem (Fig. 184d). The raw edge of a tailor's hem is overcast. (French dressmakers overcast everything!)

Catch-stitched hem (Fig. 184e) is used for woolens and heavy fabrics. Simply catch-stitch the hem to the garment over the raw edge.

Fig. 184

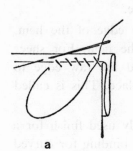

a

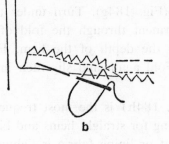

b

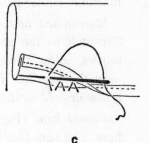

c

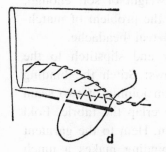

d

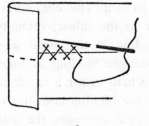

e

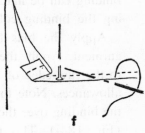

f

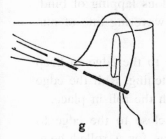

g

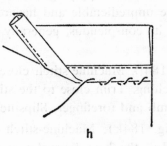

h

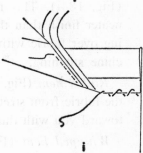

i

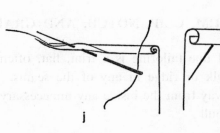

j   **k**

Edge-stitched hem (Fig. 184f) is useful as a self-finish for cotton, silk, or light-weight woolens. Turn under the raw edge and stitch by machine. Either hem or slipstitch the edge in place.

Slipstitched hem (Fig. 184g). Turn under the edge of the hem. Slipstitch to the garment through the fold of the hem. For sheer fabrics, allow twice the depth of the hem. Fold the raw edge to meet the hemline. Fold again and slipstitch in place. This is called a *double-fold hem.*

Bound hem (Fig. 184h) is the most frequently used finish for a hem. Use hem binding for straight hems and bias binding for curved hems. If the garment or lining fabric is lightweight or soft enough, binding can be made from it. This eliminates the problem of matching the binding color to the fabric, often a real headache.

Apply the bias binding in the usual way and slipstitch to the garment. Apply the straight binding as follows: Stitch the binding to the raw edge of the hem as for a regulation joining of two seam allowances. Note that the binding does *not* overlap the fabric. Fold the binding over the fabric, enclosing the seam. Hem to the garment (Fig. 184i). This method of applying the binding makes a much neater finish than the unpredictable and hazardous lapping of binding over fabric with its conspicuous, generally wavering line of machine stitching.

Rolled hem (Fig. 184j). Machine-stitch close to the edge to keep the fabric from stretching. Trim close to the stitching. Roll the edge toward you with thumb and forefinger. Slipstitch the roll in place.

Whipped hem (Fig. 184k). Machine-stitch close to the edge to prevent stretching. Roll the hem toward you as for a rolled hem. Stitch in place with whipping stitches.

HOW TO SLASH, TRIM, CLIP, NOTCH, AND GRADE

One of the hallmarks of fine tailoring is a trim, flat, often sharp edge which permits no bulk or ridge in any of the seams. This is accomplished by cutting away from the inside any unnecessary fabric which would produce the bulk.

Use small, sharp-pointed scissors for the following operations:

> slash—to cut open with a sweeping stroke
>
> trim—to cut away excess fabric
>
> clip—to make a short snip in the seam allowance close to the stitching line, using the point of the scissors at right angles to the stitching line
>
> notch—to cut a small V shape from the seam allowance as a guide in assembling pattern pieces
>
> grade seams—to trim away one seam allowance so that it is narrower than the other, giving a staggered or layered appearance

Trim It Away

After the garment has been carefully fitted and stitched, there is generally no need for a wide seam allowance. It has served its purpose and has no further function in the garment. Most seams can be trimmed to ½"; armhole seams to ⅜"; enclosed seams to ⅛", ¼", and ⅜". Sheer fabrics may be double-stitched and trimmed close to the second line of stitching (this method has its uses in other fabrics as well). Heavy fabrics and fabric which ravels easily require wider seams. If future alterations of the garment are contemplated, leave a wider seam allowance.

All darts in firmly woven, nonraveling wool over ¼" are slashed open. Slash as far as the sharp point of a small pair of scissors will go but no further than that part of the dart which is ¼" (Fig. 185a). To go beyond this point is to imperil the dart. If the fabric ravels easily, slash and overcast the edges (Fig. 185b). This may mean a little extra work but a flattened dart is essential for a trim, tailored look. It is not necessary to slash a dart which is narrow (¼" or less) or of light-weight material.

Trim the excess seam allowance of a waistline dart to ½" at its widest part. Slash the points of the darts to open them to within ¼" width. Clip the dart at the waistline so it is released to do the shaping for which it was intended (Fig. 185c).

Fig. 185

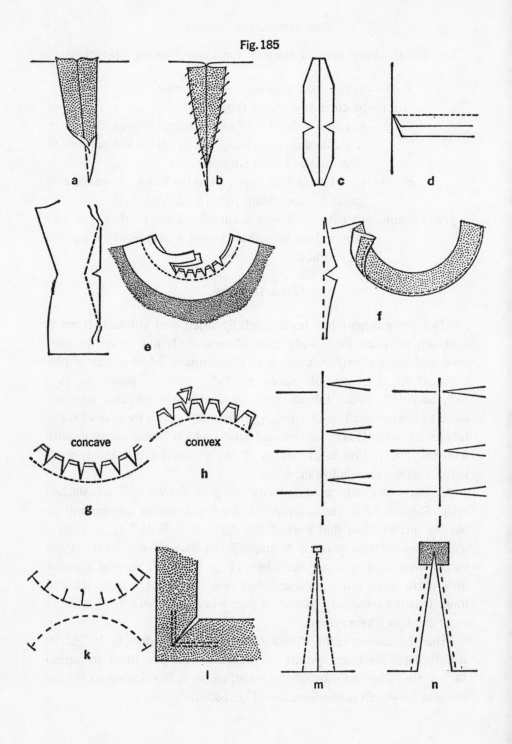

Grading

In tailoring (fine dressmaking, too) never allow two or more thicknesses to end one directly over the other. This shows up as a ridge on the right side when pressed or as a bulky seam. To prevent this, the seam allowances are trimmed so that each seam is a different width (Fig. 185d). This process is called grading (sometimes staggering or layering). This applies to as many layers of fabric as are stitched into any one seam.

The thickness of the fabric determines the amount left in each seam allowance. In medium-weight, firmly woven woolens, trim the first layer to ⅛", the second to ¼", the third to ⅜", and so on. In heavy fabrics or those which fray easily the seam allowances start a little wider and go up accordingly—⅜", ½", ⅝". Generally, the allowance closest to the outside of the garment is widest; that nearest the body is shortest. The encased seam described on page 248 is an exception to this rule.

Clipping and Notching

Whenever the outside edge of a seam allowance or fold is shorter than the seam line (Fig. 185e), clipping or notching is necessary to release the seam so that it can lie flat in the finished garment (Fig. 185f).

For an inside curve (concave)—that is, one curving toward the body—clip every inch or so close to the stitching line (Fig. 185g). Deep curves require more frequent clipping—every ½" or so. If the curve is an outside curve (convex)—that is, curving away from the body—cut notches (triangular wedges) out of the seam allowance (Fig. 185h).

Some seams, like the control seam over the bust, require clipping on one seam allowance and notching on the other. When the seam is opened flat, one seam allowance strains to lie flat. This should be clipped to release the strain. The other seam allowance ripples with excess fullness. Notch this to prevent the little darts or ripples which form when the seam is flattened. Notch between the clips so that there will not be too much strain on the stitching (Fig. 185i).

If the notches and clips are directly opposite each other only a few threads separate them from disaster (Fig. 185j).

When the seam lines to be stitched together are opposing curves (Fig. 185k), stay-stitch both, clip or notch one curve, open to match the other curve, pin together and stitch to position.

To clip a corner: reinforce the corner to be clipped with a double row of tiny machine stitches. Clip diagonally to the corner close to the stitching line (Fig. 185l).

To reinforce a line to be slashed: reinforce with tiny machine stitches (Fig. 185m) on either side of the slash or with a small square of facing at the end of the slash (Fig. 185n). For the facing use self-fabric, matching lining material, or matching seam binding.

To free corners of excess bulk: make three slashes (Fig. 186a). Slash One cuts diagonally across the corner. Slash Two cuts diagonally further into the seam allowance on one side. Slash Three does the same on the other side. Slashes are close to the stitching line (Fig. 186b). If you have any doubts about the ability of the stitching line to bear the strain, put a second row of reinforcing stitches directly over the first.

To miter a corner: turn the fabric to the outside so that right sides are together. Pinch the corner into a dart. Pin the dart diagonally across the corner (Fig. 186c). Stitch the seam, trim, and press open (Fig. 186d). Turn to the inside. In heavy fabrics, turn up the hem so the wrong sides are together. Pinch the corner into a dart, cut the excess fabric which forms the dart diagonally across the corner (Fig. 186e). Stitch the raw edges securely in place with overhand stitches (Fig. 186f).

To reduce bulk at cross seams: stitch and press the seam open. Trim the seam allowance slightly beyond the stitching line of the cross seam (Fig. 186g). Stitch the seam across the trimmed area. In very heavy fabric, the bulk is reduced by clipping the seam close to the cross seam and trimming away the entire seam allowance (Fig. 186h).

To reduce bulk in the hem: trim the seam allowance of the hem to the hemline. When the hem is folded back into position, the seam allowances are graded (Fig. 186i).

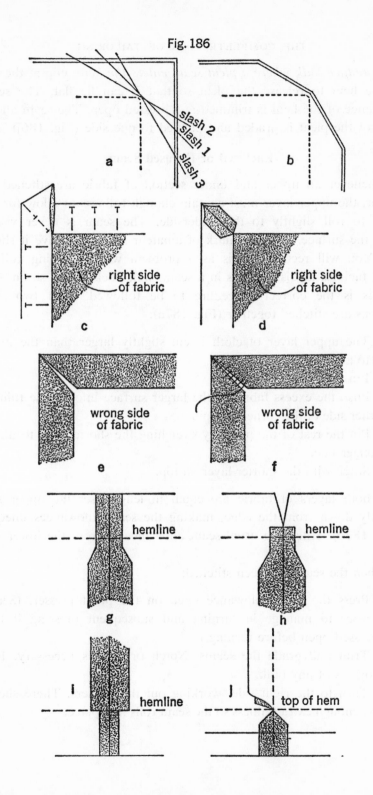

Fig. 186

slash 2
slash 1
slash 3

a

b

right side
of fabric

c

right side
of fabric

d

wrong side
of fabric

e

wrong side
of fabric

f

hemline

g

hemline

h

hemline

i

top of hem

j

To reduce bulk where a pleat seam enters the hem: clip at the top of the hem to release the pleat so that it can lie flat. The seam allowance of the hem is trimmed and pressed open. The seam allowance of the pleat is graded and pressed to one side (Fig. 186j).

Enclosed or Encased Seam

Whenever an upper and under section of fabric are stitched together, the upper layer must contain enough fullness to allow for the seam to roll slightly to the underside. The seam is never visible from the surface. It is the mark of amateur sewing to have it showing. You will recognize this as a problem when stitching collars, cuffs, facings, lapels, pockets in a seam, welt pockets and so on.

This is the correct procedure to be followed when two such sections are stitched together (Fig. 187a):

1. The upper layer of cloth is cut slightly larger than the under layer to allow for the seam roll.

2. Pin the corners together.

3. Push the excess fabric of the larger surface into a little fullness on either side of the corner and pin.

4. Pin the rest of the piece by stretching the shorter side to match the longer one.

5. Stitch with the shorter layer on top.

If both layers of fabric are equal in length, set the upper side slightly down from the edge, making the seam allowances unequal (Fig. 187b). Stitch the usual seam allowance in from the lower raw edge.

When the seam has been stitched:

1. Press the seam allowance open on the point presser. (Seams are easier to manage in turning and subsequent pressing if they are pressed open before turning.)

2. Trim and grade the seams. Notch or clip as necessary. Free the corners of any bulk.

3. Turn to the right side, working out the corners. There should be just enough extra fullness so the seam rolls into place.

Fig. 187

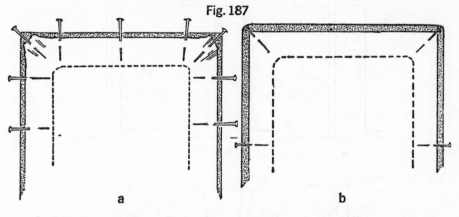

a   b

4. Steam-press the rolled edge to position. It is easier to do this from the underside so you can control the roll.

5. When the fabric is dry, edge-baste securely.

6. To ensure that the double layers remain in the proper position either top-stitch or understitch.

Joining the Seams and Darts in the Interfacing

All the seams and darts in the interfacing are lapped and stitched to prevent bulk.

To stitch the interfacing seam:

1. Lap the seam line of one section over the seam line of the other.

2. Run a double line of plain machine stitching (Fig. 188a) or zigzag stitching (Fig. 188b) close to the seam line.

3. Trim away the seam allowance close to the stitching line on both sides (Fig. 188c).

If hand stitching is used instead of machine stitching, use a cross-stitch to join the two thicknesses along the stitching line. Trim close to the stitching (Fig. 188d).

To stitch a dart in the interfacing:

1. Slash on one dart leg to the dart point (Fig. 188e).

2. Lap the slashed edge over the other dart leg (Fig. 188f).

3. Stitch close to the cut edge. Put a second line of plain stitching

Fig. 188

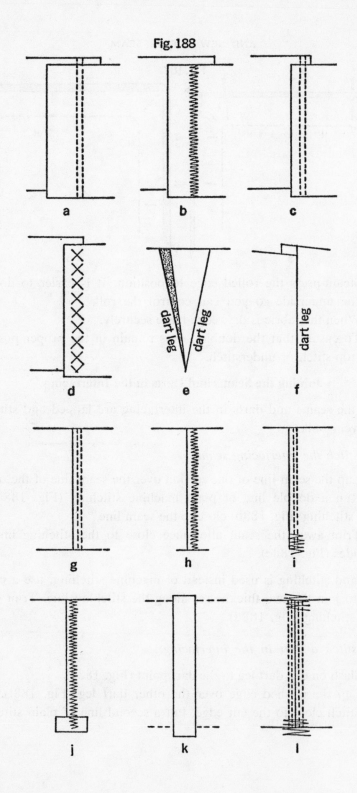

close to the first (Fig. 188g). Or close the dart with machine zig-zagging (Fig. 188h).

4. Reinforce the point of the dart with either zigzag stitches (Fig. 188i) or a patch of muslin (Fig. 188j).

5. Trim away the excess interfacing on the underside close to the stitching line.

NOTE: If you were to stitch from the outer edge to the dart point as you normally would, the presser foot would have a tendency to push the interfacing into a fold at the dart point. To avoid this, reverse the procedure for stitching a dart in the interfacing. Start the stitching at the dart point and stitch toward the outer edge.

An alternate method for joining the darts and seams in the interfacing:

1. Cut a stay of preshrunk tape or a narrow lengthwise strip of interfacing (Fig. 188k).

2. Trim away the seam allowance of each edge to be joined. Cut out the entire dart.

3. In either case, bring the newly cut edges to meet over the center of the stay.

4. Make a double row of plain stitching or zigzagging on either side of the slash (Fig. 188l), fastening the interfacing to the stay. Reinforce the end.

This is a good method for those areas which require a strong joining.

To stitch the dart in the underlining:

There are several ways in which darts can be handled in the underlining.

METHOD I

1. Cut the fabric and the underlining from the same pattern piece.

2. Transfer the pattern markings to the underlining.

3. Tailor-baste or stay-stitch the fabrics together.

4. Stitch the center line of the dart through both fabric and underlining to hold both thicknesses in place.

5. Pin and stitch the dart through both thicknesses.

6. Slash the dart and press it open.

METHOD II

1. Cut the fabric and the underlining from the same pattern piece.

2. Transfer the pattern markings to each.

3. Pin and stitch the dart in each.

4. Press the garment dart toward the center, the underlining dart in the opposite direction to avoid bulk.

5. Tailor-baste or stay-stitch the underlining to the outer fabrics.

METHOD III

1. Cut the fabric and the underlining from the same pattern piece.

2. Transfer the pattern markings to each.

3. Pin and stitch the dart in the fabric. Slash the dart and press it open.

4. Lap and stitch the underlining dart. Trim away excess material close to the stitching line.

5. Tailor-baste the underlining to the fabric.

If the underlining is sheer—organza, net, etc.—Method I can be used successfully. If the underlining as well as the outer fabric is lightweight—silks, cottons, etc.—Method II may be used. If the underlining is crisp or firm and the outer fabric is medium to heavy use Method III. Use the technique most appropriate for both fabric and underlining. If you have any doubt about which method to use, stitch test darts in fabric and underlining. Use that method which is least bulky and where the stitching is most accurate as it comes off the dart point.

And sew on—

This has been a chapter on techniques. Assuredly they are essential for fine production and one cannot minimize their worth. Tools and techniques alone do not make artists. It's what an artist does with them that matters. Practicing from morning to night undoubtedly helps but does not necessarily make of every aspiring young pianist a concert star. Stitching miles of perfect seams and doing acres of fine needlework does not alone guarantee that a suit will turn out to look like a couturier's creation. A garment could be as well built in its way as a bridge or skyscraper and yet not have style or beauty.

While anything which can come under the term "work of art" requires a knowledge of technique, technique alone never makes it such. So sew that you raise the *act* of sewing to the *art* of sewing.

CHAPTER VII

Pressing Problems

PRESSING MAKES THE DIFFERENCE

There comes a time in the sewing process when one wonders whether these limp little pieces of cloth so carefully stitched together are ever going to look like a suit or coat. This is usually just before a good pressing. Pressing makes the difference between an unfinished look and a completed one.

Fine sewing can be spoiled by poor pressing or the lack of pressing. Fair sewing can be enormously improved by a good pressing. That precisely tailored look is as much due to good pressing as to good sewing. The iron is just as important to the tailoring process as the sewing machine.

There are some home sewers—present readers excepted—who never tear themselves away from sewing long enough to do the bothersome (and often fearsome) chore of pressing. When the garment is completed, off it goes to the pressers for the final touch. Some pressing services refuse to take such work. They know how impossible it is to turn out a well-pressed garment with only one final pressing.

This is the way a well-pressed garment should look:

1. All edges on jacket fronts, lapels, collars, cuffs, welts, and flaps are thin, flat and crisp.

2. The nap, pile, or textured surface has been protected and preserved.

3. All seams are pressed flat.

4. There are no seam imprints and no press marks on the right side.

5. The garment is free from shine.

6. There is no stretch in any bias area.

7. The facings of double thicknesses of cloth are turned under slightly so that the seam is invisible from the right side.

8. All darts are pressed open. The darts are properly merged at the points so there are no wrinkles or bulges.

9. All shaping seams and darts are molded and blocked to produce a sculptured contour.

10. The collars and lapels are shaped to the body contour.

11. The sleeve cap is preshrunk, molded, and eased into the armhole.

12. Hems are smooth and flat without lumps, bumps, wrinkles, or ridges.

Can all of this possibly be done with one final pressing? The answer is obvious. *It must be press-as-you-sew for that well-pressed look.*

Every Fabric an Individual Problem in Pressing

Every fabric has a character, structure, and surface appearance of its own. Every design has style lines and shaping of its own. Just as the fabric and design determine how each garment is to be sewn, so they determine how it is to be pressed.

One cannot press a gauzy mohair coat as one would a cotton blouse; the motion of the iron would stretch it and crush it. One cannot iron a worsted suit as one would a linen suit; a hot iron applied directly to the cloth produces a shine acceptable in linen, disastrous in worsted. A velvet or corduroy jacket cannot be pressed like a smooth silk dress; the pile, which is its beauty, would be flattened and destroyed. The kind of fiber and the character of the fabric must be considered in choosing an appropriate method of pressing.

Darts and control seams produce all manner of curves in a garment—subtle ones, deep ones, in-between ones. One cannot press a shift dress like a fitted sheath; the one has very little shaping and the other very much. Even within the garment itself there are variations of contour which must be handled differently. The gentle curve which fits over the shoulder blades presents a decidedly different pressing problem from the pronounced curve which fits over the bust. The curve of the collar around the neck needs different shaping from the curve of the sleeve cap. Each of the many varied curves in a garment must be pressed and blocked in an individual manner.

Results Depend on Proper Equipment

To meet all the contingencies of design, shape, and fabric, a variety of pressing equipment is essential. In fact, a large proportion of all sewing equipment is used for pressing. Some of the following items are a familiar part of your household. Many will be new to you. Most of them can be purchased. Those marked * can be made at home from the diagrams, dimensions, and directions on the following pages.

Iron: A dry iron with heat controls will do, but a steam-and-dry iron is more generally useful.

Ironing board: Should be sturdy, of a good working height and well padded. Have it set up and ready for use when sewing.

Press board (Fig. 189a): A small ironing board that can be placed on a table. It raises the part to be pressed to a good working height. The table supports the weight of the garment so that it will not pull or stretch or trail on the floor. A press board doesn't take the room of an ironing board and is easy to store. Since most pressing is done in small units, this could replace the ironing board in your sewing room.

A sleeve board (Fig. 189b), a long, narrow, padded press board used for pressing sleeve seams. If one end of it is wide enough, the sleeve cap can be shrunk on it.

*Clapper or pounding block** (Fig. 189c). Sometimes called a spanker or beater, is a *must* piece of equipment when working with smooth, firmly woven, and hard-surfaced woolens. It is used to pound the seams flat and the edges sharp. Its special blocking and drying action prevents shine. The clapper is a heavy block of nonresinous hardwood usually about 1⅜" thick by 15½" long. It is 4" at its wider end and 2½" at its narrower end. Grooves along the sides make it easy to grip. It must be sanded perfectly smooth so that it will not snag any fabric.

Hardwood press block* (Fig. 189d), a hard, nonresinous, smooth press block used in combination with the clapper. A new, clean breadboard, cheeseboard or chopping block will do. (Needless to say, they don't travel back and forth between sewing room and kitchen.) The press block may be the size of the clapper or larger. An extra clapper is a wonderful convenience. It is just right for pressing sleeve seams. (It is much easier to buy an extra clapper than to search for the right hardwood, cut it, and sand it perfectly smooth.)

Edge and point presser (Fig. 189e), a very useful bit of equipment. Its point gets into the corners of lapels, collars, cuffs, welts, and seams otherwise difficult to reach. It is also used to prevent seam imprints on the right side of the fabric when the seams are pressed open.

Needle board (Fig. 189f), also called a velvet board, used for pressing nap and pile fabrics. It has a flexible base from which protrude closely spaced "needles." The pile is placed against the needles and steamed from the wrong side.

Cloth press mitt* (Fig. 189g), used for pounding seams and darts flat in fabrics whose nubby or napped surface would be flattened by the clapper. It is easier to use the press mitt for some curved seams and hard-to-get-at places than most of the other pressing equipment.

To make the press mitt, cut two sections double in the shape of a mitt, one shorter than the other. Stitch around the longer one leaving one side open. Pad with cotton to the depth of about one inch. Stitch the open end closed. Place the shorter unpadded section over it, matching the curved edges and stitch them together. Make the mitt of heavy unbleached muslin, duck, or drill.

Press cloth.* In pressing, the iron never comes in direct contact with the fabric. A press cloth is always placed between the cloth and the iron. It is a very important part of pressing. A rectangular strip 4" to 6" wide by 12" to 18" is easy to handle. It should be of unsized muslin or lawn, drill, linen, or cheesecloth. Wash thoroughly to make sure that all sizing has been removed so that the cloth won't stick. It should also be free of lint. Old, worn sheets, pillow cases, napkins, and Turkish towels make fine press cloths. (Turkish towels hold the steam particularly well.)

To protect the surface of woolens, a napped or nubby press cloth is necessary. Self-fabric is best for this use. There are always scraps which fall away in cutting. Any napped or nubby wool will do. Terry cloth or a Turkish towel are fine. A nubby wool-lined cotton press cloth 9" by 18" is a great convenience for wool as well as for other fabrics. Since moist heat is used in pressing, don't take any chances on color that may bleed onto your good fabric. Use white, light, unbleached, or color-fast material for press cloths.

*Steam-iron slip cover** (Fig. 189h), a device which may be slipped over the steam iron and used in place of a press cloth. It has two good features: it permits you to see what you are pressing (a press cloth hides it) and it forces one to use the lower-and-lift motion of pressing since it cannot be pushed along as in ironing. It is particularly good for right side touch-ups. The iron is set on steam.

To make the steam-iron slip cover, place the iron over the cloth to be used. This may be either cotton or wool. Perhaps you will want one of each. Trace around the iron. Extend the outline sufficiently beyond the tracing to bring the slip cover up on the iron and allow for a casing. Use elastic, a shoelace, or tape through the casing to draw up the hood to fit the iron.

Brown wrapping paper and tissue paper. Strips of brown paper slipped under the seam allowance prevent the imprint of the seam allowance on the right side. Covering the fabric to be pressed with tissue paper prevents the impression of the iron on many materials.

Small basin of water. Pressing is done with moist heat. The steam (moist heat) created by the steam iron is a standard amount. This is not always sufficient to press some woolens. More steam can be created with a damp press cloth and a hot dry iron. Keep a basin of water handy for dampening the press cloths.

PRESSING EQUIPMENT

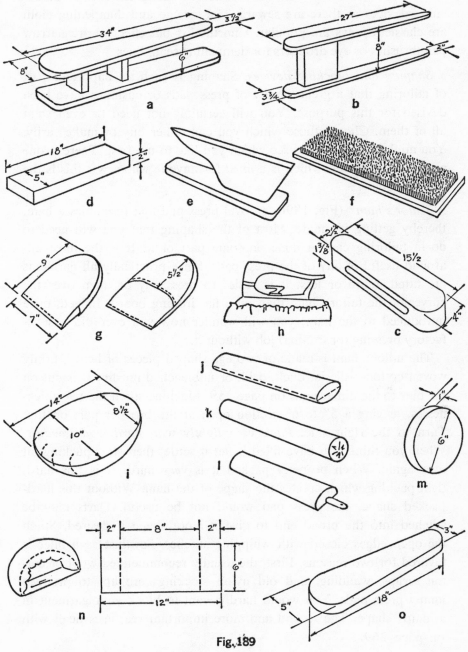

Fig. 189

Dampening devices. There are almost as many varieties of dampening devices as there are sewers. The sponge and dampening cloth are classic. Sprays are popular. Unorthodox but effective are narrow paintbrushes or eye droppers for dampening seam lines.

Shaping and blocking devices. Shaping is such an important part of tailoring that a great variety of press pads or cushions have been devised for this purpose. You will certainly not need or even want all of them. Choose those which you can either buy or make easily. You might experiment to see which you like to use best. There is one press pad, however, which is a *must* for anyone who sews: this is the tailor's ham.

Tailor's ham* (Fig. 189i), an oval press pad that resembles a ham, thereby getting its name. Most of the shaping that you will need to do in tailoring can be done on some part of it. It is the most all-around useful of any of the press pads. Since practically all garments are fitted, more or less, it is easier to press any of them over the curves of the tailor's ham than on a flat ironing board. Indeed, once introduced to the ham, you will wonder how you ever did a satisfactory pressing (or ironing) job without it.

The tailor's ham is made of two egg-shaped pieces of heavy, firmly woven cotton—silesia, duck, drill, or unbleached muslin. It is cut on the bias to the dimensions on page 259. Machine-stitch the two thicknesses, leaving a 5″ to 6″ section open at the broader part on top. Turn to the right side. *Pack very tightly with hardwood sawdust.* When you think you have filled it, let it settle, then start packing all over again. When properly packed it is *very* hard. It is this hard, tight packing which creates the shape of the ham. Without this hard-packed shape, the press pad would not be useful. Darts may be stitched into the broad end to give it more shape if desired. Stitch the open edges closed with whipping stitches. Sawdust as a filler is favored for two reasons. First, the usually recommended wool or cotton scraps, wadding, and old nylon stockings are apt to produce lumpy press pads. You would hardly want to block your garment in a lumpy shape. The second and more important reason is dealt with on page 269.

Napped, nubby, or looped fabrics must be protected when being shaped, too. Cover one side of the tailor's ham permanently with wool, terry cloth, or Turkish towel cut on the bias and slip-stitched in place. Or, make a slip cover of wool or Turkish towel that can be taken off when not in use. Put a zipper in one end for easy removal.

Assorted Rolls and Press Pads

The following press pads are used to prevent *making a seam imprint* on the right side of the fabric when seams are pressed open. The iron touches only the seam which rests on the crest of the curve. No pressure is applied to the edges of the seam allowances which drop below this high point, thus preventing an imprint.

A long seam roll* (Fig. 189j) can be made very like the tailor's ham. Cut a bias strip of fabric 9″ by 12″. Fold it in half lengthwise. Stitch the edges together, rounding the corners and leaving one end open. Pack tightly with hardwood sawdust. Close the open end with whipping stitches or slip stitches.

A tightly rolled magazine* (Fig. 189k) makes a very satisfactory seam roll. Cover a thick, tightly rolled magazine with a piece of unbleached muslin to hold its shape. Make a second cover for it either of muslin or wool.

A rolling pin* (Fig. 189l) makes a fine seam roll. It may be used either covered or uncovered. If uncovered, there is the benefit of pressing over wood when all the varnish is removed. If the rolling pin is split lengthwise you can have both—one half can be left as uncovered wood while the other half can be covered. Half a rolling pin has another advantage, too. Its flat surface rests more easily on table or ironing board.

For collar shaping. The collar can be shaped over a curve of the tailor's ham. A rolled Turkish towel curved into horseshoe shape is a simple and good device. Designed especially for this purpose are the collar press board and the collar press pad.

Collar press board* (Fig. 189m), a circle of hardwood 6″ in diameter and 1″ thick.

*Collar press pad** (Fig. 189m) is made of silesia, duck, drill, unbleached muslin, or any similar heavy firm cotton. Cut two circles of the material 6" in diameter and one 1" bias strip to join them. Pack tightly with hardwood sawdust.

Another version of a *Collar Press Pad** (Fig. 189n) and perhaps one easier to handle is made of a bias strip of heavy cotton 6" wide by 12" long. Fold this rectangle lengthwise and stitch the long side. Stuff it tightly with sawdust to within 2" of each end and hand-stitch across the pad at this point. Turn the unstuffed ends under so they overlap and stitch them securely to each other. These two-inch ends can be stiffened with cardboard or buckram, which makes it easier to hold the press pad. If you wish, the ends may be tacked to a heavy piece of cardboard or plywood 2" by 4½", so that it can sit upright.

For sleeve-cap shaping. Any of these can be used for shrinking and shaping the sleeve cap: the narrow end of the tailor's ham, the broad end of the sleeve board, or the press mitt. However, the most convenient to use are a sleeve press board or a sleeve press pad.

*Sleeve press board** (Fig. 189o) is made of wood to the dimensions on page 259. Trace the broader curve at the top from the pattern of a sleeve cap from which the ease has been eliminated. Pad the press board heavily like an ironing board. Old crib pads, bed pads, or table pads make excellent, smooth padding. Cover the padding with unbleached muslin or an old sheet.

*Sleeve press pad** (Fig. 189o) can be made the same way, using heavy cardboard as the base. Pad it heavily on both sides and across the ends.

Some General Hints on Pressing

Equipment is often a tip-off on technique. You have probably discovered some important facts about pressing: wool in construction is generally pressed with moisture and dry heat on either wood or self-fabric, the surface is protected with press cloths, needle boards, paper, and seam rolls; some force is used to flatten seams and make sharp edges whether it be pounding or patting, all manner of shaping cushions are used for blocking. Most important, the word "press"

has been used rather than "iron." This differentiation is very important in tailoring.

Pressing or ironing? In the usual kind of laundry ironing, the iron
is pushed along over the surface of the fabric. Cotton, linen, and
silk are ironed in this way. But this method doesn't do at all for wool.
In the damp stage necessary for pressing wool, it is very malleable.
It can be stretched and shrunken, pushed and pulled, molded and
straightened. If the iron is pushed along as in ordinary ironing, the
wool is easily stretched, wrinkled, and pushed out of place. Only a
careful up-and-down motion rather than a gliding one can prevent
this.

Have you ever observed a pressing machine in action? The heat
shoe is lowered, pressure is applied, the shoe is lifted. A new section
of the garment is fed into the presser and the action is repeated. This
is the same action which we use in hand pressing, too. The iron is
lowered, pressed, and lifted. It is moved to a new section of fabric
and the action is repeated. The motion of the iron like that of the
heat shoe is lower, press, lift; lower, press, lift.

Hints and helps. These are some general hints and helps in pressing
as true for cotton, linen, silk, and synthetics as for wool.

1. When sewing, keep the ironing board and tools up and ready
for use. Select the equipment necessary for pressing and shaping the
garment you are working on. Place a chair or table near the ironing
board (or vice versa). Let the garment rest on it while you are
pressing so there will be no pull or strain on the garment and to
keep it from trailing on the floor. Have the scissors handy for any
necessary trimming or clipping.

2. Test Your Fabric before You Begin
Experiment with a test seam or dart to determine

   a. the best heat setting on the iron
   b. the correct amount of moisture, if any
   c. the best method for flattening seams and edges
   d. some way in which the surface texture can be preserved
   e. if pressing produces a shine and how to deal with it
   f. how to prevent seam imprints or iron marks

*Don't begin your pressing until you are sure how your fabric will
react to the heat, moisture, and pressure.*

3. When a hot iron comes in direct contact with fabric it produces a shine. To prevent this, press fabrics on the wrong side (unless
you want the shine). Use an appropriate press cloth, the proper heat
setting and some dampness where possible. If the garment needs a
touch-up on the right side, be sure to use a press cloth to protect it.

4. Do not press the seams, darts, or any folds unless you are sure
of the fit and hang of the garment. It is very difficult, sometimes
impossible, to press out the crease marks put in by the iron.

5. Don't fold the garment in construction any more than is necessary. Keep the fabric as flat as possible. If storage or work space is
insufficient for this, roll rather than fold the pieces. As soon as possible, hang the pieces on a hanger or a dress form. (The dress form
is wonderfully useful in this respect. It makes the garment begin to
assume the contours of your figure.) Pin at the center front while the
garment is in construction. Button when the garment is finished. This
preserves the grain and permits the fabric to "hang out."

6. In combinations of fibers, the heat setting is for the most delicate fiber present, for instance: a cotton and acetate fabric is handled
as if it were all acetate. The low heat prevents the melting or fusing
of the acetate.

Heat settings from lowest to highest

low	acetate, Dynel
	Dacron, Creslan, Verel, Zefran
medium	silk, nylon, rayon, Orlon, Acrilan, Arnel
	Kodel, wash-and-wear cottons, wool
high	cotton, linen

7. Don't press over pins or bastings. Both leave marks. If basting is absolutely needed use silk thread which is less apt to leave
marks. Press as you sew.

8. Press every seam before it joins or is crossed by another. Press each construction detail as you finish it. Press each section before stitching it to another. Press all inside seams before turning. This makes it easier to turn and produces a cleaner and sharper edge. For instance, when a facing has been stitched to the garment, press the seam open before grading it and pressing it to the underside.

9. Just as there is directional stitching so there is directional pressing. To preserve the shape of the garment piece, press with the lengthwise grain in the same direction in which the garment was stay-stitched. To avoid stretching bias and curved edges, press with the lengthwise grain.

10. Press the seam or dart open with the thumb or forefinger first. Press lightly with the tip of the iron only on the stitching line. When the seam has been opened by these two operations, apply more pressure to flatten it.

11. Darts over ¼" wide are slashed open as far as the point of sharp scissors will go. Clip the seam allowance at this point so the dart may be pressed open above this. The unslashed end may be pressed as a small box pleat or to one side. A knitting needle inserted into the dart end while pressing prevents a press mark on the right side.

12. Darts and curved seams, both of which produce curves in the garment, are *always* pressed over curves. Use the tailor's ham or some other suitable press pad.

13. It is easier to do top-stitching if the edge has been well pressed first.

14. It is often easier to stitch if the section has been pressed first: the hem, the placket, pleats, a seam roll.

15. Do not press a lengthwise crease in sleeves or a sharp crease on the roll line of the upper collar or lapel.

16. Reduce the heat of the iron for slow work. Holding even a moderate iron for a length of time on one spot has the effect of intensifying the heat.

17. Avoid overpressing. Do not use too hot an iron, too much moisture, or too great a pressure, too many times.

18. The final pressing is always a hand pressing.

PRESSING WOOL

The equipment is so varied, the process so fascinating, the results so spectacular that even people who ordinarily hate ironing actually enjoy the pressing in tailoring. Here are a few general things to remember about pressing wool.

Wool is a living fiber. It must be treated so. Like any other living thing, it does not like being doused or dunked, scorched, broiled or beaten within an inch of its life. Don't subject wool to excesses of heat, moisture, or pressure, all of which in some degree are necessary to press it.

On temperature: Wool takes a moderate setting on the iron—350° to 375° F. Excessive heat directly applied causes the overlapping scales of the wool fiber to lock, thereby producing a shine. It also damages the fibers and makes them feel harsh. A hot iron should never come in direct contact with wool fabric on either right or wrong side. Between the moderate iron and the fabric there should always be a press cloth present. Sometimes the press cloth is of cotton, sometimes of wool, sometimes dry, sometimes damp, and often all of these. Even when using a steam iron a press cloth is often needed for protection of the surface. In some instances, the iron slip cover may be substituted for the press cloth.

On moisture: Wool is pressed and shaped with moist heat. The degree of moisture and heat varies with the kind of wool. Some wools require little and some require more. The use of the steam iron for a first pressing is limited to those fabrics that respond to a short, light steaming. Most woolens require the kind and amount of steam produced when a moderately hot, dry iron is pressed against a damp press cloth.

Though water cannot hurt wool (imagine sheep that weren't water-proof!) it is the press cloth rather than the wool which is dampened. Some woolens do water-spot, producing color changes. This is due to the dye which is affected by water rather than the wool. The press cloth should be damp, not wet. Wetness, plus heat, can shrink or felt wool. The cloth must be *uniformly damp* so that no part of the fabric will be subjected to more moisture than any other, hence shrinking or felting one part and not another.

Fig. 190

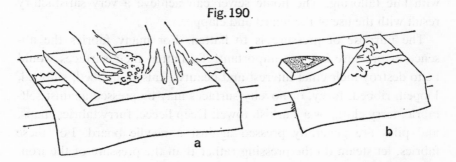

a   b

A press cloth may be dampened by either of the following methods:

1. Dip about one third of the cloth in water and wring it out. Roll or fold the rest of it around the damp third until the entire cloth is uniformly damp.

2. Rub a wet sponge or dampening cloth over the press cloth until it is moist enough (Fig. 190a). The advantage of this method over the first is that the press cloth is less likely to be wet.

Place the right side of the fabric against wood or other appropriate surface. Place a damp press cloth against the wrong side of the garment. Apply the dry iron to it with a lift-and-lower motion. Press lightly until the moisture changes to steam, then apply more pressure. Do not keep the iron too long on any one spot. From time to time allow the steam to escape by raising the press cloth (Fig. 190b). Stop pressing while the fabric is still steaming. Do not press it dry;

allow it to dry naturally. Hang it on a hanger or a dress form while it is still damp so that you do not lose the shaping.

On pressure: The word "press" implies that some weight bears down upon the fabric. Some woolens require very little pressure to flatten them—merely that brought by the ordinary up-and-down motion of the iron. A gentle patting with the press mitt while damp will suffice for other wools. For the hard-surfaced woolens like worsteds and flannels pressure amounting to force is required. In commercial production, garments are pressed on special machines which exert tremendous pressure to produce that clean, crisp, flat look associated with fine tailoring. The home sewer can achieve a very satisfactory result with the use of the board and clapper.

The purpose of pressure is to flatten. For many fabrics the absence of pressure is more important! To flatten their surfaces would be to destroy their chief interest and beauty. Raised, nubbed, slubbed, looped, ribbed, fuzzy, or novelty surfaces may be pressed against self-fabric, terry cloth, or a Turkish towel. Deep fleece, furry fabrics, naps, and piles are generally pressed against a needle board. For these fabrics, let steam do the pressing rather than the pressure of the iron. Pat or pound in shape or flatten with the press mitt while the fabric is still damp.

Each woolen fabric is a problem fabric, and presents an individual pressing problem. It is wise, before proceeding blithely with water and iron, to test your fabric to determine which combination of heat, moisture, and pressure will give the best and safest results.

How to press a straight flat seam in worsted or hard-surfaced woolen: Have all the equipment ready and handy, place the wood press board on a firm table or ironing board, the clapper on the left, the iron to the right. (Left-handed sewers, please reverse.) Have the press cloth ready, the basin of water and sponge or dampening cloth within easy reach. Using the board and clapper requires some dexterity.

Place the right side of the fabric against the wood press board. Open the seam by finger-pressing. Slip a ruler or yardstick under the seam allowance and line up the seam against it to make sure it is straight (Fig. 191a).

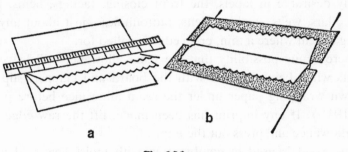

Fig. 191

Remove the ruler. Place the dampened press cloth over the area to be pressed. Only a small section is done at a time. Lower the dry iron set at WOOL onto the damp press cloth. Keep it on just long enough to create a good head of steam. Lift the iron and set it aside.

The next two actions are done in such quick succession as to be almost simultaneous. Whisk the press cloth off quickly with one hand while the fabric is still steaming; immediately slap the clapper on the seam with the other hand, bringing it down with some force. Let it rest there a minute, then remove the clapper. If the seam is not sufficiently flattened (some fabrics are stubborn) repeat the performance or beat with the clapper.

The loud sharp crack of clapper against board may be somewhat of a shock to unsuspecting members of the family. Better warn them. Especially if your best sewing time is about midnight when the rest of the family have retired.

Are you curious to know why and how this works? The clapper forces the steam into the porous surface of the press board which obligingly absorbs it. The wool is held in place by the pounding block long enough to train it flat. The absorbing quality of the wood helps to dry the fabric in the shape in which it has been pounded or shaped. This is why so much of the pressing equipment is of wood—press boards, clapper, shaping blocks, and point presser. The rest—assorted seam rolls, press pads, and the tailor's ham—are stuffed with wood (sawdust).

Whenever the fabric can take it, use the press board and clapper to achieve the very flattest seams and the sharpest edges. This is particularly desirable in lapels, the front closing, facings, hems, pleats, cuffs, collars, welts, pockets, belts, buttonholes—just about anywhere on the garment where a thin, crisp edge is called for.

If there is any possibility that the seam allowance will leave press imprints while being pressed with the board and clapper, slip strips of brown wrapping paper under the seam allowance before pressing (Fig. 191b). If any imprint has been made, lift the raw edge of the seam allowance and press out the imprint.

When wood is used in combination with moist heat and a press cloth, a hard-surfaced fabric is protected from shine.

How to press a straight flat seam in the softer woolens: Obviously the board and clapper cannot be used on any but hard-surfaced fabrics. All other woolens must be pressed in such manner that the surface is *not flattened.* One way to preserve the raised surface of woolens is by the use of a needle board. The right side of the material is placed against the "needles." The raised surface of the wool dovetails with the protruding needles. This prevents the surface from being flattened while the fabric is being pressed (Fig. 192a). Pile fabrics, heavy fleeces, and furry woolens are best pressed on a needle board.

Fig. 192

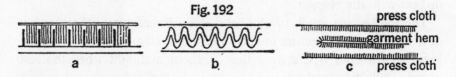

a   b   press cloth / garment hem / c   press cloth

A press cloth of self-fabric, any similar wool, or terry cloth can be substituted for the needle board with good effect on many fabrics. Place the dampened press cloth and the fabric right sides together on the ironing board. The nubs, loops, ridges, fuzzy ends, etc., of both press cloth and fabric interlock to preserve the raised surface of the wool while being pressed (Fig. 192b).

Then, too, when a napped fabric is pressed against another napped fabric, nap adheres to nap. As the fabric is raised to separate the two after pressing, the nap is lifted.

At least two press cloths are used in pressing wool. Generally, a dampened wool press cloth is placed beneath the fabric, a dry one on top. Many textured fabrics require both extra protection and extra dampness on top as well as below. For such fabrics use a dampened wool press cloth under the fabric, right sides together, a second dampened wool press cloth with right side against any turned-back surface —seam allowance, facing, or hem. By this latter method, the fabric is enclosed by wool press cloths. Should it ever be necessary to let out the seam allowance or lower a hem, the protected surface will be usable (Fig. 192c).

The use of a dampened press cloth both above and below the fabric creates steam which penetrates the fabric both from the right side and the wrong side. The upper steaming flattens where necessary, the lower steaming freshens and restores the wool. Both smooth out wrinkles, creases, or folds in the fabric.

Do a small section at a time. The motion of the iron is: lower, press, lift. Raise the press cloth from time to time to permit the steam to escape. Pat the seam flat with the press mitt. While the fabric is still damp, brush up the surface of the woolen.

SHAPING AND BLOCKING

Garments are designed to conform to the shape of the body— sometimes more, sometimes less. The style lines indicate the three-dimensional quality; the pattern is cut to produce it; the fabric is stitched to achieve it; the interfacing is designed to buttress it. Now it is the turn of the pressing to guarantee that the shape is blocked in.

Think of wool as hair that needs setting. When you set your own hair you use a setting fluid and anything from bobby pins to large rollers to produce the contour you want. Wool, too, needs a setting agent and some shaping device—water for the setting and any or all of the curved press pads for the shaping. As with your own hair, if dissatisfied with the setting, it can be reset.

Wherever there is shaping in the garment, either darts or control seams, these areas must be pressed over curved press pads. Were they to be pressed on a flat surface the fullness or shape would be shrunk out and flattened, defeating the very purpose of the darts and control seams. In addition, even straight pieces which are designed to fit curved areas—like the collar and the sleeve cap—must also be blocked to shape. (You will note that the under collar is cut on the bias and that the edges of the sleeve cap are really bias which makes this curving and shaping easy.)

The following areas are always pressed and blocked over some curved press pad: all bodice darts, dart tucks, and control seams; all skirt darts and control seams; all shaped side seams and underarm sections; the waistline seam; shoulder ease, elbow ease or darts, the sleeve cap, the armhole seam; collars and lapels; hips of skirts and jackets. Use that curve of the tailor's ham which best corresponds to the curve of the garment, or use any of the specialized press pads for a particular area.

The seams and darts of worsteds and other hard-surfaced fabrics may be pressed open with the board and clapper first, then shaped and blocked over a curved press pad. The darts and seams of woolens may be both pressed and shaped at the same time.

Keep scissors handy to clip wherever it is necessary to make the seam or dart lie in the planned curve without restraint.

Observe all the general directions for pressing woolens or hard-surfaced wools. If one side of the tailor's ham has been covered with wool it is not necessary to use an additional lower press cloth. Dampen either the press cloth or the woolen surface of the tailor's ham.

How to press a curved seam: Place the curved seam over a corresponding curve of the tailor's ham face down. Cover with a dampened press cloth. Press with the lengthwise grain and in the direction of the stitching—from the neck down, (Fig. 193a) from the underarm down, from hem to waistline.

How to press darts: Place the opened dart over a corresponding curve of the tailor's ham. Press the dart from the wide end to the point (Fig. 193b). Use a slight rotary motion at the dart point to smooth out and round out the area. It is often necessary to pull the

Fig. 193

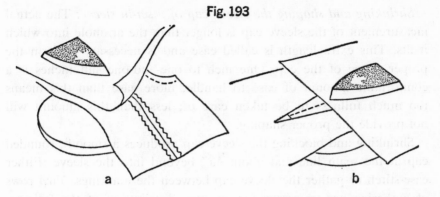

a   b

fabric taut while doing this in order to get rid of the sharp bulge at the dart point. Place the entire curved area over that curve of the tailor's ham which most corresponds to the shape of the area. Cover with a dampened press cloth and press.

Shaping the interfacing: To guarantee the permanent contour of the garment, the interfacing, like the outer fabric, is blocked to shape. Place the interfacing over the ham. Using the steam iron, press into the desired smooth, rounded shape. Pull the dart point taut. Press with a rotary motion to eliminate any sharp bulge. Allow each unit to dry to shape over the ham.

Pressing the sleeve seam: Slip the sleeve over the sleeve board, the sleeve press board, the sleeve press pad, or the clapper (Fig. 194a). The wrong side is up. Straighten the seam line against the yardstick. Press the seam allowance open in the technique best suited for the fabric.

Fig. 194

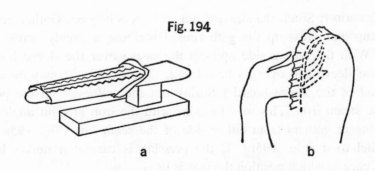

a   b

Shrinking and shaping the sleeve cap of a set-in sleeve: The actual measurement of the sleeve cap is longer than the armhole into which it fits. This extra length is called ease and is necessary to form the proper shape of the cap. One inch to one-and-one-half inches is a comfortable amount of ease to handle; more ease than this means too much fullness to be taken care of; less than this amount will not provide the proper shaping.

Shrinking and blocking the sleeve cap produces a smooth, rounded cap at the seam line and about ⅝" beyond into the sleeve. Either ease-stitch or gather the sleeve cap between the markings. *Two* rows of gathering are necessary for an even distribution of the fullness. Draw up the gathering until the sleeve cap cups over your hooked fingers (Fig. 194b). Do not worry that you will draw up too much. It can always be spread a bit to fit the armhole.

There are two methods for shrinking out the fullness in the sleeve cap. In either method use the pressing technique best suited to the fabric.

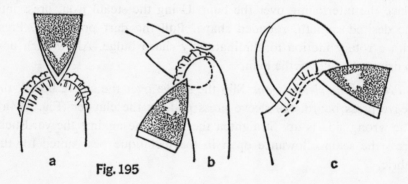

a   Fig. 195   b   c

METHOD I: Stitch the sleeve seam and press it open. Gather across the cap and draw up the gathering. Distribute it evenly across the cap. With the wrong side up, slip the sleeve over the sleeve board. Fit the sleeve cap over its broad end. (The press mitt may be used instead of the sleeve board.) Shrink out the fullness with the point of the steam iron. This may be done with the iron at right angles to the line of gathers from either side of the seam line (Fig. 195a) or parallel to it (Fig. 195b). If the pressing is careful it makes little difference in which position the iron is used.

METHOD II: Do *not* stitch the sleeve seam. Gather across the cap and draw up the gathers to cap shape. Distribute the fullness. Place the sleeve cap, wrong side up, over the tailor's ham. Shrink out the fullness with the steam iron parallel to the line of gathering. Stitch the sleeve seam and press it open.

By either method some fullness may be left in the seam allowance but there should be *none* at the seam line of the cap.

Since there appears to be such a division of opinion as to the best way in which to shrink out the fullness, choose whichever method is easier for you or whichever seems right for a particular design or fabric. It is perhaps simpler for home sewers to get a good cap shape by Method I. Whatever the method, the important thing is to shrink and shape the cap *before* the sleeve is stitched into the armhole. This is so much easier than after! And it practically guarantees a sleeve set without ripples or puckers.

How to press welts and flaps: In construction: After the welt or flap has been stitched, press the seam allowances open over the point presser (the point is inserted into the corner). Grade the seams and free the corners of bulk. Turn to the right side. Press flat with the seam rolled to the underside. Use the clapper for a sharp edge whenever possible.

For a right side touch-up on the finished garment: insert wrapping paper or a rectangle of cardboard under the flap or welt so that the pressing will not leave an imprint on the garment.

Pressing the collar: In a classic tailored suit, the collar hugs the neckline. All other collars are handled in such manner that they curve with the neckline.

In construction: When the roll line of the collar interfacing has been established by the trial fitting (page 345), make a sharp crease along the fold with the fingers (Fig. 196a). Pin the collar interfacing over the under collar and pad-stitch the roll line. From this moment on, you must treat the collar as if it really were meant to fit around the neck. You can no longer think of it as a flat surface. Hold it in a neck shape while pad stitching. Steam it into a neck shape over a rolled Turkish towel, the tailor's ham, or any of the collar press pads (Fig. 196b).

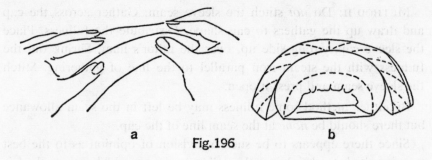

a   Fig. 196   b

When the upper collar has been stitched to the under collar, press the seam allowances open, using the point presser. When the collar has been turned to the right side, press the edges as thin and flat as the pressing technique for your fabric will permit. Be sure to roll the seam to the underside.

Shaping the completed collar: While the collar is still damp, mold it once more into a neck shape. Use any of the shaping devices (Fig. 196b). If necessary, steam along the inside curve of the neckline and stretch the outside curve. Pin the collar to position on the dress form or around one of the press pads. Allow it to dry in this position.

Pressing the lapel: In construction: the lapel is handled much the same way as the collar. However, the roll line is *never* pressed to position.

Fig. 197

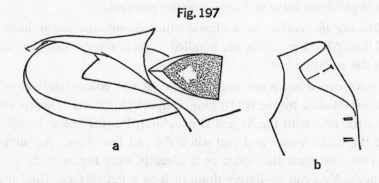

a   b

When completed, since the lapel lies over the curve of the chest, press it over a gentle curve of the ham (Fig. 197a). While it is still damp, roll the lapel to position. Pin it in place to train it so as it dries (Fig. 197b).

A beautiful lapel is distinguished by its thin, flat edges and the natural roll of the lapel.

Which way to press? Many sewers are puzzled as to the direction in which to press seam allowances and darts. The safest rule to follow is to press in that direction which produces least bulk.

Uncut darts (unless otherwise noted in the pattern), are pressed as follows: horizontal darts, down (their tendency is to fall down anyway because of gravity); elbow darts, down; vertical darts, toward the center. When an uncut dart in the lining falls directly over the uncut dart of the outer fabric, press one vertical dart toward the center and the other toward the side seam; press one horizontal dart up and the other down. This prevents bulk in any one area.

Yoke seam allowances are generally pressed away from gathers or other types of fullness.

The armhole seam: The direction in which an armhole seam allowance is pressed depends on the style of the sleeve. In a set-in sleeve the seam allowance is generally pressed into the sleeve adding to the roundness of the cap. When decorative welt stitching is used around the armhole, the seam allowance is pressed toward the garment. A sleeve set on a dropped shoulder has its seam allowance pressed open to eliminate bulk at the seam line. There is no one way. The style dictates the treatment.

The waistline seam: This, too, depends on the style and the desired effect. In a dress it may be pressed either toward the bodice, toward the skirt or opened flat—whichever direction produces the least bulk. Clip the seam allowance where necessary to make it lie flat. In a skirt the seam allowance is pressed into the waistband. The waistline seam is in reality a slight curve. Like all curves it should be pressed over the tailor's ham.

Pleat seam allowances are generally pressed together at the back of a pleat. When a hem is involved, clip the seam allowances at the top of the hem. Press the seam allowances open below the clip, and to one side above it.

OTHER PRESSING PROBLEMS

How to press bound buttonholes and bound pockets: Close the binding with diagonal bastings before pressing to assure that they are in the proper position. Use the pressing technique best suited for the fabric.

Pressing applied pockets, yokes, and lapped seams: Turn under and press the seam allowances before setting. This makes for a sharper edge and easier setting.

Pressing the zippered area: Press the fold of the seam allowance before putting in the zipper. This makes it much easier to set the zipper. It also eliminates the need to press over the metal when the zipper has been stitched. For right side touch-up, press over a heavy press cloth or Turkish towel with the tip of the iron beside the metal.

Pressing pleats: To achieve sharp pleats, each side of both upper and under folds should be pressed thoroughly.

Fig. 198

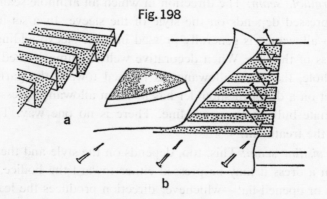

The right side is pressed first. To prevent pleat press marks on the fabric beneath, slip a strip of cardboard, wrapping paper, or tissue paper under each pleat (Fig. 198a). Pin the top and bottom of the pleats in place on the ironing board over a damp press cloth. Pin along the sides of the fabric so that its weight will not pull the pleats out of place (Fig. 198b). Pinning is preferable to basting which leaves an imprint when pressed. Remove pins as you reach the area to be pressed. Replace when pressed. Place a dampened press cloth over the pleats. Press with the grain, using lengthwise strokes. Cross-wise strokes not only displace the pleats but stretch the fabric. Press to within six inches of the lower edge. This makes it easier to set the hem. When the hem has been finished and pressed, fold the pleats into position and press. When the right side is completed, turn to the wrong side and repeat the procedure.

Whenever possible use the clapper to "spank" in a sharp edge. If the fabric has a raised surface be sure to protect it in an appropriate manner.

Sometimes in knife pleats and always in accordion pleats it is easier to press each fold separately. Place the fold of the pleat near the edge of the ironing board and press.

An easy way to make short pleats in sheer fabric is to use the tissue pattern itself as a guide. Pin the pattern to the fabric. Fold both tissue and fabric into pleats and press carefully along the line of the fold.

Pressing Other Types of Fullness

Gathering: Press gathering with lengthwise strokes working the toe of the iron into the gathers (Fig. 199a).

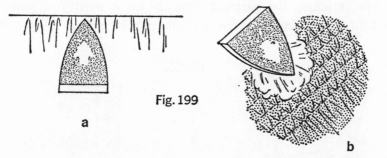

Fig. 199

a

b

Decorative shirring and smocking: Place the shirred or smocked area on the ironing board right side up. Hold the steam iron ½" to 1" above the fabric and move slowly over the area. This preserves the raised effect of the shirring or the honeycomb surface of the smocking. *Do not touch the surface with the iron,* however lightly; let the steam do the work (Fig. 199b).

Pressing the hem:

1. Press all inside seams before turning up the hem.

2. Press the hem in place *before* hemming it.

3. Press with short strokes from the lower edge up. Pressing parallel to the fold stretches the edge.

4. Press the fold of the hem but not the binding. Pressing the seam binding often produces a ridge or an obvious stitching line on the right side.

5. For a very sharp hem edge, "spank" with the clapper—if the fabric can take it.

Curved hems: The depth of the hem should be only as much as will lie flat when the fullness is shrunken out. The more circular the hem, the narrower it must be to avoid the darts, pleats, or ripples that result when the longer outer edge of the curved hem is turned up against the shorter length. Put a line of gathering along the top of the hem. Pull up the thread of the gathering until the hem fits the skirt. Distribute the fullness as evenly as possible (Fig. 200b). Then shrink out the fullness by steaming. To shrink out the hem without shrinking the garment beneath, insert a strip of paper or cardboard as a shield between the hem and the garment (Fig. 200a).

Fig. 200

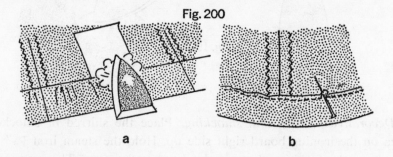

a   b

Be sure to protect the surface of both hem and garment. It may be necessary to lengthen the hem at some future date.

Touch up from the right side.

Tape Shape

When tape is used to reinforce a straight edge, it is preshrunk and pressed in a straight line. When tape is used to reinforce a curved edge it must be shaped to correspond to the curved seam line. Dampen the tape. Place the dampened tape over the pattern with the outer edge of the tape along the seam line. Set the iron on STEAM and press slowly into shape. Use one hand to swirl the tape into a curve while the other glides the iron along. Pull the outer or longer edge of the tape slightly; ease in the shorter or inner edge (Fig. 201a).

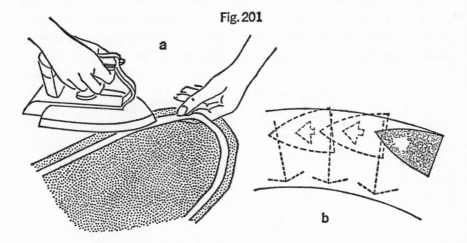

Fig. 201

If the garment itself rather than the pattern is used as a guide for the shape, place the tape beside it and parallel to the seam line to be taped. This avoids the wet imprint of tape on fabric.

Grosgrain ribbon or bias strips of fabric used as collar, binding, or facing may be shaped in a similar manner. The side of the iron is parallel to the edge of the ribbon or strip. Push the iron from the outer or longer edge to the inner or shorter edge, easing in the fullness while shaping (Fig. 201b).

Pressing Pile Fabrics

Were the iron to be pressed on velvets, velveteens, or corduroys, its weight would flatten the pile. There are two methods of "pressing" such fabrics to preserve the pile.

METHOD I: Place the pile of the fabric against the needles of the needle board. (If this is not available, use a strip of pile fabric. Place the piles together.) Steam press the wrong side using *very little* pressure. Press over the center of the needle board; pressing too close to the edge may leave an imprint. Press with the nap.

Protect the right side of the pile fabric when it is turned back to the wrong side in seam allowances, hems, and facings. Whenever possible use a top needle board. This is similar to the flat needle board except that shorter needles are attached to a heavy flexible cloth which allows the steam to penetrate. If a top needle board is not available use a strip of pile fabric as an upper press cloth (Fig. 202a).

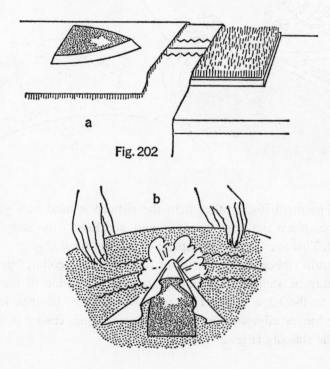

Fig. 202

METHOD II: Stand a hot dry iron on end. Cover it with a damp cloth. This creates steam. Draw the wrong side of the velvet against the steaming iron (Fig. 202b). Handle lightly to prevent finger marks. (Finger marks on velvet can be steamed out and brushed up while steaming.)

Both of these methods press seam allowances open and steam out wrinkles. Hang the garment on a hanger or a dress form while drying.

THE FINAL PRESSING

Before Inserting the Lining

If the garment has been carefully and properly pressed during the construction it should not need very much of a pressing now. However, one final hand pressing is necessary before inserting the lining. This is your last chance to get at any part of the inside of the garment before it is covered by the lining.

Press both inside and outside of the garment. Press both sides of double surfaces, the underside first. Use the steam iron and wool press cloths. Be very careful to maintain the original shaping of the garment. Use the same press pads as were used for the construction pressing.

This is the order in which the garment is pressed (Fig. 203):

Press the outer edges of the collar, lapels, fronts and hem. Press the facing first, making sure that the seam is rolled to the underside; then press the right side.

Press the body of the garment as follows:

1. left upper front, **2.** left bust and underarm, **3.** left pocket, if any, **4.** left lower front, **5.** left lower back, **6.** left upper back, **7.** right upper back, **8.** right lower back, **9.** right lower front, **10.** right pocket, **11.** right bust and underarm, **12.** right upper front.

Press the sleeve and shoulder:

13. hem, **14.** lower sleeve, **15.** upper sleeve, **16.** shoulder.

Press the collar and lapels:

Place a strip of paper between the collar and the garment to prevent an imprint. Press the collar from the outer edge to the roll line over a press pad. Make sure that the lower edge of the collar covers the neckline seam by at least ¼". Press a soft roll (not a sharp crease!) into the collar and continue for one inch down on the lapel.

Fig. 203

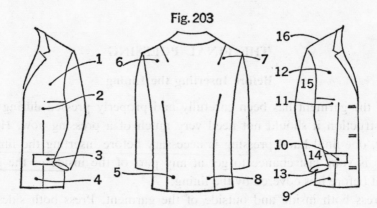

Pressing the Lining

Before inserting the lining in the garment press all seams open. Since the lining is generally silk or rayon, follow the general directions for pressing these fibers on pages 286 to 288.

After the lining has been attached to the garment place the garment over the tailor's ham with the lining up. Use a moderately warm iron and a dry press cloth to prevent scorching and shine. Press so that a soft fold of the lining covers the stitching line along all the edges where the lining is attached to the facings and hem. Press the hem of a free-hanging lining separately. Press a sharp pleat at the center back.

Slip the sleeve over the sleeve board with the cap over the broad end. The lining is up. Press a soft fold along the edge slipstitched to the sleeve hem. Press the sleeve upward toward the cap. Press the sleeve cap.

Right Side Touch-Up

Turn the garment to the right side. It should need very little other than a touch-up. This is a good place to use the steam-iron slip cover (Fig. 204a). Press lightly over the same press pads as during the construction pressing. Use very little or no steam and, of course, the ever-present press cloth, preferably of self-fabric. Button or pin at the front closing and hang up.

Fig. 204

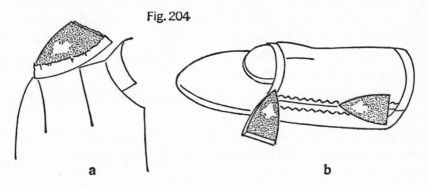

a   b

Pressing the Skirt

Use the pressing technique best suited to the fabric. If the skirt has a free-hanging lining, press each separately. Slip the skirt over the ironing board, wrong side up. Press from the hem up. Slip the ham under the hip area and press all darts and curved seams. Press the placket with the zipper closed. Press the waistband. Turn to the right side and touch-up.

The skirt is pressed with the lengthwise grain, the iron parallel to the seam lines of the skirt and the waistband (Fig. 204b).

FIRST AID

Careful as one is, there are casualties sometimes—here's what to do:

To remove shine: Sponge with a cloth slightly dampened in a solution of two tablespoons of vinegar to a quart of water or one tablespoon of ammonia to a quart of water. Steam-press using a wool press cloth. Brush with a stiff brush to raise the nap.

To restore the nap: Brush the surface of the fabric using a hard brush for worsteds, a soft brush for wools. Press the brushed surface lightly using a wool press cloth to help raise the nap. If the nap has been worn down, rub gently with fine sandpaper or a suede brush.

To remove an unwanted bulge: Lay the bulging area over a flat surface right side up. Place a damp press cloth over the area. Steam until the fullness has disappeared. This type of shrinking takes a somewhat damper press cloth, a little more steam and a little more pressure than generally used. Wool is one fiber that responds well to this type of reshaping.

To remove chalk marks: Remove the marks left by waxy tailor's chalk with cleaning fluid.

To remove cosmetic marks: Cosmetic marks acquired during fittings can be removed with cold water and a light detergent.

PRESSING SILK

The most difficult fabric to press is silk. It requires great care to protect its delicate, frequently high luster, and often raised surface.

On heat: Like wool, silk deteriorates under excessive heat. Always use a moderately warm iron.

On moisture: Some silks are washable and may be pressed while damp. Most are damaged by water and should never come in direct contact with it. Some silks tend to water-spot. Don't use a sputtering or drippy steam iron on them.

Most silks are pressed dry. If dampness should be necessary for pressing, the silk must be protected with a dry press cloth or several layers of tissue paper which absorb the moisture. Press either with a steam iron or on a slightly damp press cloth, placed over the dry press cloth. Even when pressed dry, silk should be protected by a dry press cloth. If the iron is applied directly to silk fabric it produces a shine.

On pressure: To prevent iron marks on smooth silk, press over a dry press cloth, tissue paper, or wrapping paper. Do not keep the iron too long over one spot.

Crinkled, blistered, puckered, embossed, and similar surfaces are best left unpressed by the iron lest the raised surfaces be flattened. To open seam allowances on such fabrics, merely finger-press. If the fabric can take it (this requires testing), hold the steam iron about ½″ above the fabric and move it slowly over the area. Some of these fabrics may be pressed lightly over well padded terry cloth or Turkish towel.

Follow all the general rules for pressing outlined earlier in this chapter. Press silk garments on the wrong side first, then touch-up the right side. Use the tailor's ham for pressing shaped areas. Use any other suitable press pad for pressing curved or shaped sections. In general, silk *cannot be molded*. The exception to this is raw silk which can be handled much like wool.

Unlike other washable silks, pongee is best pressed when dry to avoid stiffness and shine. Fabrics made of tightly twisted yarns, like crepe, must be very carefully pressed, both to prevent pressing out the crinkly surface and to avoid shrinking. It is sometimes wise to steam crepe before cutting because of its tendency to shrink when steam-pressed. Press satins and brocades with a light touch on the wrong side. With many silks it is impossible to get flat seams or sharp, crisp edges. Don't force the issue. Settle for a reasonable pressing.

PRESSING RAYON

Rayon is treated like silk. Since it has a great tendency to shine, press lightly on the wrong side, using a press cloth. Place the fabric over a folded Turkish towel or a soft pad. Rayon is very sensitive to heat; the fabric may be injured or scorched if the iron is too warm. Use a relatively cool iron. Check the setting indicated on your iron.

Steam discolors some rayons; others water-spot. Many rayons shrink with moisture and yet require it for flattening seams. Therefore, use a very slightly dampened press cloth or several layers of tissue paper between the fabric and the damp press cloth.

If sizing sticks to the iron leaving brown streaks, press over tissue paper.

Be careful not to stretch the seams in pressing.

PRESSING COTTON

The easiest fabric to press is cotton. It doesn't require a bit of the tender loving care lavished on wool, silk, and rayon. In fact, cotton is treated in just the opposite way. It may be pressed with either the steam iron or a dry iron directly applied to the right side. A press cloth is unnecessary. Cotton is pressed while well dampened. It is pressed until dry.

There are a few precautions, however: White and light colors are pressed on the right side; dark colors or dull finishes are pressed on the wrong side to prevent shine.

Crinkled, embossed, puckered, and like surfaces are left either unpressed or steam-pressed above the surface as suggested for similar silk fabrics. Embroidered cottons are pressed with the right side against a Turkish towel to prevent flattening the raised surface. Sheer cottons take slightly lower heat; too hot an iron will scorch them.

A tailored cotton garment cannot be treated as an ordinary laundry ironing problem. You would hardly want to sprinkle your good suit, roll it up, and allow it to set until evenly damp, like a simple wash dress. Treat it like a tailored garment. Dampen the surface with a wet sponge or a damp press cloth. Press the shaped areas over appropriate press pads. Press the seams, darts, facings, and hem on the wrong side first, then press the right side. Press in the same order as suggested for a woolen garment. Press carefully in construction so that it will not need much in the way of a final pressing.

PRESSING LINEN

Linen takes a little more doing than cotton but responds easily and beautifully to pressing. Ironing produces a shine. Press on the right side when you want the shine. Press on the wrong side when you don't want it. Press seams open on the wrong side first, then press the garment on the right side. Press over suitable press pads. The linen should be well dampened; the iron, hot. Use either the steam iron or dry iron. Press until dry or it may muss before you get a chance to hang it up.

White and light colors may be pressed on the right side but dark colors or dull finishes are pressed on the wrong side. Embroidered linen is pressed with the right side against a Turkish towel to prevent flattening the raised surface.

PRESSING SYNTHETICS

There are so many new fabrics of man-made fibers that it is a little difficult to suggest pressing techniques for them. In general, they are all sensitive to heat. They take very little ironing with a cool iron on the wrong side. It would be best to check the label that comes with the fabric for correct pressing procedure.

This chapter should give you some idea as to why the pressers in clothing factories are often more highly paid than the sewers. Pressing is a specialized skill. But, by following the rules, you can learn to do a very creditable job. There is no doubt that pressing makes the difference between a half-done look and a precise, trim, tailored look. It is worth the effort.

CHAPTER VIII

Tricky Trio—Buttonhole, Pocket, Zipper

Otherwise brave, hardy souls have their moments of apprehension when confronted with the necessity for making a buttonhole, applying a pocket, and inserting a zipper. There is the winter coat which needs buttonholes. You can't put them off much longer or the first robin will appear before your last stitch. Cut that buttonhole? But it's so final! And there it is, good result or bad, plunk out front for all the world to see!

This time you'd really love to put pockets in that suit. You've been making suits without pockets for years. There is a limit to the number of fake pockets or pocketless suits a wardrobe can contain.

And then there is that perfectly gorgeous raw-silk dress with its mauled closing. You've put the zipper in and taken it out so many times, it has become a way of life. But you always end with that same miserable, wobbly line of machine stitching. Little wonder that beginners and experienced sewers alike put off the awful moment of attempting these three until it is literally impossible to proceed without them.

THE ZIPPERED CLOSING

So accustomed are we to seeing zippers either at a side or center-back seam that one might suppose an orthodoxy in relation to their placement. Zippers can be placed anywhere they are convenient to operate and anywhere consistent with the design of the garment. Why have an arbitrary side-seam zipper if the design offers other opportunities? The zipper can just as well be set in a style line at side back, side front or center front. It can be hidden under a pleat or in a fold. In a dress it can even be set in a long waistline dart. If at all possible it is better hidden from view. It should at the very least be as inconspicuous as possible. The best way to do this is to *put the zipper in by hand* rather than by machine.

Better by hand: Hand stitching looks well, holds well, and is done quickly. Elegant fabrics deserve something better than a hard, rigid line of machine stitching. Fragile and sheer fabrics look prettier when the zipper is put in by tiny hand stitches. Stretchy fabrics, bias, and curved seams are easier to control with hand stitching. (Most zippers are placed on curved or bias seams.)

Hand stitching actually takes less time. By the time you've pinned, basted, looked for your zipper foot and set it in place for machine stitching you could have had the entire zipper put in by hand. This doesn't even count the time it takes to rip out that aesthetically jarring line of machine stitching plus the struggle to put the zipper in more neatly the second time. If done right, hand stitching is strong. Using a single thread, take a tiny backstitch on the right side of the fabric and a somewhat longer stitch on the underside. The stitches need not be set in a continuous line like machine stitching, but can be spaced at small intervals.

There are two standard methods for inserting the zipper—the regulation zipper construction (Fig. 205a) and the slot-seam zipper construction (Fig. 205b).

Fig. 205

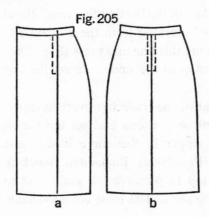

a   b

Both methods are acceptable for any closing, anywhere, on the garment. The regulation zipper is generally used on side seams while the slot-seam zipper is used at back seams and neck openings. The advantage of the first method is that fabric, particularly sheer fabric, is less likely to catch in the zipper when opening and closing. The merit of the second method is that it appears to be a narrower closing.

Most zippers can be set right into the seam allowance, generally ⅝" to ¾". If the seam allowance has been cut a little wider to accommodate the zipper as previously suggested, there will be no problem at all. Should the seam allowance be too narrow, attach a length of seam binding to each edge, ½" longer than the opening. This provides additional facing width.

The regulation zippered closing: When fitting the skirt, carefully pin-fit the opening placket. With tailor's chalk, mark the seam line on the wrong side where pinned. Transfer the markings to the right side with basting thread. The garment should close at this line of basting. The metal pull is placed ¼" below the waistline seam line. The placket opening is the length of the zipper from this point down. Work from the right side both in setting the zipper and in stitching it.

In order to conceal the zipper when the garment is closed on the seam line, the underlap is set ⅛" in from the line of basting, then:

1. Clip the seam allowance of the underlap at the end of the opening to within ⅛" of the basting line (Fig. 206a).

2. Carry this ⅛" marking from the clipped edge to the top. Fold to the underside along this line and press (Fig. 206b).

3. Fold the overlap to the underside on the line of basting. Press (Fig. 206b).

4. Place the fold of the underlap over the right side of the zipper as close to the teeth as you can and yet have it work (Fig. 206c).

5. Holding the zipper in the curve it will assume on the body, pin it to position (Fig. 206c). Backstitch. Work from the bottom of the zipper to the top to preserve the grain and to ensure a smooth and continuous side seam. The most common fault in the setting of a zipper is the ripple at its end caused by stitching which starts at the top and has no place to go by the time it reaches the bottom of the opening.

6. Place the folded edge of the overlap so it meets the seam-line basting of the underlap. This will enclose and conceal the stitching of the underlap. Pin the folded edge in position.

7. Holding the seam in a curve over one hand, backstitch the zipper in place with the other (Fig. 206d). Start at the bottom and work to the top. Slide the tab down while stitching the lock of the zipper. This makes stitching easier and permits a continuation of a narrow welt throughout the length of the zipper.

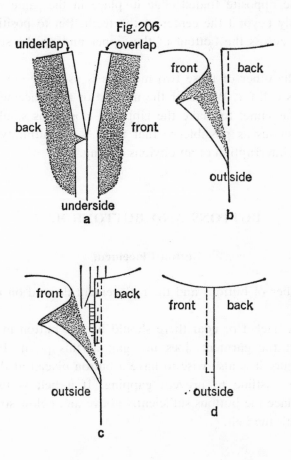

Fig. 206

The slot-seam zippered closing:

1. Fold each side of the placket opening along the line of basting to the underside. Press.

2. Pin one folded edge a little beyond the center of the closed zipper. This slight correction takes care of the pull of the stitching away from center. Were the fold on dead center, the pull of the stitching would expose the metal.

3. Holding the zipper in the curve it will assume on the body, backstitch to position. Work from the bottom to the top. The stitches should be as close to the teeth as will permit the zipper to open easily and close enough to make a narrow welt.

4. Set the opposite folded edge in place in the same way as the first—slightly beyond the center of the teeth. Pin to position.

5. Stitch across the bottom of the zipper and up the second side.

One or the other of these two methods is used for any placement which styles call for. Whatever the method or the placement the aim is always the same: to make the zippered closing as small, as neat, as inconspicuous as possible so that there is a continuity of design without the interruption of an obvious closing.

BUTTONS AND BUTTONHOLES

Button Placement

The number of buttons and their placement depend on the following factors:

In a fitted jacket or coat there should be one button at the waistline so that the garment does not gap at this point. In a large-bosomed figure it is also wise to have a button placed at the heaviest part of the bustline to prevent gapping. If a belt is used at the waistline, place the buttons sufficiently above and below so they don't interfere with the belt.

In an unfitted coat or jacket, these considerations are desirable but not essential. In such garments, buttons are placed where they are most effective for the design. Many current fashions feature few buttons widely spaced. Covered snaps are used between the buttons to ensure a perfect closing.

The location of the top button is always determined by the style of the garment. In a high closing, either with or without a collar, the top button starts at least a button's width down from the finished edge (the neck seam line). In a style that has shaped lapels it is best not to raise or lower the position of the top button since this necessitates a pattern change of style line. Such alteration is too difficult to make unless one knows pattern making. However, if the line of the lapel is a continuation of a straight vertical front line, the position of the top button may be changed to make the lapel break where you desire it.

Buttons may be grouped or spaced at intervals between the fixed positions determined by style or figure. Use the number of buttons best suited to the design or the amount of available space. Choose a number easily divided into equal parts without getting into higher mathematics. It is permissible to shift the position of a button up or down one half inch to simplify the division. A length of string equal to the distance between two fixed points is helpful in making the division. Fold the string in half, quarters, eighths, etc., for an uneven number of buttons or into thirds, sixths, etc., for an even number of buttons. Don't forget to count the button at each end of the string.

In order to ensure that the garment buttons directly on the closing line a slight correction must be made for the shank of the button. The shank may be part of the button or one created by thread (Fig. 207a). The pattern maker allows ⅛" for its width. Therefore the buttonhole begins ⅛" beyond the closing line toward the outer edge of the right front and extends inward the length of the buttonhole (Fig. 207b). You have undoubtedly noticed this placement on your patterns and perhaps even wondered why. The button itself is stitched to the left front *on* the closing line.

Vertical buttonholes are placed directly on the closing line.

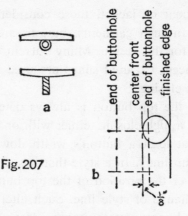

Fig. 207

The Buttonhole

The buttonhole should be long enough to slide the button through easily. It is a tragic discovery to find that several painstakingly made buttonholes are too small for the buttons. The length of the finished buttonhole is equal to the width of the button plus ⅛″ (Fig. 208a). For thick, high, or bumpy buttons, the length of the buttonhole is equal to the button's width plus the button's height or thickness. Do remember that when the buttonhole is worked it will be slightly smaller than the slash. It is wise to make a test slash to see if the button slides through easily. Better yet, make a test buttonhole. You can then decide the proper length and width for your buttonhole. You will also have a chance to test the behavior of the fabric.

Fig. 208

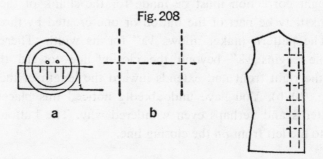

A good part of the success of bound buttonholes is due to careful measurement and marking. Use contrasting thread to mark the placement of the buttonhole, its beginning, and its end (Fig. 208b). When doing a number of buttonholes mark the entire row to be sure they line up (Fig. 208c).

Beautiful Bound Buttonholes

Bound buttonholes are always made *before* the facing is stitched to the garment. They should not be made through heavy, stiff, or resilient interfacing. To do so would produce a bulky buttonhole and one too difficult to press flat. Buttonholes may be made through any of the soft or light-weight interfacings or underlinings.

When canvas or other similar interfacing has been used, remove a section of it where the buttonhole is to be constructed and substitute one of the lighter weight interfacings in its place. Use muslin, lawn, batiste, etc. You may also use any of the new iron-ons if the garment fabric can take the heat required for bonding. In those instances where soft or light-weight underlining has been used as well as interfacing, cut away the interfacing and make the buttonhole through the underlining.

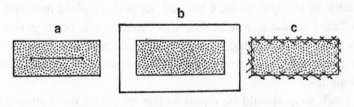

Fig. 209

1. Transfer the buttonhole marking on the outside to the interfacing on the underside.

2. Draw a rectangle around this line about ⅜″ away from it (Fig. 209a). Do not make this too large an opening—just large enough to take the width of the buttonhole comfortably.

3. Cut out the rectangle of interfacing.

4. Place the cut-out rectangle on the new backing material as a guide. Trace around it.

5. Cut a rectangle of the replacement material making it at least ¼″ larger all around (Fig. 209b).

6. Either insert the new backing in the opening or place it on top of it. The tracing marks of the original rectangle can be used as a guide for placement. Catch-stitch the replacement to the interfacing (Fig. 209c).

METHOD I

The easiest method for making a bound buttonhole is the two-strip method, which follows:

Fig. 210

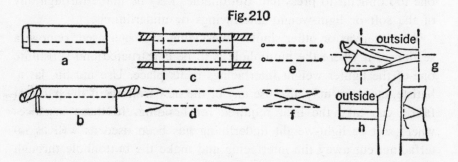

1. Cut or tear a strip of your fabric about ¾″ wide. This strip is usually on straight grain. Checked, striped, or plaid material should be matched to the garment. For this reason, it is often easier to use a bias strip and eliminate the matching. Effective buttonholes may be made if the strip is a contrasting color, when this is consistent with the design.

2. Each strip should be equal to the length of the buttonhole plus 1″. Each buttonhole needs two strips.

3. Fold each strip in half lengthwise with the right side outside. Press.

4. Make a row of hand or machine basting slightly more than ⅛″ from the folded edge (Fig. 210a). A beautiful buttonhole results when cording or even ordinary string is inserted in the fold (Fig. 210b).

5. Trim the strips along the raw edges so that each strip equals ¼″ in total width.

6. Place the strips on the right side of the garment so the cut edges meet at the horizontal buttonhole marking. The folded edges are away from the center of the buttonhole. This is opposite to the position which they will assume in the finished buttonhole. The strips extend ½″ beyond the marking for the beginning and the end of the buttonhole (Fig. 210c).

7. Baste each strip to position directly over the previous basting.

8. Machine-stitch each strip to the garment between the two end markings ⅛″ away from the folded edge and parallel to it. This makes the stitching lines ¼″ apart, the width of the finished buttonhole.

Now turn to the wrong side:

9. The two parallel rows of machine stitching are clearly visible. Pull the end threads through to this side at all four corners (Fig. 210d). These threads should end directly across from each other to produce square corners. Should the stitching go beyond the line of marking, pull back several stitches; if they are short of this line, thread a needle with the ends and backstitch to the marking.

10. Tie each pair of threads (Fig. 210e) with square knots. This is a more satisfactory method of securing the ends than back-and-forth stitching on the machine which is apt to be inaccurate.

11. Make a *small snip* at the center between the rows of stitching. Make *long slashes* diagonally to the corners just to the stitching (Fig. 210f). Proper slashing is most important. Long points are very much easier to handle than short ones which tend to ravel too easily and too quickly leaving you nothing to catch against the strips.

Turn back to the right side:

12. Remove any basting that shows or extends beyond the stitching.

13. Take the ends of both strips and push them through the opening gently.

The folded edges of the strips are now brought into their proper positions. They meet at the center of the buttonhole (Fig. 210g). If accurately stitched and slashed there should be no overlapping of the buttonhole pipings. Sometimes just a little coaxing or rearranging is all that is needed to make them lie side by side.

14. Use diagonal basting to hold the folded edges together. This places the strips in the correct position for fastening across the ends. Skipping this step produces a buttonhole that gaps.

15. Fold the fabric back over the buttonhole so that the little triangle which lies against the two strips is visible. Stitch across the ends through both triangle and strips (Fig. 210h). Stitch as close as possible to the fold of the fabric. If you stitch too far away you will have an ugly hole at the end of the buttonhole; if you stitch over the fold you will include some of the garment and end up with tucks or pleats in the corners.

16. Press the buttonholes.

While this is an easy and foolproof way to make beautiful and uniform bound buttonholes, the strips are difficult to manage in some fabrics. They are too tiny and too flimsy to handle in sheer material. They are too narrow and too bumpy in heavy material. And, they are too much of a risk in material which ravels easily. Following is a variation of Method I which is more satisfactory for problem fabrics.

METHOD II

Make the strips:

1. Cut strips the desired length of the buttonhole plus 1″ by *at least* 2″ wide.

2. Fold the strips in half lengthwise with the right side outside and press.

3. Place cording in the fold if you wish. (Optional.)

4. Place a row of basting slightly more than ⅛″ from the folded edge (Fig. 211a).

Additional marking needed:

In Method I, the ¼″ width of each strip and its placement on the center slash line automatically put the stitching line in the right place—⅛″ from the folded edge and ⅛″ from the center slash

Fig. 211

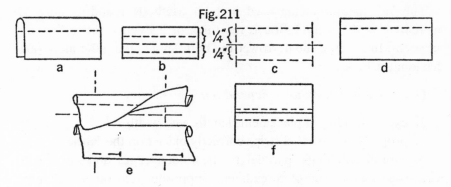

line (Fig. 211b). Because of the increased width of the strips in Method II, additional guide lines are necessary to place them in the same relative position. Use bastings to indicate where the folded edges of the strips are to be placed. One line of basting will be ¼″ above the slash line, the other ¼″ below the slash line (Fig. 211c).

Placement of the buttonhole strips: Because of the width of the strips only one at a time is basted and stitched to the garment.

5. Place one strip so that the folded edge is against the upper marking and baste it to position over the previous basting (see step 4).

6. Stitch the strip to the garment between the two end markings and ⅛″ away from the folded edge (Fig. 211d).

7. Fold the strip back over the folded edge and pin. This will expose the rest of the marking (Fig. 211e).

8. Place the second strip in like manner against the lower marking. Baste to position and machine-stitch. *Do not stitch across the ends.*

9 through **14** are the same as for Method I.

15. Note the wide extension of the buttonhold strips (Fig. 211f) on the wrong side. Grade the thicknesses of the extensions so there will be no bulk and no ridge.

16. Fold back the garment so that the little triangle of fabric is visible resting against the strips. Stitch across the ends through both triangle and strips.

The ⅛″ measurements used in both Methods I and II may be increased to ¼″ if the fabric is too thick or heavy for the ⅛″ measurement. In general, the narrower the buttonhole piping the more professional it looks.

Good bound buttonholes depend on:

1. exact marking of placement, length, and width
2. properly constructed strips correctly placed on the fabric
3. careful stitching—parallel to the folded edges and parallel to each other; each pair of threads ends opposite each other. Stitching across the ends is neither too far away from the end of the buttonhole nor too far into the fabric
4. effective slashing—long points cut diagonally to the corners
5. diagonal basting to hold the folded edges of the piping together to prevent gapping

Finishing off the underside of the bound buttonhole: This is finished on the underside after the facing is stitched to position. There are several ways in which this may be done. Choose that method easiest to manage in any particular fabric.

METHOD I

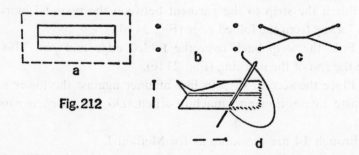

Fig. 212

1. Pin or baste around each buttonhole to keep the facing in place (Fig. 212a).
2. Push a pin through each corner of the finished buttonhole so that the point emerges on the facing (Fig. 212b). This serves as a guide for turning under the raw edges.

3. Slash through the center and clip diagonally to each corner making two small triangles (Fig. 212c).

4. Turn under the raw edges to form a rectangle (Fig. 212d).

5. Hem tentatively to position with a few quick stitches so that the opening is set. Then go back and hem neatly and securely (Fig. 212d).

METHOD II

Fig. 213

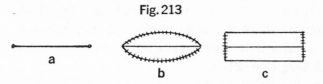

a   b   c

1. Pin or baste around each buttonhole to keep the facing in place.

2. Push a pin through each end of the buttonhole opening as a guide (Fig. 213a).

3. Slash from one pin to the other (Fig. 213a).

4. Turn under the raw edges to form an ellipse (Fig. 213b).

5. Hem quickly to position; go back and hem more securely in place.

In some fabrics this type of slash may be pushed into the rectangular shape of Method I with the point of the needle. Overhand-stitch these ends to prevent fraying (Fig. 213c).

METHOD III

The third method requires more care and more work but gives a very beautiful finish. It is particularly good for fabrics that ravel easily. Method III provides a facing for the buttonhole opening applied to the facing of the garment.

1. Locate the position of the opening in the facing. This must be the exact length and width of the finished buttonhole. Mark it with basting thread. Mark the center opening (Fig. 214a).

2. Cut a rectangle of lining material at least 1½″ wide and 1″ longer than the buttonhole.

3. Fold the lining in half lengthwise and press or crease along the fold.

4. Place the right side of the lining against the right side of the garment facing. Match the fold of the lining and the center marking of the facing (Fig. 214b). An equal amount is left on either side of the buttonhole. Pin in place.

5. Transfer the markings for the center, the length, and width of the buttonhole to the lining (Fig. 214c).

6. Stitch a rectangle through both facing and lining equal to the length and width of the finished buttonhole (Fig. 214d). Keep the corners square. Take the same number of stitches across each end.

7. Slash through the center and clip diagonally to each corner close to the stitching (Fig. 214e).

8. Turn the lining to the wrong side of the facing through the slash. This creates a faced rectangle on the facing (Fig. 214f). Press.

Fig. 214

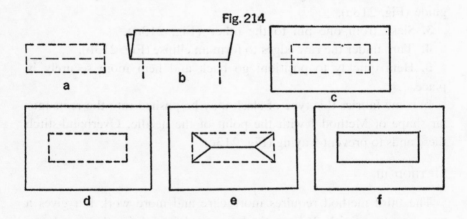

9. Place the opening against the bound buttonhole and hem to the stitching lines of the buttonhole.

Practice making bound buttonholes in your fabric until you are satisfied with the result. It is certainly worth the effort to learn to make them well since they are the accepted closing in women's fine clothing.

Hand-Worked Buttonholes

Hand-worked buttonholes are classic but less frequently seen on women's clothing than bound buttonholes. They may be made either horizontally or vertically and are much easier to work if they are on either straight grain. This buttonhole is made *after* the facing is attached to the garment. It is worked through both garment and facing. When canvas or other similar interfacing has been used, remove a rectangular section where the buttonhole is to be constructed and substitute a strip of lining fabric as a replacement in the same way as for the bound buttonhole.

The vertical buttonhole is made with a bar at each end as a reinforcement (Fig. 215a). The horizontal buttonhole is reinforced with a bar at the left end and a fan at the right end, the end nearest the finished edge of the garment (Fig. 215b). This is a point of stress for the shank of the button pulls against this end.

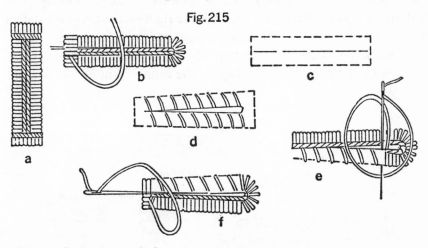

Fig. 215

To work the buttonhole:

1. Mark the exact placement of the buttonhole and its length. Use contrasting basting thread.

2. Reinforce the buttonhole by machine stitching—16 stitches to the inch. Place the stitching 1/16″ away from the slash mark on both sides and directly over the ends (the exact length of the buttonhole) (Fig. 215c).

3. Slash along the center marking.

4. Overcast the slashed edges (Fig. 215d).

5. Work buttonhole stitches from right to left. Place them close together so the purls cover the raw edges (Fig. 215e).

6. Fan the stitches at the right end; work a bar across the left end (Fig. 215f).

7. Bring the thread through to the wrong side. Fasten and clip.

To make the bar: Take two or three stitches across the end. Work very small overhand, buttonhole, or blanket stitches over the end threads.

To make the fan: Take 5 to 7 buttonhole stitches around one end; stitches are evenly spaced with the center one in line with the slash.

Tailor's Buttonholes

The tailor's buttonhole is usually found on men's suits and coats but it could be used equally well on women's tailored clothing. The bottonhole is made with an "eyelet" at the right end to accommodate a large shank. It is worked through the wool *and* the interfacing.

1. Mark the length of the buttonhole and the position of the eyelet. The center of the eyelet is directly on the center front of the garment (Fig. 216a).

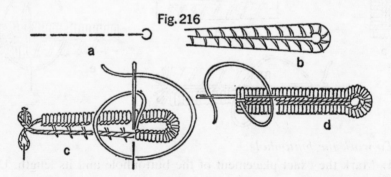

Fig. 216

2. Punch a hole at the right end of the buttonhole with a stiletto. Trim away any excess fabric to make a perfect circle.

3. Slash on the center slash line.

4. Overcast the cut edges (Fig. 216b).

5. Pad the slit with strands of gimp, linen, or cotton thread (⚹10 pearl) of the same color as the fabric. Fasten the strands at the end on a pin. Carry across each side of the slash and around the eyelet as you work the buttonhole (Fig. 216c).

6. Work the buttonhole stitch from right to left over the padding.

7. Fan the stitches around the circle at the right end. Finish with a bar at the left end (Fig. 216d).

8. Bring the thread through to the wrong side and fasten.

Precision Closing

If you've ever made a suit or coat with a parade of a dozen or more buttonholes down the front you've undoubtedly longed for a return to that paradise where clothing was simply slipped over the head or wrapped around the body. Getting in and out of clothing can be a problem from the standpoint of design as well as convenience. As you study fashions you become aware of an endless array of ingenious openings, closings, and fastenings. However, the complete separation of right and left sides necessary for a suit or coat makes the buttonhole and button the easiest type of closing to use (to date). Anything that opens like the front of a tailored garment must close precisely in order to maintain the design and the fitting. For this reason the correct location and the proper sewing on of the buttons becomes very important.

To Locate the Buttons

Close the garment with right front over left front. Match the center-front markings. Match the cross lines of the design—neck, break of lapel, waistline, and hem. Match any cross lines of the fabric design. Use a safety pin for the marking; it won't fall out as a straight pin may. Mark the position of each button on the left front through the buttonhole opening directly on the center line.

Mark and sew on the first button. Button the garment. Locate the next button. Sew it on. This locate-and-sew procedure assures an accurate placement of each button, thereby a perfect closing for the garment.

The buttonhole is made through several thicknesses of fabric—garment, interfacing, facing. The buttonhole itself may be thick—double fabric plus the cording of each piping. If the button is to sit comfortably on the surface of the right front it must be as far away from the left front as the several thicknesses of fabric. This is the function of the shank of the button. It acts as a bridge between left front and right front. Its length depends on the thickness of the opening edges. The thicker the area through which the button is to be slipped, the longer the shank must be; the thinner the area, the smaller the shank may be.

A button may have a metal shank or one made of fabric. A button which has no shank must have a shank created for it. The most commonly created shank is one made with the thread by which the button is sewn to the garment. A shank may also be created by threading the eyes of the button with a loop of self-fabric or other material (see page 310). The eyes of the button must be large enough to take the fabric for this type of shank.

To sew on the button, use a single strand of matching thread. This may take a few more stitches to sew the button on but it eliminates the uneven pulling up of a double thread. Use any thread—silk, cotton, linen, heavy-duty, or buttonhole twist. Color and shine are factors to consider. Any thread may be strengthened by pulling it through a piece of bees wax.

Fasten the thread on the right side at the button marking with a few tiny overhand stitches. The stitches which fasten the button to the garment go through the outer fabric and the interfacing. They *do not*

Fig. 217

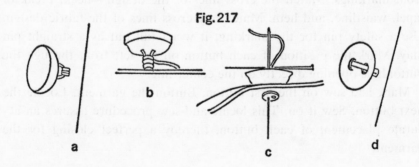

a   b   c   d

come through to the facing. Finish off with a few tiny stitches at the base of the shank through one thickness of fabric only.

The shank button: Sew the button on through the loop of the shank with small overhand stitches. The row of stitches is parallel to the edge of the fabric (Fig. 217a).

A button which has no shank by which to attach it to the garment has holes or eyes instead. Hold the garment over the forefinger. Fasten the thread. Stitch alternately through the holes of the button and through the fabric. Keep the stitches loose; there should be space between the button and the garment. Holding the garment in this position assures this. Take sufficient stitches through the button to hold it on securely—how many depends on the size of the button, the size of the hole, and the thickness of the thread. When the stitches are completed, wind the thread around the loose stitches which attach the button to the garment. This creates the shank (Fig. 217b). Finish off with tiny overhand stitches at the base of the shank.

A stay button: When a button is subjected to great strain the fabric at the base of the shank is apt to tear. To prevent this a smaller button is used as a reinforcement. This is attached to the underside of the garment directly under the first button (Fig. 217c). Both buttons are stitched in one operation.

A fabric loop: Stitch and turn a strip of fabric to the right side. Cut it to the proper length for the loop. Thread the loop through the eyes of the button. Use overhand stitches to fasten the ends of the loop to the garment (Fig. 217d).

OTHER FASTENINGS

There are other types of fastenings that can be used but these are usually associated with dressmaker-type garments rather than strictly tailored ones.

Fabric or braid loops: Make the fabric loops of strips of bias stitched right sides together and pulled through to the right side. They may be corded or self-filled with the seam allowances which are not

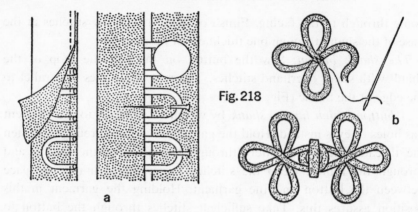

Fig. 218

trimmed away. The loops are inserted in the seam that joins facing to garment (Fig. 218a). They should be large enough to take the buttons with ease, identical in size, and evenly spaced.

Frogs are made of cording or bias tubing. Shape either into a design. Fasten with small stitches on the wrong side at the crossings (Fig. 218b). Place the two frogs opposite each other. Often they fasten on the same button (Fig. 218b). Leave one loop free to slip over the button; fasten the other loops with small stitches on the underside.

No discussion about fastenings could ever be complete without some mention of those old faithfuls—snaps, and hooks and eyes.

Snaps: Mark the placement of the snaps accurately to maintain the lap. They should be placed slightly in from the edge for a true closing.

Sew the ball on first. Chalk the ball and press against the opposite edge to locate the exact position for the socket. Use a single thread. Sew with overhand stitches through the small holes at the edge (Fig. 219a). The stitches *do not* come through to the right side.

Covered snaps are a custom touch when used in places where they are exposed to view, for example, between widely separated buttons. These are large metal snaps covered with fabric. They come in a number of standard colors. But you can make them yourself of any fabric or color to match your garment. Cover the entire snap but ex-

Fig. 219

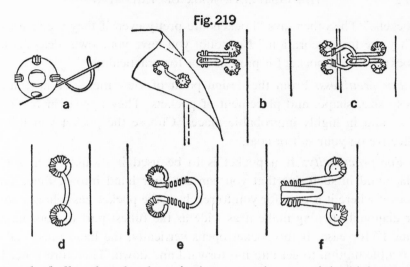

pose the ball and socket by snipping away the material which covers them.

Hooks and eyes: Mark the position for the hooks and eyes carefully. Set the hook close to the edge of the garment for a true closing. Use straight eyes where the edges overlap (Fig. 219b). Use round eyes where the edges meet (Fig. 219c). Extend the eye slightly beyond the edge for this latter type of closing (Fig. 219c).

Sew the hook first. Sew the eye exactly opposite it. Sew through the rings with overhand stitches (Figs. 219d, e, and f). Overhand-stitch the hook end so it, too, is fastened to the garment (Fig. 219f). Because there is considerable strain on hooks and eyes they should be fastened securely. The stitches *do not* come through to the right side.

There are often times when buttons and buttonholes ruin the over-all effect of an elaborately decorated fabric. A fine invisible closing can be obtained with the use of furrier's hooks and rings in an appropriate color.

PICK A POCKET

There are two schools of thought about pockets. One says "No pockets unless they are real and are meant to be used. No fake pockets." The other says "Pockets are pretty even if they aren't used. They are fine decoration." No doubt you have your own ideas about pockets. Pick a pocket for prettiness or for practicality.

For prettiness: From the design point of view there are no limits as to size, shape, and placement of pockets. They appear in baffling sizes and in highly improbable places. Choose the pocket you think effective on your suit or coat.

For practicality: If a pocket is to be used it should be in such place and in such size that you can get your hand into it. Place the pocket where it is easy for you to reach. If the pocket has a horizontal or diagonal opening make it as wide as the fullest part of your hand plus 1" for ease. If the pocket opens vertically, the hand must make a double motion to get into it—forward and down. Therefore it needs a little more ease. Make vertical openings as wide as the fullest part of your hand plus 2".

The anatomy of a pocket. Though varied in design, structurally, pockets fall into two categories—those that are applied to the right side of the garment and those that are inserted into a slash or seam of the garment. The kind of pocket is determined by the pattern. In many cases the designer could just as easily have used one of a number of pockets. Perhaps this idea has occurred to you, too, and you would prefer another type. There is no reason why you cannot substitute one pocket for another if it is consistent with the design. Many suits and coats are so simply cut that they offer considerable leeway in the choice of pocket designs.

Make your own design for a pocket. Experiment with paper cutouts or scraps of fabric until you get the size and shape you like. Hint—the shape of a pocket is more pleasing if its lines are in harmony with the lower edge of the jacket and the shape of the lapels.

The Patch Pocket

The patch pocket is a completed pocket applied to the right side of the garment. To make it:

1. Decide the style, size, and placement of the pocket.

2. Cut the pocket of the fabric. This is generally cut on the same grain or nap as the garment. If the fabric has a surface design, the pocket should match the garment. Plaids, checks, and stripes may be used on the bias for decorative effect and to eliminate the problem of matching.

3. Cut the pocket lining and interfacing (if any). The amount and kind of interfacing will depend on the style effect desired. The lining should be about ½″ smaller than the pocket so that the joining seam can be rolled to the undersurface.

4. Attach the lining to the pocket. There are several ways of doing this, depending on how the completed pocket is to be fastened to the garment.

TYPE A—a finished pocket slipstitched to the garment

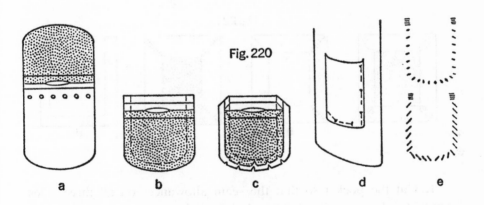

Fig. 220

1. Stitch the lining to the hem of the pocket, leaving a small opening at the center of the seam (Fig. 220a). Press the seam open.

2. Fold the pocket at the fold line of the hem; the right sides of both pocket and lining are together (Fig. 220b).

3. Stitch around the remaining three sides of the pocket. Clip, notch, trim, grade seams as needed (Fig. 220b and 220c).

4. Turn the pocket to the right side through the opening at the edge of the hem. Close the opening with slipstitches.

5. Press the pocket, rolling the seam to the underside.

6. Pin the pocket to position, allowing a little ease so that you can get your hand into it. The pocket should not be flat and taut against the garment; it should stand away from it slightly (Fig. 220d).

7. Slipstitch the pocket to the garment on the right side. Make the stitches a *tiny* bit in from and under the finished edge. If the pocket is to get hard wear, it may be further secured with hemming stitches on the underside. In either case, the corners are reinforced with over-hand stitches on the underside (Fig. 220e).

When the pocket is to be attached by top stitching an even distance in from the edge, it should be faced with the outer fabric since a facing of lining would show.

TYPE B—a top-stitched, straight-sided pocket

Fig. 221

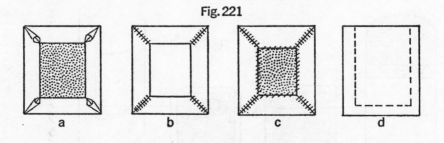

a   b   c   d

1. Cut the pocket so that the seam allowances on all three sides are wider than the top-stitching line.

2. Turn the hem and the seam allowances to the underside and press to position. If the garment has more than one pocket of the same size, press them over a cardboard pattern in the size and shape of the completed pocket. This assures that they are identical (Fig. 221a).

3. Miter the corners. Cut away the excess fabric. If the fabric is lightweight, miter by machine. If the fabric is heavy, it is easier to slipstitch the miter (Fig. 221b).

4. Cut the lining to fit the unfaced portion of the pocket.

5. Turn under the seam allowance of the lining and slipstitch to the pocket wrong sides together (Fig. 221c).

6. Set the pocket in place. Top-stitch either by hand or by machine (Fig. 221d).

TYPE C—a top-stitched curved pocket

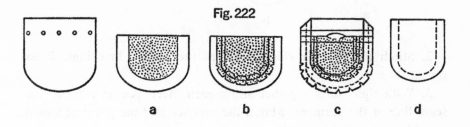

Fig. 222

a   b   c   d

1. Cut the pocket. Cut a facing for the pocket. Make it wider than the distance in from the edge at which it is to be top-stitched. Cut the lining to fit the unfaced portion of the pocket (Fig. 222a).

2. Stitch the lining to the facing. Clip, notch and trim the seam. Press it open (Fig. 222b).

3. Attach the lining-facing to the pocket in the same way the lining was attached in Type A (Fig. 222c).

4. Set the pocket in place and top-stitch (Fig. 222d).

The Pocket Set in a Seam

This pocket consists of two shaped pieces several inches longer than the pocket opening. It should be deep enough to rest the hand comfortably in it. This kind of pocket can be put into any seam whether the pattern calls for it or not. Fig. 223a is the pattern shape for a pocket stitched into the side seam and the waistline seam. Fig. 223b is the type frequently found in coats.

1. Cut the pocket of lining fabric. Face the edges at the side seams with outer fabric so that one may see fabric rather than lining at the pocket opening (Fig. 223c).

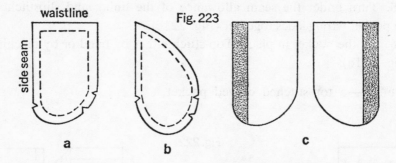

Fig. 223

waistline

side seam

a   b   c

2. Stitch the coat or skirt as far as the pocket markings. Press open.

3. With right sides together stitch each faced pocket edge to the seam line of the garment. Match the notches and the point at which the side-seam stitching ends.

4. Stitch the pocket sections together. Press the pocket and the seams to the front.

5. In the case of a skirt pocket, baste the top edges of the pocket to the waistline of the skirt and catch in the waistline seam. Grade the seam allowances.

The Pocket Set in a Slash

In a bound, welt, or flap pocket, the opening of the pocket is slashed right into the garment. You can't change your mind once the fabric has been cut. A little planning beforehand can save a lot of heartache. The pocket is composed of two parts. One part is seen from the outside as a binding or piping, a welt or a flap. The other part is the pouch which is attached to the underside. The pouch is composed of an upper pocket (front) and an under pocket (back). The under pocket is longer than the upper pocket to compensate for the depth of the opening. Both are as wide as the opening plus ½″ seam allowance on either side.

Whenever a slash is made in the garment fabric in order to insert another section, the opening is reinforced with a strip of light-weight interfacing applied to the underside. For the pocket set in a slash make this reinforcement 2″ longer than the pocket, 1″ on either side.

The Bound Pocket

If you have learned how to make a beautiful bound buttonhole, you will have no trouble making a bound pocket. The method is the same. The binding of the pocket may be a little wider than that used for the buttonhole. It is not corded. The pouch of the pocket is attached to the raw edges of both top and bottom strips.

When the pocket opens there should be a continuous appearance of the garment's outer fabric. To get that all-one-color and all-one-fabric look, the under pocket may be made of self-fabric if the material is light enough in weight. Should the garment fabric be heavy or bulky it is better to make the pocket of lining material. If lining is used, the top edge should be faced with a strip of the outer fabric. Make the strip wide enough to extend to a safe depth. Use a selvage edge where possible so there will be no need to turn the facing under for a finished edge. Lap the facing over the lining and stitch (Fig. 224a). Another way to solve this problem is to use the garment fabric for the under pocket, and lining for the upper pocket. Though not necessary, it is a nice touch to use the depth of the bottom strip as a facing for the upper pocket (Fig. 224b).

How to make a straight bound pocket:

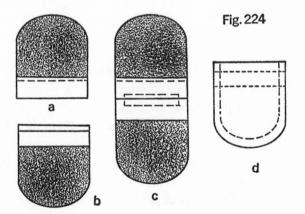

Fig. 224

1. Mark the placement of the pocket.
2. Reinforce the area with interfacing.

3. Construct the bound opening. Use Method II for making bound buttonholes.

4. Cut the upper and under pockets. Face where necessary.

5. Trim the top strip to seam-allowance width. Attach the faced under pocket to it (Fig. 224c).

6. Attach the upper pocket to the bottom strip (Fig. 224c).

7. Stitch the upper and under pockets together (Fig. 224d) to form the pouch.

How to make a curved bound pocket:

A curved bound pocket is a very decorative touch especially if the lower edge of the jacket is curved, too.

Fig. 225

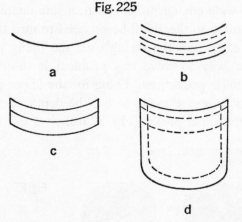

a   b

c

d

1. Mark the placement of the pocket (Fig. 225a).

2. Reinforce the area with interfacing.

3. Cut two bias strips for the bindings.

4. Steam the bindings into shape and set them in place at the marking (Fig. 225b).

5. Construct the bound opening using Method I for bound buttonholes (Fig. 225c).

6. Attach the faced under pocket to the top strip.

7. Attach the upper pocket to the bottom strip.

8. Stitch the upper and lower pockets together to form the pocket pouch (Fig. 225d).

The Welt Pocket

The welt pocket is made by inserting a completely finished welt into a slash of the garment. Every bit of sewing skill—stitching, trimming, clipping, notching, grading, and pressing—goes into the making of each welt. The welt is generally made of the same fabric as the garment. It is cut on the same grain and same nap. All checks, stripes, plaids must match that part of the garment where the welt is to be placed. This problem can be eliminated by cutting the welt on the bias (if the design will permit).

If a facing is stitched to a shaped welt, be sure to allow enough fabric on the upper welt so the joining seam may be rolled to the underside.

If the style has more than one pocket of the same size and shape, cut a paper tracer in the shape of the completed welt. Pin or baste the tracer to the cloth. Stitch very accurately on the stitching line. This is also a good method to follow when stitching a welt of a difficult shape.

A fake welt pocket:

This really isn't a pocket at all but merely a welt attached in such fashion as to simulate a welt pocket.

1. Mark the position of the welt on the garment.

2. Cut a strip of fabric the length of the welt and twice its width plus seam allowances.

3. Fold the welt in half crosswise with the right sides together and stitch across the ends.

4. Press the seams open on the point presser. Clip the corner seam allowance and grade the seams.

5. Turn to the right side. Press.

6. Pin the finished welt to position on the right side of the garment. The correct position in which to place the welt is opposite to that which is desired in the finished garment (Fig. 226a). Were it to be laid in a reverse position, the welt would end up as a flap (Fig. 226b).

7. Stitch the welt to the garment. Secure the ends of the stitching.

Fig. 226

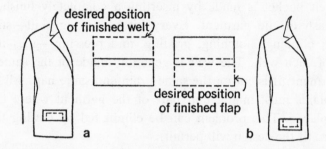

desired position
of finished welt

desired position
of finished flap

a   b

8. Trim the seam allowance of the welt very close to the stitching.

9. Press the welt to its desired position.

10. Slipstitch the ends of the welt to the garment concealing all stitching.

The above directions hold for a fake flap except that the stitching in Step 10 does not continue all the way down the sides. The flap really should be able to flap or it wouldn't be what its name implies.

How to make a straight welt pocket:

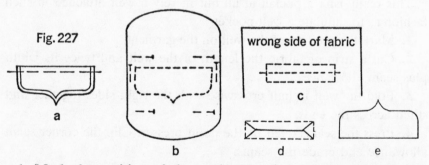

Fig. 227

wrong side of fabric

a

b

c

d

e

1. Mark the position of the pocket opening on the right side of the garment. Reinforce the area to be slashed on the wrong side with a light-weight interfacing.

2. Make the welt. If interfacing is used for the welt, make it lightweight; it may be stitched in the seam. Stitch, trim, grade, clip, or notch as necessary. Press the seam allowance open. Turn to the right side and press once more, rolling the seam to the underside.

3. On the right side of the garment, place the welt in a position opposite to that of the finished pocket. Place the stitching line of the welt slightly below the mark for the opening (Fig. 227a).

4. Stitch the welt to the garment. Secure the ends. Trim the seam allowance close to the stitching.

5. Use a strip of lining material for the pocket. Make it equal to the length of the welt and twice as long as the pocket pouch. Add the seam allowances. Mark the pocket opening at the center of the lining strip.

6. Place the pocket lining over the welt right sides together. Match the center marking of the lining with the stitching line of the welt. Pin in position securely (Fig. 227b). (The broken lines in the illustration indicate the welt under the lining.)

7. Turn to the wrong side. Using the previous line of stitching as a guide, stitch the lining to the welt and garment directly over the original stitching and ⅛" *in from each end.* Stitch a rectangle the other side of which is parallel to this line of stitching and ¼" away from it. Stitch across the ends. This rectangle will be the opening of the pocket (Fig. 227c). Note that it is smaller than the welt so that it will be completely concealed by it.

8. Slash through the center of the rectangle to ¼" from the ends. Clip diagonally to the corners (Fig. 227d).

9. Turn the pocket to the wrong side by slipping it through the opening. The welt will automatically turn to its proper position on the right side (Fig. 227e).

10. Stitch the upper and under pockets together.

11. Slipstitch the ends of the welt to the garment.

This method has three distinct advantages:

1. The complete length of the welt is attached securely without involving the pocket itself.

2. Because the welt has already been attached, the rectangular opening may safely be made smaller. This means that when the welt is turned to its proper position, the pocket opening is completely concealed. No holes at the ends!

3. When the pocket lining is stitched to the welt and garment from the underside using the previous line of stitching as a guide, one can be sure it is correctly done. No guessing and no X-ray eyes necessary as when stitching blindly from the right side of the garment.

How to make a curved welt pocket:

Fig. 228

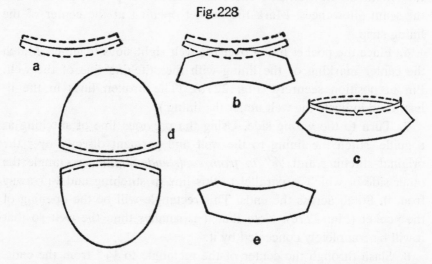

1. Mark the position of the pocket opening on the right side of the garment.

2. Reinforce the wrong side of the area to be slashed with light-weight interfacing.

3. Stay-stitch 1/16" either side of the marking. Take a stitch across each end (Fig. 228a).

4. Make the welt. If interfacing is used keep it lightweight.

5. The correct placement of the welt on the right side presents a problem. Placed as it should be the welt and the marking are two opposing curves—very difficult to pin and even more difficult to stitch (Fig. 228b). However, if the reinforced curve of the fabric is slashed to within 1" of each end, the pinning and stitching may be done more easily (Fig. 228c). When the welt has been stitched to the garment, slash the rest of the opening to within ⅛" from each end.

6. Cut two separate pocket pieces for the upper and under pockets. Match the curve of each pocket top with the corresponding curve of the opening. Add seam allowances.

7. From the right side, stitch the upper pocket to the bottom of the opening right sides together. Stitch to within ⅛″ from the edges (the end of the slash). Stitch the lower pocket to the top of the opening in like manner (Fig. 228d).

8. Pull the pocket through the opening to the wrong side. The welt will turn up in its right position (Fig. 228e). The pocket opening is concealed.

9. Stitch the under and upper pockets together. Slipstitch the ends of the welt to position.

A simple welt formed within a faced opening of a pocket:

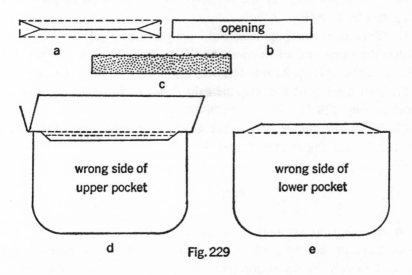

Fig. 229

1. Mark the position of the pocket opening.

2. Reinforce the underside of the opening with light-weight interfacing.

3. The welt and pocket strip are cut in one piece of garment fabric. Make it one inch wider than the pocket and twice the depth of the pocket plus 1″ for a ½″ welt. Add seam allowances.

4. Mark the pocket opening with basting on the pocket strip. The opening is 1″ below the center to allow for the ½″ welt.

5. Place the pocket strip over the garment right sides together, matching the markings for the openings. Pin securely to position.

6. Stitch a rectangle ¼″ from the opening line on either side and directly across both ends as marked. Count the number of stitches across the ends to make sure they are equal (Fig. 229a).

7. Slash through the center of the rectangle and diagonally to all corners (Fig. 229a).

8. Turn the pocket to the wrong side through the opening. Press the rectangular opening so all four sides are flat and all corners are sharp (Fig. 229b).

9. To form the welt: bring the upper pocket up in a pleat to fill the entire width of the opening (½″). The fold of the pleat will be along the upper edge of the rectangle. Hold the welt in place with diagonal basting (Fig. 229c).

10. Turn to the wrong side. Fold the garment back over the welt. Stitch the open end of the welt to the seam right over the previous line of stitching (Fig. 229d). This will close the bottom of the welt.

11. Pull the top of the strip straight down to form the back of the pocket (Fig. 229e).

12. Stitch the under and upper pockets together catching in the welt and the triangles at each end.

Flap Pockets

A fake flap pocket may be made in the same way as a fake welt pocket except that the position in which it is stitched is reversed. This is used merely for its decorative effect. A flap may be used in the same way over a patch pocket to conceal the opening of the pocket. Stitch it to position ¼″ above the opening to enable the hand to get into the pocket (Fig. 230a). Trim the seam allowance close to the stitching line. Press the flap down. Often a line of decorative stitching is added just below the seam line making it look like a welt seam (Fig. 230b).

Fig. 230

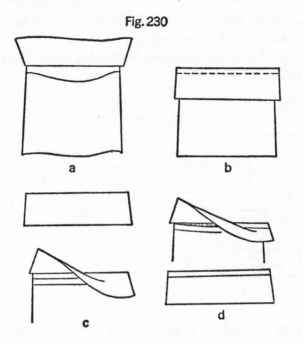

a   b

c   d

The flap pocket can also be made with a bound-pocket opening. The flap is inserted in the top seam of the binding either above it (Fig. 230c) or below it (Fig. 230d). Make the flap of garment fabric cut on the same grain and nap as the garment. If the fabric is checked, plaid, or striped, the flap must match that part of the garment where it is to be placed. Cut the flap facing of the garment fabric. If the fabric is too heavy or too bulky, make the facing of lining material instead. If interfacing is used it should be light in weight. As with any slash made in a garment, the area in which it occurs should be reinforced.

Flap pocket with a welt strip:

1. Mark the opening of the pocket.

2. Reinforce the pocket opening. Make the reinforcement 2″ longer than the flap and at least 1½″ in depth.

3. Make the flap. Use all stitching, trimming, and pressing skills.

4. Pin the flap to the right side of the garment in a position opposite to that of the finished pocket. Place the stitching line of the flap ⅛″ above the marking for the opening (Fig. 231a).

5. Stitch the flap to the garment. Secure the ends. Trim the seam allowance close to the stitching line.

Fig. 231

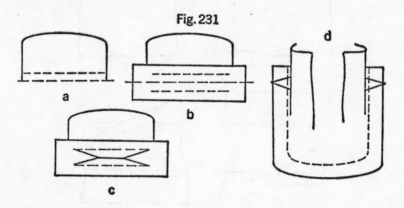

6. Pin strips of binding in place as for a bound buttonhole. The stitching line of the upper strip is directly over the stitching line which joins flap to garment (Fig. 231b).

7. Stitch the strips to the garment and flap. The stitching ends ⅛″ in from each edge so that the flap may completely cover the bound opening.

8. Snip at the center between the rows of stitching and slash diagonally to each corner, making large triangles at each end (Fig. 231c).

9. Turn the strips to the wrong side through the opening. Note that the flap is automatically brought into its right position (Fig. 230c above).

10. Use diagonal basting to hold the strips together at the opening.

11. Cut both upper and under pockets. Face as necessary or as desired.

12. Attach the pockets to the seam allowances of the binding strips.

13. Stitch the pockets together, catching in the binding and the triangles (Fig. 231d).

Men's Coat Pocket

1. Mark the opening of the pocket.

2. Reinforce the area to be slashed.

3. The bound opening is made like a bound buttonhole with this exception: stitch the upper strip the full length of the opening; stitch the lower strip to within ⅛″ in from each end. The lines of stitching are parallel but the lower stitching tapers in (Fig. 232a).

Fig. 232

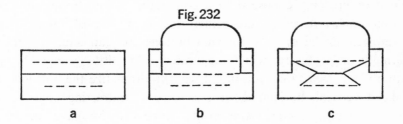

a   b   c

4. Make the flap.

5. Pin the flap over the top binding strip, right sides together, matching the seam line of the flap with the seam line of the strip. It is, of course, in the reverse position it will be when finished (Fig. 232b).

6. Stitch the flap in place for its entire length. This line of stitching is exactly that of the binding strip. Secure the ends.

7. Snip at the center between the rows of stitching and slash diagonally to the ends. Note that because of the unequal lines of stitching, the upper part of the triangle is longer than the lower part (Fig. 232c).

8. Pull the flap and the strips through to the wrong side through the opening. Note that the flap automatically turns down in its right position (Fig. 230d). There is one narrow welt above the flap and one below it.

9. Fold the garment back over the pocket and stitch the triangles at each end to the strips. This will be a slanting rather than a vertical line of stitching.

10. Attach the upper and under pockets to the seam allowances of the strips.

11. Stitch the pocket sections together catching in the binding strips.

Zippers, buttonholes, and pockets become elements of design: It has been said that necessity is the mother of invention. This is certainly true of design. When it comes to zippers, buttons, buttonholes, and pockets, you can be your own designer and as inventive as you would like. If there *must* be a zipper, use it cleverly, whether you hide it or brazenly expose it in a contrasting color. If buttons and buttonholes *are necessary* make them the focal point of interest. Use the most beautiful or most unusual buttons you can find. Use them sparingly or profusely, widely separated or in little groups. If the button is inconspicuous, you might want to dramatize the buttonhole. Make it vertical, horizontal, or bias. Use a contrasting color, contrasting texture, or contrasting grain. Make it a tiny sliver or giant size. The same philosophy applies to pockets. Go ahead and make sensible ones that you really can use. But remember also the ones that are mere conversation pieces.

Whatever you choose to do with zippers, buttons, buttonholes, or pockets, never let them look as if you didn't know or couldn't do better. By all means make them look as if you had some very special design idea in mind. If you can learn to make some decorative use of these necessities then you will be amply compensated for the time and trouble of making them.

CHAPTER IX

All's Well That Ends Well

This chapter is like the last chapter of a mystery story. (Perhaps you've already peeked back here to see how it all comes out!) This is the time when all disjointed bits of information are pieced together for the final, speedy, and satisfactory (we hope) conclusion of the story.

After careful planning and deliberation, the outer fabric has been cut, marked, and stay-stitched. With due consideration for the design effect and the fabric, the interfacing and the underlining have been cut and marked. The techniques of stitching and pressing have been studied and selected for this garment. All the equipment and findings needed to assemble and press the garment are ready and handy.

Each unit of the garment must be stitched, pressed and blocked before being joined to another. So the work must be assembled and completed in units. Each unit consists of all the pieces which make up: each front, the back, the sleeves, and the collar. This is true whether it be jacket, coat, bodice, or skirt.

The interfacing, underlining, and skirt lining are worked in units as well as the outer fabric.

Place all of the pieces together which belong to each unit. If there is an underarm section in place of a side seam, join the underarm section to the back.

The First Fitting—A Pin Fitting

Before stitching, we want to make sure that the darts and seams are in the right place in the garment fabric. This should be just a simple matter of checking since the trial muslin presumably took care of all major changes. There will be several other fittings to refine the fit before we are through, not to mention the number of times you will try the garment on merely to admire yourself.

Pin-fit the shell of the garment only. Do not include set-in sleeves, collars, facings, or any other double thicknesses of fabric. Do all fitting from the right side. This gives a true fit for each side of the figure. Corrections are transferred to the wrong side.

Pin the darts and shaping seams in both fronts and the back on the wrong side just as they will be stitched in the finished garment. Pin the shoulder seams and the side seams on the right side to facilitate the fitting. Try on the garment. Pin it as it will close. If shoulder pads are to be used, set them in place.

Examine the fit. Refresh your memory by referring to Chapter III. Check the position of the darts and shaping seams. Check the ease and fullness. Keep in mind that the hang of the garment will be different after pressing, blocking, and the addition of the interfacing or the underlining.

If changes are necessary, repin. When satisfied with the fitting, remove the garment. Mark with tailor's chalk on the wrong side of the material where pinned. These marks are the new stitching lines. Be sure to make similar corrections in the interfacing and/or underlining.

SO SEW!

Using all the sewing techniques outlined in Chapter VI, join all darts, seams, sections, insets, etc., which complete each unit of the jacket, skirt, coat, or dress. This goes for outer fabric, interfacing, underlining, and skirt lining. (A great deal of work is disposed of in these two short sentences.)

Each unit of the outer fabric is separate from every other. Each unit of the interfacing, underlining, or skirt lining is separate from every other. The outer fabric and understructure are separate from each other. Trim, clip, notch, and grade where necessary. Using all the pressing techniques outlined in Chapter VII, press each unit of the garment, interfacing, underlining, and skirt lining. Using suitable press pads, shape all areas of the garment and underpinnings which require it.

Joining the Garment Fabric and Understructure

The outer fabric and the supporting fabric now are joined as one with tailor basting for the rest of the time the garment is in construction.

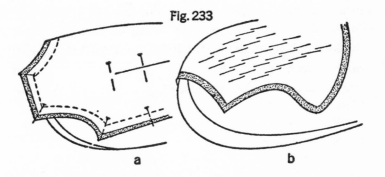

Fig. 233

a   b

How to apply the interfacing or underlining to the front of the garment:

1. Place the blocked interfacing over the tailor's ham.

2. Place the blocked outer fabric over the interfacing right side up.

3. Match the darts and shaping seams.

4. Pin the two thicknesses together at the dart point or the highest point of each shaping seam. Smooth the fabric over the interfacing toward the outer edges. Pin along the seam allowance (Fig. 233a). Work over the curve of the ham with the fabric and the interfacing in the same relative position they will assume when worn. This automatically adjusts the necessary length and width of the interfacing. Generally a small margin of it will extend beyond the edge of the garment fabric (Fig. 233a).

5. Join the entire front fabric to its interfacing with *tailor basting.*

Start at the dart point or high point of a shaping seam and work to the outer edges (Fig. 233b). Use large "easy" stitches to avoid a quilted effect.

6. Trim away the excess interfacing.

Underlining may be applied to the outer fabric in the same way.

If both underlining and interfacing are used, first join them to each other with tailor basting or stay stitching, then join them to the garment fabric with tailor basting. The underlining is placed directly against the wrong side of the fabric. The interfacing is placed against the underlining. This method of joining ensures that the shaping of both fabric and understructure correspond. Hold up the front and see the permanently built-in shape of the completed unit. The garment now exhibits the contour and body which you've planned all along.

Caution: If needles and pins leave permanent marks or bruises on the fabric (satins, brocades, velvets, etc.) *do not join the units with tailor basting.*

Join as follows:

1. Place the interfacing or underlining over the ham.

2. Place the outer fabric over the supporting fabric, matching darts and shaping seams. Start at the high point and smooth toward the outer edges.

3. Pin along the outer edge within the seam allowance.

4. Either baste or stay-stitch where pinned.

5. Trim away any excess interfacing or underlining.

Use this alternate method only where absolutely necessary. The first method is more accurate, therefore preferable.

How to apply the interfacing or underlining to the back of the garment:

The method for joining the back interfacing or underlining to the outer fabric is the same as for the front, with this exception: start the matching and tailor basting at the center back and work toward each side, smoothing the fabric toward the outer edges.

How to join the skirt and the half back lining:

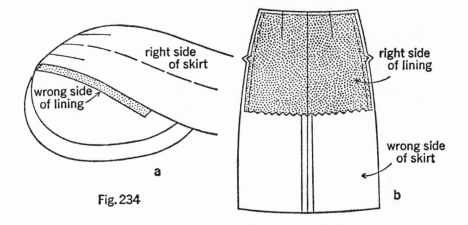

Fig. 234

1. Place the skirt lining over the tailor's ham *wrong* side up.

2. Place the skirt fabric over the lining *right* side up. This places the wrong sides together (Fig. 234a). The finished side of the lining is toward the body. The finished side of the skirt is, of course, toward the outside (Fig. 234b).

3. Match the center lines and the shaping seams.

4. Pin the two thicknesses together at the center. Smooth the fabric toward the outer edges and pin along the seam allowances.

5. Work over the tailor's ham (Fig. 234a). With fabric side up, tailor-baste the skirt to the lining, starting at the center lines and working toward the side seams.

6. Stitch the skirt front to the skirt back, catching the lining in the side seams (Fig. 235a). The seam allowance of the lining may be trimmed back.

7. Insert the zipper in the garment fabric only.

8. Snip the seam allowance of the lining about ¼" at the end of the placket opening. Fold it under and press.

9. Place the folded edge against the tape of the zipper. Hem to position (Fig. 235b).

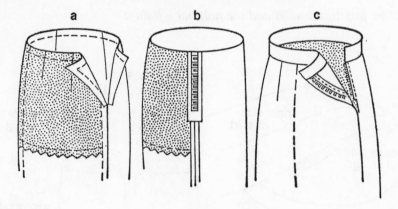

Fig. 235

When the skirt band is stitched to the skirt, the lining is also caught in the waistline seam (Fig. 235c). Grade the seam allowances leaving the lining widest.

How to completely line the skirt:

A complete lining in a skirt is best when it is used as a free-hanging half slip joined to the skirt only at the waistband and the zipper. Wool and silk "give" differently. If the less-likely-to-stretch silk is treated like an underlining, the wool may "balloon" over it. A free-hanging lining avoids this.

1. Fit, stitch, and press the skirt. Insert the zipper.

2. Fit the lining as if it were a slim basic-fitting skirt.

3. Stitch the lining leaving the placket open.

4. Clip the seam allowances of the lining at the end of the placket about ¼". Fold under and press.

5. Press the rest of the lining.

6. Slip the skirt over the lining with both *wrong sides* toward the body.

7. Baste the skirt and the lining together across the waistline (Fig. 236a).

8. Place the folded edge of the lining placket opening against the tape of the zipper. Hem to position (Fig. 236b).

9. Stitch the waistband to the skirt, catching the lining in the seam.

10. If the lining has been cut on the horizontal grain, the selvage may serve as the hem finish for the lower edge. If the lining has been cut on the vertical grain, a regulation hem is used in the lining. It is turned up in the same direction as the skirt hem, that is, toward the body. It is generally 1″ shorter than the skirt hem. Use any hem finish appropriate for a silk lining.

Fig. 236

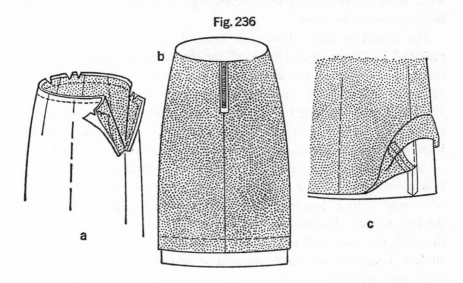

Optional: If you wish, you may fasten the side-seam allowance of the lining to the side-seam allowance of the skirt with permanent, very loose basting stitches in matching thread. Stop the stitches about 6″–8″ above the hem (Fig. 236c). This prevents the lining from slipping around inside the skirt.

NOTE: Both the half lining and the full lining are completed apart from the skirt itself. To do so means that all darts can be stitched with precision. Were the fabric and lining treated as one, it would be too difficult, if not impossible, to stitch a dart which tapers perfectly off the dart point and blends into the fabric without a pucker or a pleat.

All about Waistbands

The waistline of the skirt needs some finish. Usually this takes the form of a waistband. However, there are many times when the design of a skirt would be improved by using a concealed inside band of grosgrain ribbon or French belting instead. Narrow waistbands— ¾″ to 1¼″—are best for fit; they hug the waist. If a waistband gets wider than this some shaping is necessary on the side seams to fit the indentation of the waist.

The length of the waistband is equal to the waist measurement plus ½″ to 1″ for ease, plus 1½″ for the underlay, plus 1″ for the two seam allowances. For example, the length of the waistband for a 26″ waist will total 29″. The band is generally cut on the lengthwise grain to match the design or the nap of the fabric. It may also be cut on the crosswise grain, in which case the selvage may be used as a finished edge. Since fabric does not stretch in the length, this has the added advantage of acting as a stay. A bias waistband gives an excellent fit but care must be taken in reckoning its length. Make the waistband 1″ to 2″ less than the actual measurement to accommodate the bias stretch. The heavier the fabric and the wider the sweep of the skirt, the more pull exerted on the waistband and the greater the stretch. Therefore, the larger amount should be subtracted from the waist measurement.

The easiest way to handle the waistband is to cut the length of fabric double the width of the band plus seam allowances. When the fabric is heavy this makes a bulky band. To eliminate the extra thickness, cut a band to the length and width of a single thickness of the fabric plus seam allowances. Cut grosgrain ribbon the single width of the band and the same length. Lap the ribbon over the right side of the skirt band a little above the upper seam line. Proceed as for the previous band. The finished edge of the ribbon eliminates the necessity for turning under seam allowances, thereby further reducing unwanted thickness. Incidentally, this also adds just a bit of firmness, too—enough to keep the waistband from rolling over and not so much as to make a stiff band.

Ribbon waistbands: One often longs for some relief from the monotony of the miles of self-fabric waistbands encountered during a lifetime. Surely there must be some other finish for a skirt and there is! An attractive variation is the use of ribbon for the entire waistband. The contrast in texture between ribbon and wool can be quite decorative. The colors should match. A contrasting color is better than one which does not match. The ribbon should be wide enough to fold lengthwise. The finished ends of the ribbon are lapped over the fabric on both right and wrong sides. This avoids the bulkiness of turned-under seam allowances. The placket end may even be finished with a small cocarde or bow (Fig. 237a).

Fig. 237

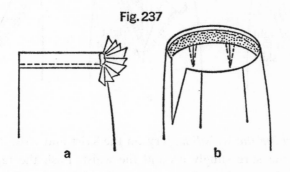

a   b

Another variation is the skirt with no visible waistband. Use grosgrain ribbon or French belting for the inside band. Mark the waistline seam on the skirt. Swirl the ribbon into the waistline curve and steam it into shape. To finish the ends turn them under and stitch. Lap the ribbon over the right side of the skirt a little above the waistline seam. Stitch. Press to position, clipping the seam allowance where necessary to achieve a flat turning. Tack the ribbon to the seams and darts of the skirt to keep it in place (237b). Or, top-stitch along the fold of the skirt. Fasten the ribbon with hooks and eyes.

Interfacing for the waistband may or may not be used, depending on your personal preference and the character of the fabric. Any regulation interfacing may be used. When interfacing is used, cut it to the length of the waistband and half the width, excluding seam allowances. Catch-stitch this single thickness of interfacing in place on the underband (the part of the band that will be next to your body). Place one edge along the fold line and the other edge at the seam line (Fig. 238a).

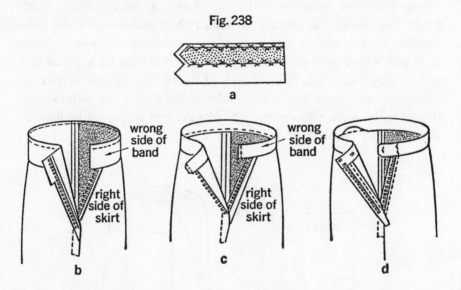

Fig. 238

a

wrong side of band

right side of skirt

b

wrong side of band

right side of skirt

c

d

To determine the waistline: Try on the skirt and close the placket. Pin a tape measure snugly around the waist. Push the tape into the waistline or into such position as you would like the waistline to be. Pin along the bottom of the tape. This is the position of the waistline seam. Remove the skirt and replace the pins with basting. The skirt band is stitched to the skirt along this line of basting.

Use this easy method to attach the waistband to the skirt:

1. Pin the right side of the waistband to the right side of the skirt back, allowing the underlay and seam allowance to extend beyond the finished edge of the placket opening (Fig. 238b).

2. Pin the other end of the waistband to position, allowing the ½″ seam allowance to extend beyond the skirt-front placket opening (Fig. 238b).

3. Pin the waistband to the skirt between the ends, easing the skirt into the band as necessary.

4. Stitch the band to the skirt, catching in the skirt lining (Fig. 238b).

5. Press the seam open first, then into the band.

6. Grade the seam allowances.

7. Fold the band in half lengthwise, right sides together, and stitch across the ends (Fig. 238c).

8. Trim, grade, and press the seam allowances open. Free the corners of bulk (Fig. 238c).

9. Turn the band to the right side and fold it lengthwise along the fold line. Make sure that the band is equidistant from the seam line along its entire length. Press along the fold line and across the ends, rolling the end seams to the underside.

10. Turn under the seam allowance of the loose edge and hem to the skirt along the stitching line (Fig. 238d).

This setting of the skirt band makes the underlay the extension of the skirt band used for closing. The overlap end is flush with the side seam making a very neat finish. It is fastened with hooks and eyes or large covered snaps.

To make a top-stitched waistband:

Fig. 239

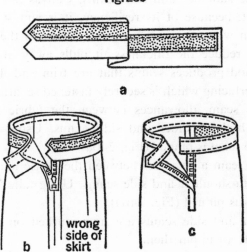

a

wrong
side of
skirt
b

c

1. Machine-stitch the interfacing to the skirt band (Fig. 239a).

2. Stitch the right side of the underband to the wrong side of the skirt (Fig. 239b).

3. Fold the band in half lengthwise, right sides together, and stitch across the ends. Trim and grade the seam allowances. Clip across the corners. Turn the band right side out. Press.

4. Turn under the seam allowances of the loose edge and pin to the right side of the skirt covering the stitching line. Press to position.

5. Top-stitch (Fig. 239c).

Perfecting the Fit of Jacket or Coat

Pin the shoulders and side seams on the right side of the garment. (All fittings and adjustments are made from right side and transferred to the wrong side.) Try the garment on over the dress, blouse, sweater, or suit with which it is to be worn. If shoulder pads are to be used, slip them in place. Pin the garment closed from the top button to the bottom of the garment, matching the center markings. Perfect the fit following all the guides set forth in Chapter III.

How to Eliminate Bulk in the Seams

If hair or wool canvas has been used for the interfacing it is *not* stitched into the shoulder and side seams. Canvas not only makes a bulky seam but, because of its resiliency, it is almost impossible to press flat. Often when it is trimmed away close to the stitching line in an effort to reduce the thickness, it pulls away in wearing. The following method produces seams that are trim and flat without involving the interfacing which is securely fastened separately.

1. Open the seam allowances between the fabric and the back interfacing of both shoulder and side seams. Using tailor's chalk, mark where the seam is pinned (Fig. 240a).

2. Open the seam allowances between the fabric and the front interfacing of both shoulder and side seams. Using tailor's chalk, mark where the seam is pinned (Fig. 240a).

The shoulder and side seams are now marked on all four thicknesses. It is safe to unpin them.

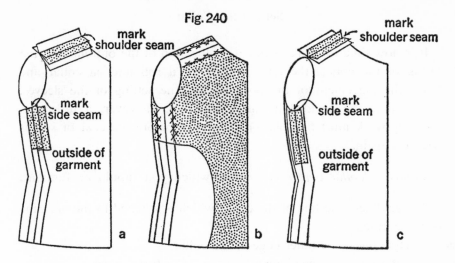

Fig. 240

3. Trim away the interfacing on the seam line where marked.

4. With the right sides of the outer fabric together, pin and stitch the shoulder and side seams.

5. Press the seam allowances open as flat as possible. Use the pressing technique determined best for the fabric. This places the open seam allowance over the loose edge of the interfacing.

6. Catch-stitch the seam allowance to the interfacing securely. This is what holds it in place (Fig. 240b). Be careful that the catch stitching does not come through to the right side of the garment.

If the interfacing or underlining is lightweight and not resilient it may be stitched into the shoulder and side seams.

1. Open the seam allowances between the interfacings (Fig. 240c).

2. Mark the interfacing with tailor's chalk. Unpin.

3. With the right sides of the fabric together, stitch the seams through all four thicknesses—outer fabric and interfacing (or underlining).

4. Trim and grade the seam allowances.

5. Press the seam allowances open as flat as possible, using the pressing technique determined best for the fabric.

Setting the Collar

It is now time to think of the exact location of the buttonholes, the fitting of the collar, the establishment of a roll line on collar and lapel, the placement of the pockets, and the setting of the sleeves. This can all be decided in the next fitting. However, a little preliminary work must be done on the collar before the coat or suit is tried on again.

Terms in collar construction with which you should be familiar:

1. neckline—the line of the collar which is stitched to the neckline of the garment.
2. style line—the outer edge of the collar
3. roll line—the line along which the collar turns down
4. rise—the part of the collar from the neckline to the roll line
5. fall—the part of the collar from the roll line to the style line
6. stand—the amount of the rise
7. break—the point at which the collar turns back to form a lapel

Shapes and stands: Any collar that conforms to the shape of the neck lies flat like a Peter Pan collar (Fig. 241a). When the collar neckline curves in an opposite direction to the curve of the neckline, the stand is deeper like that of the classic notched collar (Fig. 241b).

Fig. 241

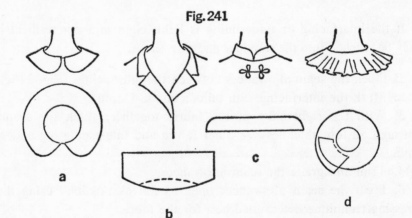

a

b

c

d

The straighter the neckline of the collar, the more it will stand. The mandarin collar is an example of a standing collar (Fig. 241c). When the collar neckline is more curved than the neckline of the garment, the outer edge will ripple like a circular, ruffled collar (Fig. 241d).

The rise and fall of the collar: The neckline of the collar may be just a little bit smaller (⅜" to ½") than the garment neckline. As the collar neckline is stretched to fit the suit or coat neckline, it pushes the collar into a slightly deeper stand. The reverse is true. If the collar neckline just fits the garment neckline or is a little larger than it, this reduces the stand. The upper collar should always be slightly larger than the under collar so the joining seam may be hidden on the underside. The fall of the collar should always be deeper than the stand of the collar so that the neckline seam is hidden—¼" is acceptable, ½" is preferable.

The under collar of a notched or shawl collar is cut on the bias so it can be eased around the neck for a perfect fit.

Compare the collar neckline with the suit or coat neckline:

1. Place a line of basting at the neck seam line of the garment. The thread goes through the outer fabric only. Make long floats on the right side.

2. Measure the neckline of the garment from the center back to the point at which the collar joins the neckline at the front. In a notched tailored collar (Fig. 242a) or a separate shawl under collar (Fig. 242b) this will be at the point where collar and lapel meet. In a Peter Pan collar (and variations) this point is generally at center front (Fig. 242c).

3. Measure the neckline of the under-collar pattern from center back to the point of joining.

4. Compare the collar measurement with the garment measurement.

5. Make any necessary adjustments to the collar. An adjustment at the center back is generally sufficient for a small change—up to ⅝". If any special styling or shaping is involved, the changes on the collar should be made in the same place as they were on the garment.

Fig. 242

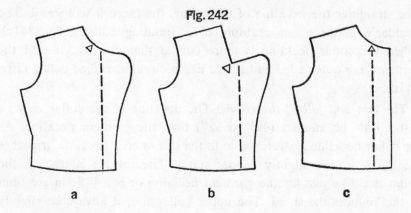

a   b   c

This will preserve the style line as well as the size of the collar. Do not make too large an alteration in any one place. This will destroy the over-all shape of the collar. Make several small changes instead.

Test the under collar:

Fig. 243

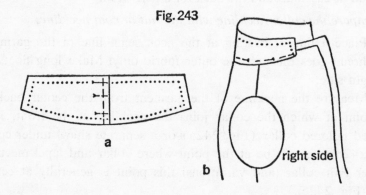

a

b   right side

1. Cut the collar interfacing from the corrected pattern. Transfer *all* the pattern markings. Use dressmaker's carbon paper and the tracing wheel.

2. Overlap and pin the center-back seam of the collar interfacing. Place the pins horizontally (Fig. 243a).

3. *Lap* and pin the neckline of the collar (as it is marked in carbon) *over* the neckline of the garment (the line of basting). Match center backs and the points at which the collar joins the neckline in front. Ease between these points. Place the pins horizontally along the seam line (Fig. 243b).

Try on the garment. Slip the shoulder pads into position. Pin the center front closed from the top button down. This places the collar and the lapels in the proper position.

Moment of Decision

Stand before the mirror. Does it begin to look like a suit or coat? Encouraging, isn't it? Now decide whether the neckline is too tight, too loose, or just right. Decide whether the stand of the collar looks and feels comfortable. Would it be improved if it were made higher or lower? The stand of a collar varies with style and with one's figure. Examine the fall of the collar. Does it safely cover the neckline seam? Does the roll line of the collar flow in a continuous line into the roll line of the lapel?

This is your big chance to get a collar that really fits *your* neck. You can see all of these things for yourself in the mirror. Remove the garment, make any necessary adjustments and try it on once more. Examine it in the mirror again. Mark the roll line of both collar and lapel. If the under collar is of tailor's linen, crease the roll line on one side. If the under collar is of any other interfacing, pin along the roll line since it won't crease as easily. Pin along the roll line of one lapel. It is only necessary to mark one side—the side easiest for you to reach. The other side will be duplicated.

On buttonholes and pockets: Determine where the buttonholes are to be placed. Follow the suggestions for placement previously given.

Decide the best placement of the pockets. Mark the position with a line of safety pins. (Of course, you may not have much choice about placement if the style is a very special one. The designer has already decided this for you.)

On sleeves: Decide where on the shoulder seam the sleeves are to be set. How far out on the shoulder the sleeve sits is primarily a matter of what is fashionable in any particular year. Secondly, it is a matter of your figure. When a narrow-shouldered look is "in," the sleeve is set further in on the shoulder. When a wide-shouldered look is fashionable, the shoulder is broadened. If there is such a thing as a classic setting for a tailored garment, it is that point ½″ beyond the shoulder bone. (This takes care of some light shoulder padding and the fact that a suit or coat is worn over another garment. If heavier shoulder pads are used, the shoulders are extended an amount equal to the thickness of the pad.) Whether you are narrow-shouldered or broad-shouldered must also be taken into consideration. What to do about it and yet look fashionable is a personal decision.

Stand before the mirror. Slip the stitched, pressed, and shaped sleeve over your arm. Experiment for placement on the shoulder. See where the sleeve looks best on you. Keep current styling in mind. When you have made your decision, place a safety pin on the shoulder seam at the armhole to mark the place where the sleeve is to be set. It is only necessary to do this at one shoulder since the other one must be made to match.

Transfer the Markings

Having made these weighty decisions and admired your handiwork, remove the garment, remove the collar, and transfer all the markings to the other side of the garment—collar, lapel, shoulder seam, and the position of the pockets.

Mark roll line of the collar and lapel with pencil, tailor's chalk, or dressmaker's carbon paper, making the right and left sides identical.

Mark the sleeve setting at the other shoulder with basting thread or a tailor's tack. Measure the shoulder seam from neck to armhole. Make both shoulders identical in width.

Replace safety-pin marking at the pockets with a line of basting.

Using the corrected interfacing as a guide, cut the under and upper collars of garment fabric. Set the collar aside for the time being.

Now the time has certainly come to test your new-found techniques. Make the buttonholes. Construct the pockets. Refresh your memory by rereading Chapter VIII.

Hold That Line—Applying Tape

Edges of a garment which get a great deal of wear tend to stretch, ripple, or get pulled out of shape even when these edges are inter-

Fig. 244

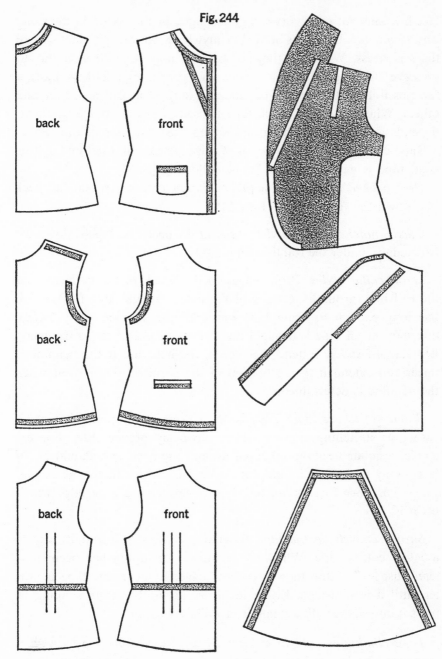

faced. Seams cut on a curve, a great angle, or bias react in the same way. Such trouble spots may be anywhere on the garment where there is stress. Wherever they occur, tape may be used as a stay to preserve the original measurement and shape. Fig. 244 suggests a few possibilities for the use of tape as a stay. You will no doubt find others. Where and how much tape is used in any particular garment depends on the cut of the garment and the character of the fabric.

Tape can be used in any or all of these places. In a tailored suit or coat, tape is generally used in the following places:

High-necked style either with or without collar: Around the neck and down the front edges (Fig. 245a).

Classic notched-collar styles: Around the neck and lapels, down the front edges, under the roll line (Fig. 245b).

Shawl-collar styles: Front edges to the break of the collar, under the roll line, around the back of the neck; cut the tape for the roll line long enough to bring it in line with the shoulder (Fig. 245c); this extra bit of tape is brought up on the roll line of the collar when it is set. *All styles:* Extend the tape to the hemline. If the hemline is uncertain, extend it to the bottom of the garment. Trim it off when the hemline is determined.

When not to use tape: Tape is never used in any place that needs easing or stretching since it would obviously prevent this. For example, a collar needs to be eased around the neck and shoulders. In fact, many under collars are cut on the bias to facilitate this easing. The collar, therefore, is *not* taped, even though the neck edge which fits it is.

Shrink and shape the tape: Beginning tailors will find it easy to use ½" cotton tape. When the technique of taping has been mastered, use ¼" cotton tape for a finer edge. Immerse the tape in water until it is saturated. Either let it dry naturally before shaping or press it into shape with a steam iron while yet damp.

Tape eliminates bulk in a seam: In addition to its use as a stay, tape may also be used to eliminate bulk at any seam where the inter-

Fig. 245

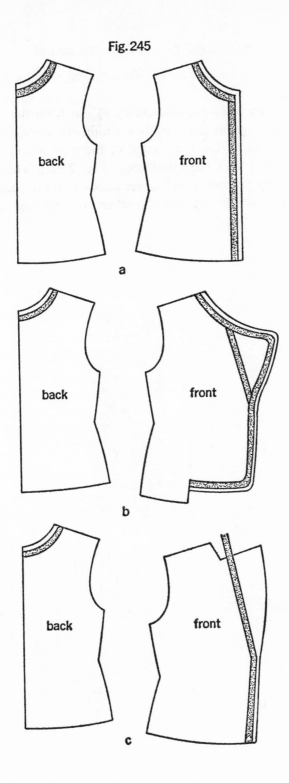

a

b

c

facing would otherwise be caught—the neck edge, the lapel, and the front closing.

To do this, trim away the interfacing ¾″ in from the raw edges. Place the outer edge of the tape just within the seam line (⅝″ in from the edge). Place the inner edge of the tape over the interfacing. The tape straddles the interfacing (Fig. 246a). This is in line with the tailoring practice which never allows two thicknesses of any material to end one directly over the other. In other words, this edge is graded, too.

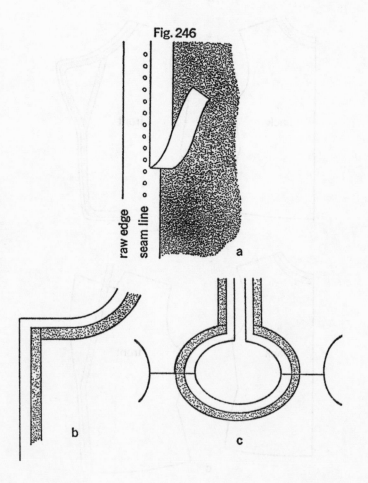

Fig. 246

Cut the tape at the end of each seam and lap any adjoining tape (Fig. 246b). This makes for a sharp, flat corner. Tape is *never* darted or mitered at corners.

Swirl the tape into shape around the neck (Fig. 246c) or any other curved edges.

Tape must be the *actual measurement* of the edge to be taped. If it is applied too tightly, the edge will be drawn up. If it is applied too loosely, it will ripple and, what is much worse, it will not act as a stay.

Stitching the tape to the garment: Use a single strand of matching thread and a No. 8 or No. 10 crewel needle. Stitch the outer edge of the tape to the fabric with tiny, "easy," invisible hemming stitches, lifting only a single thread of the fabric at a time. Hem the inner edge of the tape to the interfacing. Catch *only* the interfacing; do not come through to the garment fabric (Fig. 247a).

Here is another method for attaching the tape: trim off the seam allowance of the interfacing. Place the tape over the interfacing even with the trimmed edge. Machine-stitch the tape to the interfacing along the inner edge. Trim away the interfacing close to the stitching line. Hem the tape to the seam line (Fig. 247b).

By either method the tape is attached before the facing is stitched to the garment. *Neither tape nor interfacing are caught in the joining seam.*

Fig. 247

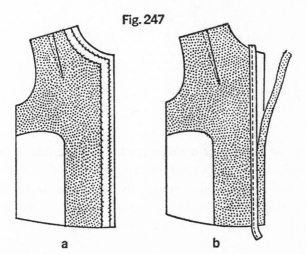

a   b

Tape used at the roll line of the lapel: Place the tape under the roll line of the lapel. The outer edge of it is about ⅛″ in from the roll line on the garment side of the interfacing (Fig. 248a). This setting stays the roll line but does not interfere with the roll. When pinning the tape to position, pull it slightly taut so that the measurement of the tape is slightly shorter than the actual roll line. This tends to throw the lapel back in a soft roll and keep it back in this position. Pad-stitch both sides of the tape.

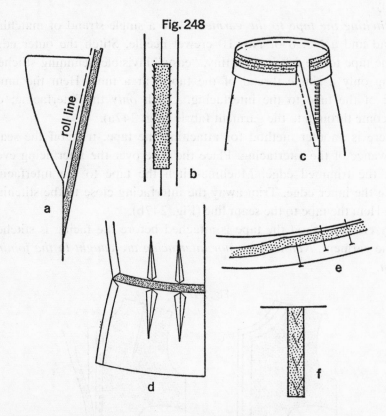

Fig. 248

Tape used on a seam at a sharp angle: Cut preshrunk tape to the desired length. Place the center of the tape directly over the seam. Pin at the top, bottom, and center of the seam. Pin sections between. Stitch each side of the tape to the seam allowance (Fig. 248b). The stitches do *not* come through to the right side. Alternate method: the

edge of the tape may be stitched into the seam if this does not produce too much thickness.

Tape used in a waistband: Cut preshrunk tape to the desired
length. Swirl into a waistline curve. Catch the edge of the tape in the
waistline seam (Fig. 248c). Press the tape into the waistband so that
it will be concealed.

Tape at a fitted waistline: Cut preshrunk tape to the desired length.
Swirl into a waistline curve. Tack firmly at the waistline to all seams
and darts (Fig. 248d).

Tape at a hemline: Cut preshrunk tape to the desired length. Swirl
into the hemline curve. Pin one edge along the hemline, the other
to the hem (Fig. 248e). Hem both edges of the tape so the stitches
are invisible from the right side.

Tape used to reinforce a dart or seam of the interfacing: Use preshrunk tape. Place the center of the tape over the seam line of either
dart or seam. Stitch the tape to the interfacing either by machine or
by hand. When done by hand use strong diagonal basting (Fig.
248f).

How to Complete the Collar

The classic notched collar:

1. Join the fabric under collar at the center-back seam. Trim the
seam allowances and press them open.

2. Overlap and stitch the center-back seam of the collar interfacing. Trim the seam allowances close to the stitching line.

3. Place the interfacing over the wrong side of the under collar.
Pin to position.

4. Using matching thread, make a row of uneven horizontal basting stitches (⅜" to ½") along the roll line. The long floats lie on
the surface of the interfacing. The needle catches only a thread of
the collar fabric through the interfacing as in pad stitching.

5. Crease the collar on the roll line. Curve it into a neck shape
(Fig. 249a). The subsequent handling and stitching of the collar
should confirm this shape.

6. Pad-stitch the stand of the collar with parallel rows of similar uneven horizontal basting. Work with the interfacing up. The stitches are about ⅜″ to ½″ long. The rows about ⅜″ to ½″ apart. Stitch to the seam line only. Do each row separately. Tug the thread *slightly* at the end of each row so that a neck shape begins to be apparent (Fig. 249b). (Caution: don't overdo this.)

7. Pad-stitch the fall of the collar with rows of pad stitching following the grain line. Hold the collar over the hand in a neck shape while working. The stitches are ½″ long. The rows are ½″ apart. Pad-stitch to the seam line.

Fig. 249

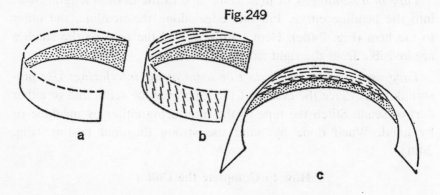

a   b

c

8. Trim away all the seam allowances of the interfacing.

9. Trim, clip, and turn up the neck-edge seam allowance of the under collar over the interfacing. Catch-stitch in place (Fig. 249c).

10. Attach the upper collar to the under collar by hand or by machine. If you can handle the stitching well by machine, this is preferable. Use all the tailoring techniques for easing, stitching, trimming, grading, and pressing in Chapter VII, particularly the directions for the encased seam.

If you have any doubt about your ability to negotiate the corners by machine, then by all means attach the collar by hand. There are some fabrics—men's wear, worsted, heavy coating—which present difficulties in achieving sharp corners while allowing enough fullness for the seam roll. When dealing with such fabrics, it is wiser to attach the upper collar successfully by hand than to botch the collar with imperfect machine stitching. In general, curved collars are easier to stitch by machine. For most home sewers, collars with sharp corners are easier to do by hand.

To attach the upper collar by hand:

Trim all the under-collar seam allowances to ⅜" to ½". Turn up all the under-collar seam allowances over the interfacing and catch-stitch to position (Fig. 250a). Clip where necessary. Miter the corners. Turn under and baste the seam allowances of the upper collar allowing enough for the seam roll. Miter the corners (Fig. 250b). Pin the upper collar to position over the under collar and slipstitch the edges (Fig. 250c).

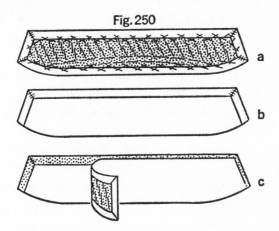

Fig. 250

Whether stitched by hand or by machine, the neck edge of the collar remains open. The neck edge of the under collar is finished. The neck edge of the upper collar is not.

11. Press all the edges of the collar as flat as possible. Use the pressing technique determined best for the fabric.

12. Steam and shape the completed collar over an appropriate press pad.

13. Edge-baste all finished edges of the collar to hold the seam roll in position.

When correctly stitched and shaped a classic tailored collar hugs the neckline. Recent styling has used this collar on a dropped neckline, producing a modified, non-neck-hugging version of it. This has a softer roll so that it is not necessary to crease the roll line. The steaming and shaping will depend on the particular design of the collar.

Peter Pan collars and variations thereof are distinguished by a low, soft roll away from the neck. Peter Pan collars are handled in much the same way as the notched collar with this difference: since there is very little or no stand there need be no roll line, no crease, and no pad stitching of a stand. The pad stitching of the entire collar follows the grain of the interfacing. This is always a safe rule to follow for pad stitching: when in doubt as to the direction of the stitching, follow the grain of the interfacing.

The shawl collar is handled differently because of its cut. The difference is more in the sequence of operations than in actual construction.

The shawl collar starts at the break (top button of the garment) and continues around to the center back. *All* of this is collar. The back part of it stands like a notched collar; the front part of it turns back like a lapel. The upper collar and the front facing are usually cut all in one (Fig. 251a). The under collar may be cut in one of two ways: all in one with the front of the garment (Fig. 251b) or as a separate under collar (Fig. 251c). While the under collar of each type requires a procedure of its own, the upper collar and facing are always applied in the same way.

TYPE I Collar-in-one with the jacket or coat front (Fig. 251b).

1. Pin the center-back seam of the garment fabric. This is the only place where any minor adjustments can now be made. It is to be hoped that important changes were taken care of in the trial muslin.

2. Overlap and pin the center-back seams of the interfacing. Place the pins horizontally.

3. Clip both the fabric and the interfacing at the neckline where indicated on the pattern. (Reinforce the point of the slash.)

4. *Lap* the collar *over* the neckline of the suit or coat matching the seam lines. Place pins horizontally.

Fig. 251

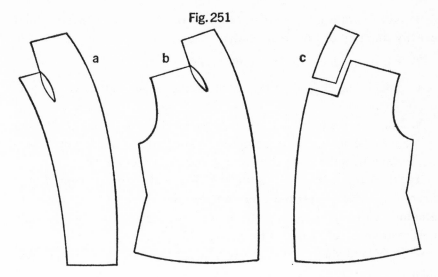

5. Try on the garment. Pin it closed from the top button down.

6. Make any necessary adjustments.

7. Establish the stand and the roll line of the collar from the center back to the break.

8. Mark the entire roll line on one side of the collar with pins.

9. Remove the garment. Mark the corrections. Mark the roll line. Unpin the collar. Trace the roll line on the opposite collar.

10. Stitch the corrected center-back seams in both fabric and interfacing.

11. Pad-stitch the roll line (uneven horizontal basting), the stand (rows of uneven horizontal basting), and the rest of the collar (pad stitching which follows the grain of the interfacing).

12. Trim away the interfacing seam allowances of the entire collar both at the neckline and the style line.

13. Trim the fabric seam allowance at the neck edge to ½″ to ⅜″.

14. Turn up the fabric neck-edge seam allowance over the interfacing (clipping as necessary) and catch-stitch.

TYPE II Separate under collar (Fig. 251c). Treat this under collar exactly like that of the notched style.

To complete the collar for both types:

1. Attach the finished neck edge of the under collar to the garment (page 356).

2. Make any similar adjustments to the back seam of the facing as were made for the interfacing and under collar. Stitch the center-back seam, trim the seam allowances, and press them open.

3. Stitch the facing to the under collar and garment front in one operation. Observe all the tailoring techniques for easing, stitching, grading, clipping, notching, trimming, pressing, and edge basting, particularly those directions for an encased seam.

4. Press and shape the completed collar over an appropriate press pad.

Standing collars are used on dressmaker rather than tailored designs. Styling is an important feature of these collars and often calls for special handling. Be guided by the construction directions in the pattern. Feel free to substitute any tailoring techniques which will produce a trimmer and flatter collar.

The interfacing of a standing collar is stiffly quilted by machine stitching to ensure a firm stand. It may be attached to the collar facing by catch stitching at the fold or seam line of the upper edge, along the seam lines of the lower edge and the ends. There is no pad stitching of interfacing to facing as for those collars which have an upper and under collar, the latter being hidden from view. In the standing collar both collar and facing are exposed and must be treated accordingly. Unlike the other collars which are attached to the garment by hand, this collar is attached to the garment at the neckline by machine.

To complete the lapel:

1. Pad-stitch the lapel from the tape at the roll line to the tape at the outer edge. The stitches follow the grain of the interfacing. They are ⅜″ to ½″ long and the rows are ⅜″ to ½″ apart (Fig. 252a).

Fig. 252

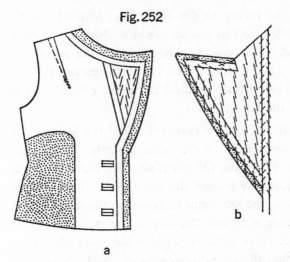

a   b

    2. Machine-stitch the facing to the front edge of the garment from the hem to the point at which the collar joins the lapel. The line of stitching is ⅛″ beyond the seam line toward the outer edge. This provides the necessary fullness so the seam can be rolled to the underside. Heavier fabrics may require a wider margin. Ease the facing around the lapel for the same reason. This utilizes some of the seam allowance. Clip the seam allowances almost to the stitching at the point where collar and lapel join and at the break. The former makes it easier to set the collar; the latter is necessary for the changed direction of the seam roll below the break (see Step 5 below).

    As with the collar, it may be necessary in some fabrics to attach the facing of the lapel by hand. When this is so, machine-stitch the facing to the garment as far as the break. Trim, clip, and turn the garment seam allowance up over the lapel. Catch-stitch the seam allowance to the tape (Fig. 252b). Turn under the seam allowance of the facing at the lapel, allowing sufficient for the seam roll. Pin the facing to position over the lapel and fasten with slip stitching.

    3. Press the seam allowance open, using the point presser in the corner of the lapel. Free the corner of bulk. Trim and grade the seam allowances making the one against the garment narrower than that of the facing.

4. Turn the facing to the right side. Steam-press the edges with the seam rolled into its proper position. Note the change of direction at the break. The seam is rolled toward the garment on the lapel; the seam is rolled toward the facing on the garment.

5. Edge-baste firmly to hold the seam roll in position for the remainder of the construction.

To complete the Peter Pan collar and similar types, stitch the facing to the front edge of the garment from the hem to the point at which the collar joins the neckline. The line of stitching is ⅛″ beyond the seam line toward the outer edge. Ease the garment around any corners so the seam can be rolled to the underside. Clip the seam allowance almost to the stitching at the point where the collar joins the neckline. Press, trim, clip, grade the seam allowances; turn, press with the seam roll in the proper position, and edge-baste.

A convertible collar is treated as if it were a Peter Pan collar even though the closing is sometimes turned down to form a lapel.

The back neck facing (if the garment has one) is stitched to the front facing at the shoulders. Trim the seam allowances and press them open.

Decision, Decision!

Despite all that we have done to assure that the seams which join the garment to the facing or the under collar to the upper collar are concealed on the underside, it is possible that in wearing the seam will emerge from hiding. It must be fastened permanently either by top stitching or understitching. Decide which of the two is more appropriate for the design. Whichever it is to be, don't skip this important step. There is nothing which gives away amateur sewing more than a seam which sits in full view on a double thickness of fabric.

If you choose to do understitching (page 230), now is the time for it—before the collar is joined to the garment and while it is still possible to get at the inside of each.

When to do top stitching (page 229) depends on the style and the method of joining collar to garment. Generally, it is done at such time that the stitching can be in a continuous line.

How to Join the Collar to the Garment

The collar is joined to the garment by hand stitching. This is a custom-tailoring method. Home sewers will find it easier, quicker, and more accurate than machine stitching.

Work from the right side.

1. Slip the finished edge of the under collar over the raw neck edge of the garment. This lapping will bring it to the line of basting which marks the neck seam line. The garment neck-edge seam allowance extends into the collar.

2. Pin at each point where the collar joins the neckline or lapel. Pin the center back. Ease the areas between and pin. Do *not* catch the front facing either in the pinning or in the stitching.

3. Make sure that both ends of the collar are the same size; make sure that both lapels are the same size.

4. Attach the *under collar only* to the garment with tiny, vertical hemming stitches (Fig. 253a).

Turn to the inside of the garment.

5. Trim, clip, and turn down the loose neck-edge seam allowance over the neckline tape. Press it open with the tip of the iron. Fasten it to the tape with either permanent basting or catch stitching (Fig. 253b).

Turn back to the right side.

6. Turn the collar into the position it will assume when worn. This allows the length required for its normal roll. Make sure that the upper collar is long enough to avoid pulling or exposing the underside. Pin both sides of the collar temporarily in this position (Fig. 253c). Do the same at each lapel (Fig. 253d).

JOINING THE COLLAR TO THE GARMENT

Fig. 253

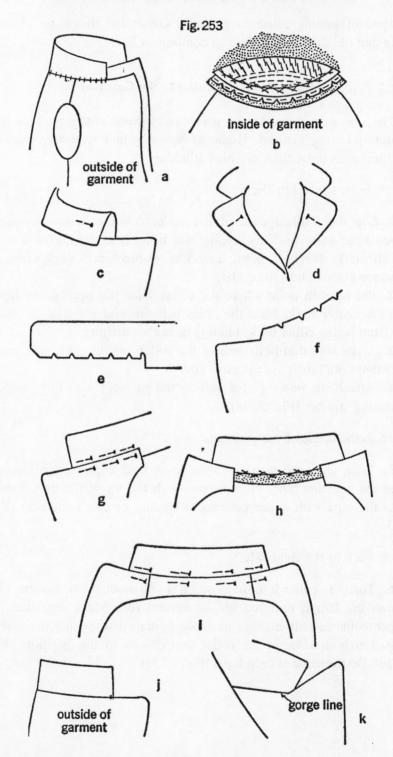

inside of garment

b

outside of
garment
a

c

d

e

f

g

h

i

j

outside of
garment

gorge line

k

To join the facing to the upper collar:

7. Diagonally snip the seam allowances of both lapel facing and upper collar at the point where they join. This frees the corners of bulk. Trim and clip both seam allowances (Fig. 253e and 253f).

When there is no back neck facing: Clip the seam allowance of the upper collar at the shoulder.

When there is a back neck facing: Continue to trim and clip the entire back neck seam allowances of upper collar and back neck facing.

8. Turn under the seam allowances of both upper collar and lapel facing so that the fold lines meet directly over the under seam line. Pin or baste them to this position (Fig. 253g). Make sure that the seam allowance of the collar is turned back toward the collar and the seam allowance of the lapel is turned back toward the lapel.

When there is no back neck facing: bring the upper-collar seam allowance down over the back neckline tape from shoulder to shoulder, clipping as necessary to make it lie flat. Fasten to the tape with either permanent basting or catch stitching (Fig. 253h). The lining will cover this.

When there is a back neck facing: continue to turn under the seam allowance of the upper collar back into the collar and the back neck facing back under the facing (Fig. 253i).

Either way, pin or baste collar and facing to position.

9. Remove the pins which are holding the collar and lapels in their rolled-back positions.

10. Use matching thread and a No. 8 crewel needle. Secure the thread with several strong over-and-over stitches on the underside of the collar where it joins the lapel (Fig. 253j). Bring the needle through to the right side at the seam line between the folds. Slipstitch the gorgeline (Fig. 253k). Don't draw the stitches up too tight. Catch an occasional stitch in the seam below to anchor the upper seam in place. When the stitching is completed secure the ends of the thread with several strong over-and-over stitches on the underside.

11. Remove the edge basting.

12. Press all the edges as sharp and flat as possible. Use the pressing technique determined best for the fabric.

This hand method of attaching the collar to the garment may be adapted to dressmaker as well as tailored garments. It may also be used for styles with other types of collars. Use it wherever and whenever it facilitates the setting of a collar.

There are several variations of this method.

VARIATION I

When the lapel and the upper collar are each joined to the underfabric by hand, this variation suggests a more logical procedure.

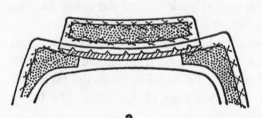
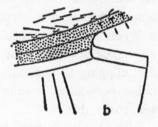

a   b

Fig. 254

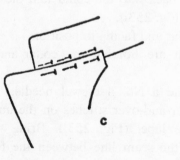
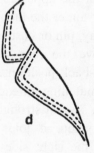

c   d

1. After the under collar has been pad-stitched and the interfacing seam allowance has been trimmed away, trim all the under-collar seam allowances to ⅜″ to ½″.

2. Turn up *all* the under-collar seam allowances over the interfacing and catch-stitch to position. Clip where necessary. Miter the corners.

3. Construct the lapel in the same way.

4. Attach the under collar to the neckline of the garment with vertical hemming stitches.

5. Open, trim, clip, and fasten the garment neck seam allowance to the tape (Fig. 254a).

6. Attach the facing to the front edge of the garment as far as the collar break by machine.

7. Trim, clip, and turn under the seam allowances of the facing. Slipstitch to the lapel. Continue turning under the neck-edge seam allowance of the facing and fell to the neck seam of the garment (Fig. 254b). Clip as necessary.

8. Complete the collar by slipstitching the upper collar to the under collar on all but the neck edge. Clip the seam allowance of the upper collar at the shoulder.

9. Fold under the seam allowance of the upper collar so its fold meets the fold line of the facing (Fig. 254c). Slipstitch the collar firmly to the front facing at the gorgeline.

VARIATION II

This is a useful joining for a style which can use top stitching.

The procedure is the same as for the first method until Step 8.

Instead: bring the seam allowance of the upper collar straight down over the tape all along the lapel and neckline. Fasten with permanent basting. Turn under the seam allowance of the lapel facing. Clip as necessary. Lap the folded edge over the upper collar and pin. To fasten, top-stitch (Fig. 254d).

VARIATION III

If you've ever had a chance to examine a woman's classic tailored coat made by a men's tailor you will recognize the following method of constructing and applying the collar. It is particularly well suited to heavy coatings.

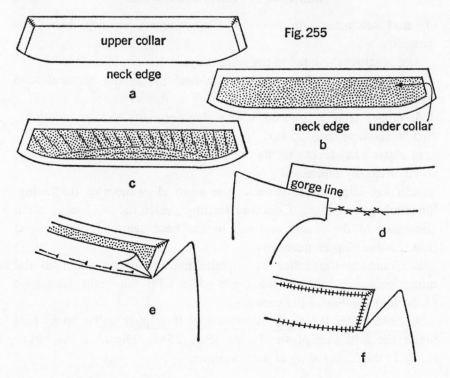

Fig. 255

1. Stitch the facing to the front of the coat as far as the point where collar and lapel join. Trim, grade, press, edge-baste.

2. Turn under and press all upper collar seam allowances except that at the neck edge. Miter the corners and whipstitch (Fig. 255a).

3. Place the under-collar interfacing over the under collar and pin in position.

4. Trim away all seam allowances of the interfacing (Fig. 255b).

5. Pad-stitch the roll line, the fall, and the stand to within ¾″ of the edges (Fig. 255c).

6. Clip the neck-edge seam allowance of the upper collar at the shoulder.

7. Turn under the seam allowance of the upper collar at the gorgeline. Bring the back neck seam allowance down over the back neckline tape. Pin in place.

8. Turn under the seam allowance of the lapel facing at the gorgeline. Pin.

9. Slipstitch the gorgeline. Catch-stitch the back neck-edge seam allowance to the neckline tape (Fig. 255d).

10. Trim away the seam allowance of the under-collar fabric at the neck edge.

11. Lap the cut edge of the under collar over the back neckline and pin in place.

12. Slip the remaining loose edges of the under-collar interfacing inside the turned-back seam allowances of the upper collar. The interfacing is really locked to the upper collar by this action (Fig. 255e).

13. Trim the remaining three seam allowances of the under-collar fabric just short of the folded edges of the upper collar. Pin the under collar to the upper collar at all edges.

14. Whipstitch all the cut edges of the under collar to both upper collar and neck edge (Fig. 255f). Use buttonhole twist or heavy-duty thread in a matching color.

How to Join the Cuffs to the Garment

Construct and apply the cuff in the same way as the collar.

1. Lightly pad-stitch the under cuff.

2. Join the cuff to the facing either by machine or hand stitching. In either case allow sufficient fullness to roll the seam to the underside.

3. Attach the cuff to the raw edge of the sleeve by machine stitching. Or, slipstitch the finished edge of the cuff to the finished edge of the sleeve. The cuff is a little larger than the sleeve and must be eased into it. This permits the cuff to stand away from the sleeve slightly, rather than be plastered against it.

Setting the Sleeve

Setting the sleeve is one of the last important operations in the construction of the garment. A well-set sleeve is one of the hallmarks of fine tailoring. That home sewers find difficulty in setting sleeves is due in large part to the inadequate sewing advice which they have been following. When you start to set a sleeve at the under-arm and work your way up to the cap, there is bound to be trouble This method of setting can only work *if* the armhole, the shoulder, the side seam, and the sleeve are still exactly as they were in the original pattern and *if* the fabric used can be comfortably eased at the sleeve cap. Should any one of these depart from the standard (and where is the garment in which at least one of these doesn't?) this method will no longer work. By the time you reach the shoulder you may end up with a handful of fabric at the cap which has no place to go except into a leg-o'-mutton puff. It does seem more logical to start setting the sleeve at the sleeve cap. Then any adjustments which need to be made can be done at the underarm where there is some room for change.

Before the actual setting of the sleeve, it is necessary to check or perhaps to re-establish the stitching line of the armhole. Use your pattern as a guide for the shape of the armhole.

1. Pin the shoulder seam of the pattern front on the shoulder seam of the garment front. Set the armhole seam of the pattern at the newly established shoulder point.

2. Pin the side seam of the pattern on the side seam of the garment. Let the underarm of the pattern fall as much below the armhole of the garment as is necessary for the pattern to lie flat and still touch the side seam.

3. Mark the new cutting line of the front armhole with tailor's chalk.

4. Repeat the procedure for the back. The back shoulder seam must match the front shoulder seam. The back side seam must match the front side seam.

The solid lines in the illustration (Fig. 256) represent an armhole which needs changing. The broken lines represent the pattern placed in position to make the necessary changes.

5. Cut out the new armhole.

6. If, in fitting, the shoulder seam has been brought forward,

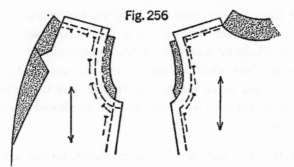

Fig. 256

lengthening the back armhole, then the shoulder notch on the sleeve cap must be brought forward, too.

Set the sleeve in the armhole: The sleeve has already been stitched and pressed; the cap shirred and shaped. It is now ready to be set into the sleeve.

1. Insert the sleeve into the armhole, right sides together. Match the shoulder notch at the cap with the shoulder seam. Pin. (All pins are placed horizontally to give a true seam line.) Hold the sleeve toward you so that its fullness can be eased into the armhole.

2. Ease the cap on both sides of the shoulder. There is a great temptation to eliminate all ease at the cap. At least 1″ ease is absolutely necessary to accommodate the curve of the shoulder and the upper arm. An insufficient amount of ease not only makes the upper sleeve look flat but causes the sleeve to pull across the arm. One inch of ease means ½″ on each side of the shoulder. This is an area which is largely bias. There should be no trouble in easing so small an amount of any fabric into this bias cut. Distribute the fullness evenly across the cap (Fig. 257a).

3. Try on the garment. Check the position of the grain. The vertical grain should be at right angles to the floor. The horizontal grain should be parallel to the floor. All horizontal lines, checks, plaids, stripes, etc., should match those of the body of the garment. Check the cap of the sleeve for just-right fullness.

4. Note any adjustments which should be made. Remove the garment.

5. Make the necessary changes. Try on the garment once again. Unless you are fortunate enough to have someone set the sleeve for you, this will likely be a matter of trial and reset.

6. When satisfied with the fitting, pin the entire sleeve into the armhole. This time place the pins at right angles to the seam line to facilitate the stitching. The sleeve underarm should match the garment underarm.

If the sleeve still does not fit the armhole, let the underarm fall where it will on the body of the coat or suit. This drop may be as much as ½″ to ⅝″ (in rare instances, more). When the underarm of the sleeve has been pinned to position, trim away the excess coat or jacket fabric using the underarm of the sleeve as a guide.

Stitch the sleeve into the armhole:

1. Stitch with the sleeve toward you so that you can control the easing. It is not necessary to baste the sleeve into the armhole. If basting is used, make the stitches as small as running stitches.

2. Catch the interfacing into the seam. This is the only place in the garment where this is so. The interfacing is used to provide a little extra firmness at the sleeve cap.

3. While it is easier to stitch the sleeve into the armhole with the sleeve up, a more perfect stitching line is accomplished when the

Fig. 257

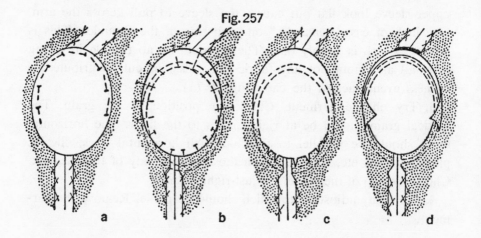

a   b   c   d

garment is up. Since the underarm needs to be reinforced with a double line of stitching (for obvious reasons), it is a good idea to stitch the entire armhole twice. The first stitching eases the sleeve accurately into the armhole. It is done with the sleeve up. The second stitching reinforces the underarm and corrects the stitching line across the cap. It is done with the garment up (Fig. 257b).

4. Clip the underarm. Each clip is made close to the stitching line (Fig. 257c). The underarm seam allowance of some fabrics can be safely trimmed away close to the double line of stitching (Fig. 257d). Either of these ways is necessary to release the strain at the underarm. The sleeve should fit at the seam line, not at the edge of the seam allowance.

5. Grade the seam allowances of the cap. Make the sleeve seam allowance narrowest, the interfacing widest and the garment somewhere between.

The Kimono Sleeve

There are an astonishing number of sewers who, fearful of tackling a set-in sleeve, limit their pattern selections to kimono-sleeved styles. In these designs the sleeves are obligingly cut all in one with the bodice. They present but one difficulty in construction and that easily surmounted.

Kimono sleeves are not only easy to sew, they are also easy to wear. This explains their universal and timeless appeal. The very deep sleeves of the Japanese kimono are most comfortable of all (Fig. 258a). The depth of the sleeves allows free movement of the arms while wrinkling under the arms is no real problem. Were an outer garment to be worn over the Japanese kimono it would have to have equally deep sleeves. Such sleeves, comfortable as they are, are not suited to our climate and our way of life.

As the depth of the sleeve lessens and the kimono sleeve becomes more fitted, problems develop. A fitted kimono sleeve extending straight out from the shoulders provides movement, but when the arms are brought down to the side in a more natural position there is considerable wrinkling under the arms (Fig. 258b). Since none

Fig. 258

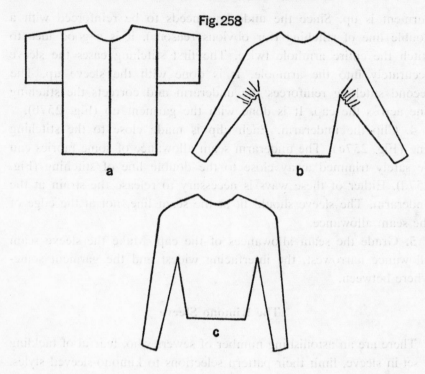

of us has the time, energy, or inclination to stand like a scarecrow forever with arms at shoulder height, the sleeve necessarily needs some modification in cut. As the kimono sleeve is cut at an angle which more nearly approximates the normal position of the arms, it also eliminates some of the movement (Fig. 258c). How to eliminate wrinkling and yet permit movement is the real problem in a kimono sleeve.

One solution to this problem was the invention of the set-in sleeve. A set-in sleeve does hang naturally at the side and does provide movement. Another solution was the invention of a hinge known more familiarly to us as a gusset. A gusset in a fitted kimono sleeve does permit the sleeve to hang in a normal position and does provide movement, while preserving the soft shoulder line and the simplicity of construction. For most home sewers the only difficulty about a kimono sleeve is sewing the gusset. This difficulty is very easily handled if the stitching is by hand.

1. Mark the seam line on the gusset very carefully with basting thread so it is clearly visible from the right side.

2. Stay-stitch the gusset opening for reinforcement.

3. Stitch the underarm and side seams. Press the seam allowance of each open.

4. Slash the gusset opening.

5. Turn under the seam allowance of the slashed opening. Press or baste in position.

6. Lap the folded edge of the slash over the right side of the gusset, bringing the fold to the line of basting which marks the seam line. Pin.

7. Using matching thread, slipstitch the gusset where pinned. Reinforce the points of the gusset with tiny whipping stitches.

This is an easy method for inserting the gusset. The stitches are invisible from the right side but make a continuous row of tiny stitches which can be seen on the wrong side. From the wrong side one can also see that the seam allowance of the slashed opening is tapered. The seam allowance of the gusset is standard. These seam allowances can be trimmed on all four sides.

If you don't feel confident that this hand stitching will hold, make a second row of slipstitching. Or, machine-stitch directly over the slipstitching on the wrong side. (Top stitching on the right side makes the gusset look like a patch.) Do each side separately for sharp corners. Do not attempt to stitch around all four sides of the gusset in one continuous line of stitching.

There are many variations of gussets used in styling. Be guided by the directions for any particular style but keep the ease of hand stitching in mind for those corners which are too worrisome to do by machine.

Kimono-sleeve variations:

The kimono-and-yoke combinations (Fig. 259a) and the kimono-and-armhole combinations (Fig. 259b). These sleeves meet the underarm at a point.

Fig. 259

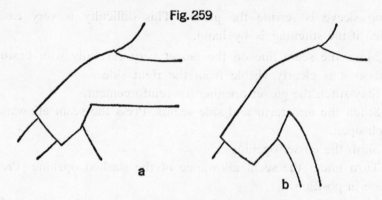

a

b

1. Reinforce the point with stay stitching.

2. Do one side at a time. Pin the seams right sides together. Match the markings at the point.

3. Bring the machine needle down on the *point* and stitch *away* from it. Pull the ends of the thread through to the under side and tie them.

4. Clip the seam allowance at the point to facilitate the pinning and stitching of the other seam.

5. Once more bring the needle down into the point and once more stitch away from it in the opposite direction. Pull the ends of the thread through to the under side and tie them.

Stitching each seam so assures an accurate joining at the point. If adjustments are necessary they can be made at the other end more easily. If you start at the other end and stitch toward the point you may have some extra fabric to worry about when you get there.

Raglan Sleeves

The curved seam line of a raglan sleeve is easily pulled and stretched out of shape. Be sure to stay-stitch immediately on removing the pattern. As you will recall of the curved welt pocket, it is easier to pin curved edges together if the seam allowances are clipped first. Pin sleeve and bodice together with right sides inside. Stitch. Press the seam allowance open. The seam may be taped to prevent stretching if you desire it.

Attaching the Shoulder Pads to the Coat or Jacket

For a set-in sleeve:

1. Slip the pad in place on the inside of the coat or jacket. The shoulder line of the pad matches the shoulder seam of the garment. The squared part of a shoulder pad is the front; the triangular part is the back. The edge of the pad extends ½" into the sleeve.

2. Holding the garment and pad in a normal wearing position with one hand, pin the shoulder pad in place with the other. Pins are placed on the right side at the armhole and at the neck.

3. Locate the point at which the tip of the pad meets the front armhole seam. Pin. Let the pad go off the seam any place that is necessary for a perfectly smooth and flat shoulder area.

4. Use the same procedure for placing the back of the pad.

5. Using matching thread fasten the pad securely on the wrong side where it meets the armhole seam. Bring the needle up to the right side directly into the armhole seam. Take a tiny stitch on top, push the needle into the seam, send it through the pad, bring it up into the seam about ½" away, and repeat until the entire pad is fastened into the armhole seam. Keep the stitches loose. Turn the garment to the wrong side and fasten the thread securely.

6. Should the pad be too wide across the shoulders, trim it down to the proper size at the neck end. Fasten this end of the pad with a French tack,* running from the seam line of the pad to the shoulder seam of the garment.

7. Fasten any other loose ends of the pad to the interfacing with French tacks.

---

* A French tack (suspension tack, swing tack) is used to hold two surfaces in place and yet provide some play and freedom of movement for each. They may be any size, depending on their use.

To make the French tack, take a tiny stitch in one piece which is to be held together and then directly opposite in the other. Pull up the thread to the desired length. Repeat making several such stitches (Fig. 260a). Work blanket stitches over the long threads, being careful not to catch the long threads or the loops (Fig. 260b). Blanket stitches are not necessary if the tack is a short one.

The French Tack

Fig. 260

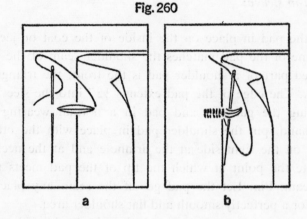

a   b

For kimono or raglan sleeves or designs with dropped shoulders:

Use a dropped-shoulder pad. This is one which cups the shoulder.

1. Try on the garment. Slip one shoulder pad into position. Pin on the right side. Remove the garment.

2. Measure the distance from the neck edge to the shoulder pad. Measure the same distance on the other shoulder.

3. Since there is no armhole seam in which to fasten the pad, it is fastened with tiny stitches in the shoulder seam.

4. Fasten the loose ends of the pad to the interfacing with French tacks.

When the shoulder pads have been set in place, pin the facing to position at the shoulder. Hang the garment on a hanger or dress form.

Hemming—the End in Sight

When you get to putting up a hem—the end is surely in sight. In fact, if you run true to form, you are probably planning your next project.

Let the garment "hang out" before setting the hem—at least overnight for a straight skirt and as much as a week for a circular or bias skirt. This gives the grain of the fabric a chance to settle so that the hem when finally marked will be accurate. Hems which are set too soon dip unevenly as the fabric settles.

Wear the foundation garment and shoes of the heel height you plan to wear with the garment. Choose a length most flattering to you within the current fashion. There is usually enough leeway within any style period to accommodate individual taste.

Despite all the advertised gadgets, it is really too difficult if not impossible to mark a hem accurately on yourself. Train someone to do this for you. Set the marker the distance from the floor you wish your hem to be. Stand still while the one who does the marking moves around you. If you change your position or shift your weight while turning, the skirt will be marked unevenly. Place the pins about 3″ apart on straight skirts. The more circular the skirt, the closer the pins should be placed to give an accurate hemline.

Jacket hems are usually set by the style. However, if the hem looks uneven or wrongly placed for you, set a new hem by measuring from the floor. You will need a yardstick for this.

Turn under the hem along the pinned line correcting any irregularities as you go along. (Pin markings sometimes do seem to be rather jumpy.) Press along the fold of the hem, removing the pins as you come to them. Working flat on a table, measure the hem to an even depth from the fold. Use a gauge for accurate marking.

Choose the hem width suitable for the style (Chapter IV). Use the pressing technique suggested in Chapter VII. Choose the hem finish which suits the type of garment and the fabric which has been used (Chapter VI). Whatever the choice, the hemline should be inconspicuous. This will depend on the right choice of hem finish, fine hand stitching, and the proper pressing technique.

Hems of Jackets, Coats, and Sleeves

The hems of coats, jackets, and their sleeves are usually interfaced to add body and to prevent stretching at the lower edges.

In those areas where hair canvas or other heavy interfacing is present:

Trim off the interfacing at the hemline.

In those areas where underlining is present:

The underlining may be trimmed away at the hemline for a crisp effect. This is usual in a tailored suit or coat.

The underlining may be folded back into the hem as extra padding when a soft unpressed effect is desired. This treatment is often used in a silk suit.

In those areas where neither interfacing nor underlining is present, the hem is interfaced with a bias strip of muslin.

When the suit or coat lining will be attached to the hem:

1. Cut a strip of bias muslin ¼″ to ½″ wider than the hem.

2. Steam-press the muslin into the curve of the hemline. (The hem of a suit or coat is a slightly curved line.)

3. Place the muslin strip inside the hem so that one edge lies along the fold line of the hem and the other edge extends beyond it. The end of the muslin interfacing slightly overlaps the front interfacing (Fig. 261a).

4. Catch-stitch or baste one edge of the bias interfacing to the top of the hem and the other to the bottom of it (Fig. 261a).

5. Fold the hem to position. Catch-stitch the protruding muslin to the garment (Fig. 261b) or baste it permanently (Fig. 261c).

When the lining hangs free of the coat or if the garment is unlined:

1. Cut the bias muslin strip ¼″ narrower than the hem.

2. Steam-press it to shape.

3. Catch-stitch (or baste) each edge of the strip to the hem (Fig. 261d).

4. Choose the desired hem finish and stitch it to the garment, concealing the muslin interfacing (Fig. 261e).

For a little extra support in a hem of this type:

1. Turn under a seam allowance on one edge of the bias muslin strip. Crease or press.

Fig. 261

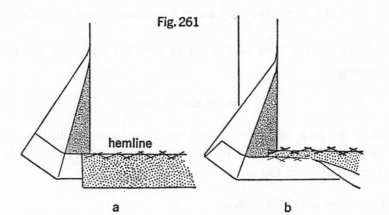

a

b

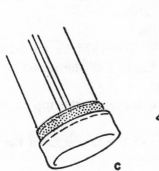

c

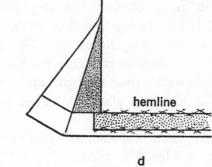

d

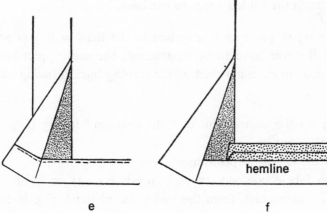

e

f

2. Pin the fold of this strip along the hemline and slip-stitch (Fig. 261f).

3. Turn up the hem and stitch to position enclosing the muslin interfacing.

Fasten the Facing

After the hem has been completed, turn back the facing against the jacket or coat and catch-stitch to position. This may create the problem of bulk in the lower corner.

To eliminate this in a jacket:

1. Cut away the seam which joins the facing to the garment to within ½" to ¾" of the hemline (Fig. 262a).

2. Grade the facing hem (Fig. 262b).

3. Fold the facing to position (Fig. 262c). Make the hemline of the facing slightly shorter than the hemline of the jacket so that it will not be visible from the right side.

4. Clip the seam allowance of the facing at the top of the hem (Fig. 262c).

5. Fold under the seam allowance of the facing from the clip to the bottom edge (Fig. 262d).

6. Slip-stitch the folded edges to the hem.

If the lining of the coat is attached to the hem or if you are sure the coat will never have to be lengthened, the same procedure may be followed. A more usual method for turning back a facing in a coat is as follows:

1. Turn up the entire hem of both coat and facing (Fig. 262e). Fasten to the coat.

2. Fold the facing to position.

3. If the fabric does not ravel, it needs no further finish. Simply make a suspension tack from the underside of the facing to the hem (Fig. 262f).

4. If the fabric does ravel easily or if a finished edge is desired,

Fig. 262

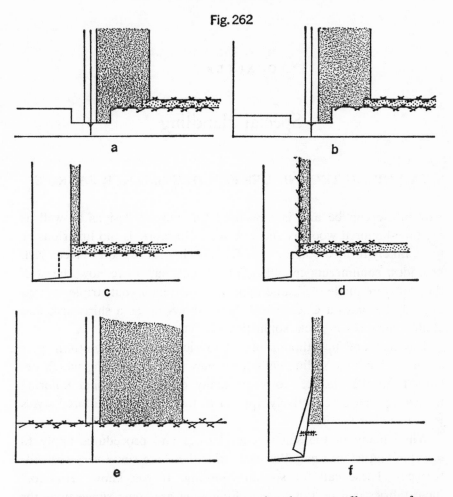

clip the facing as for the jacket; turn under the seam allowance from the clip down and slip-stitch to the hem.

It can't be long now!

All that is left to be done now before inserting the lining is to fasten all the facings to the interfacings with catch stitching, remove all the tailor bastings, and give the suit or coat a final light pressing.

CHAPTER X

Special Handling

TAILORING TECHNIQUES FOR DRESSMAKER FABRICS

Any fabric can be and is now used for tailored designs as well as the time-honored woolens and worsteds. No fabric is too luxurious or too unlikely to be a coat or suit. Glimmering satins, soft velvets, rich brocades, shimmering metallics, and fragile laces are now the stuff that suits are made of. Lamé appears as a trench coat; triple-layered organdy becomes a Chesterfield. Satin shows up as a shirtwaist, and chiffon surprises in slick, sophisticated styles.

This new and unorthodox use of fabric for tailored clothing plus the more feminine styling calls for a new type of tailoring which departs from the classic. However, many of the traditional tailoring techniques can be effectively applied to these new semitailored styles in dressmaker fabrics.

While many of the same general rules and procedures apply to dressmaking as well as tailoring fabrics there are some very real differences. These call for special handling. If you know "How-to," these fabrics can be fun to sew. Following are some suggestions for the special handling of dressmaker fabrics currently being much used for suits and coats.

New Woolens

Gauzy woolens and fuzzy mohairs are light and airy beauties with interesting surfaces that are best used for unfitted styles. Choose designs with simple lines and few pattern pieces. Intricate seaming is lost in their fuzzy textures.

To prevent interfacings and inner structure from showing through their open weaves they should be underlined throughout with organza or china silk of a matching color.

To prevent slipping, place the fabric on a flat surface over tissue paper. Pin along the outside edges.

Pin the pattern to the fabric with pins close to each other. Use sharp shears for cutting. Mark with tailor's tacks in thread of a contrasting color. Other markings will not show up on the textured surface.

Stitch slowly, being careful that the presser foot does not catch any loops of the fabric. Use 12–15 stitches to the inch.

Press on the wrong side over a needle board or self-fabric using the steam iron. Brush up the nap after pressing.

Finish the seams with overcasting or seam binding. Make a French dressmaker's hem for an invisible, flat finish.

Knit fabrics: The chief difficulty in sewing these fabrics of silk or wool jersey, bulky and novelty knits is *stretch*.

If you like the sweater comfort of knits and would like to preserve the stretch, do *not* line the garment. For complete control of the stretch, *do* line it. For additional body with some control, underline with *bias* fabric, which also has some stretch.

Sponging is optional. Because of the stretch of the fabric, shrinkage is presumably no problem. Use your judgment.

The folds in a tubular knit are not necessarily the vertical grain. In fact, they are very rarely and only accidentally so. Cut tubular knits open on the vertical grain, following one lengthwise rib or wale. Establish the horizontal grain with any right angle placed against the vertical grain. It is easier to establish the grain of looped or soufflé knits on the wrong side where the wales and courses are more clearly visible.

It is difficult to press out the original fold in knitted fabric. Place the pattern on the fabric with this in mind.

Stay-stitch all bias and curved edges immediately on removing the pattern. Work on a flat surface to prevent stretching. Use a fine machine needle and 10 to 12 stitches to the inch. Hold the fabric firmly.

Pull slightly as you stitch, so stitching will have some give. Avoid ripping, which is difficult and hazardous. Tape with bias binding for controlled stretch; use plain seam binding for no stretch. Tape the waistline seam. Double-stitch any points of stress.

Face necklines and other edges with taffeta, cotton, or silk.

Avoid buttonholes when possible. Use some other type of fastening. If buttonholes must be used, try the new iron-on interfacings to stabilize the area in which the buttonhole is to be made.

Finish the seam allowances with overcasting, edge stitching, or pinking.

Allow the garment to hang out 24 to 48 hours before setting the hem. Make a tailor's or French dressmaker's hem for a flat, invisible finish.

Press with a steam iron over a dry press cloth.

Double knits—double pleasure: Some of the common fears in sewing jersey are completely absent when working with the double knits. They have no right or wrong side. They are easy to cut because they lie flat without curling. They are firm and stable; easy to stitch and easy to press. They tailor beautifully.

The selvage is the vertical grain. Establish the horizontal grain with a right angle placed against the vertical grain.

Stay-stitch the cut edges immediately. Use a normal stitch and normal tension for sewing. Do *not* stretch the fabric while stitching. Tape all bias seams and the waistline seam with seam binding. Interface the buttonhole area with an iron-on or other soft fabric. Press with a steam iron over a dry press cloth. The iron applied directly to the fabric produces a shine.

Finish the seam allowances with overcasting or seam binding. Make a tailor's or French dressmaker's hem.

Silk—"Sweet Evening Stars"

Silk in all its variety is now used for the most glamorous of the new suits, coats, and ensembles.

Satin: Don't attempt satin unless you have a sure hand in sewing and an accurate eye for fitting. It is a fragile fabric that bruises easily and water-spots dreadfully. A trial muslin is a must. The fit must be perfect before stitching. Ripping marks show forever. The fabric needs plenty of ease, for it has no give. It has considerable seam slippage. A tight, overfitted garment will end up with you, like June, "bustin' out all over."

The direction of light striking the directional weave of satin affects its color and sheen. All pattern pieces must be placed, going in one direction from neck to hem (see Chapter IV for further directions). Needles, pins, and tracing wheel all leave hole marks in satin. Use silk pins (as few as possible) and place them close to the cutting line to make certain they are in the seam allowance only. Use tailor's chalk for marking. Avoid anything that will leave a permanent mark—this goes for basting, pad stitching, and ripping. Use a sharp, thin machine needle and normal stitches. Stitch slowly.

Satin needs some moisture for pressing but unfortunately it water-spots. This makes matters difficult. Use a steam iron over a dry press cloth. Don't hold the iron too long in any one spot. Don't try for sharp edges; satin looks better without them anyway. Settle for what you can get with a light pressing. If you must press from the right side, use tissue paper as a press cloth and a moderately warm dry iron.

The hems of satin suits and coats (dresses, too) look best when softly turned, unpressed, and slightly padded with cotton flannel or wadding. Use a variation of the tailor's or French dressmaker's hem for a finish.

Variation of the French dressmaker's hem for use on all silk garments that have been underlined:

Fig. 263

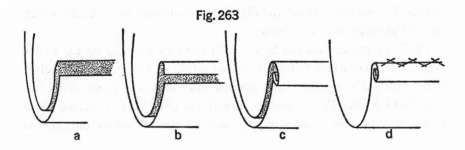

a   b   c   d

1. Turn the underlining up with the hem, allowing it to extend ½" beyond the top of the hem (Fig. 263a).

2. Fold under ¼" of the ½" extension (Fig. 263b).

3. Bring the folded edge down over the top of the hem, enclosing it (Fig. 263c). Slipstitch the underlining to the hem along the fold.

4. Fold back the finished edge of the hem ¼" toward the hem (Fig. 263d).

5. Use a running hemming or a catch stitch to fasten the hem to the underlining along the fold. The stitches *do not* come through to the outside of the garment (Fig. 263d).

Brocaded fabric is generally made on a satin ground. Everything that is true of satin is also true of brocade plus the additional care of its ornamented surface. In pressing, place the right side of the brocade against terry cloth or Turkish toweling to protect the raised surface. Should the brocade be woven with metallic thread, treat it like a metallic fabric.

Metallics have a strong tendency to ravel. Avoid any details like buttonholes or pockets which slash into the material. Work quickly. Overcast all edges or bind with seam binding. The metal threads are permanently creased by pressing. Press very little with a warm dry iron. Dampening may cause tarnish. As with satin, pin and needle marks show. Pin within the seam allowances. Be certain the stitching lines are in the correct place; ripping will show. Treat this fabric tenderly; it's probably your most expensive purchase.

Velvet: The nap of velvet which gives it a very special beauty also makes it a problem fabric to handle. Choose a design with little seaming so its beautiful surface remains unscarred. Remember that velvet drapes beautifully. Avoid details like buttonholes or pockets which require slashing into the fabric.

Place the pattern on the fabric with the nap running up for richer color. Use a complete pattern to avoid a fold of fabric. Folding velvet with right sides together, pile against pile, makes a problem in cutting. See Chapter IV for further directions. Use silk pins placed close to the cutting edge so they appear in the seam allowance only. (Fine hand needles are even better if you have that many of them.) Use silk thread for basting but baste in as few places as possible. The pile of velvet "creeps" when either hand- or machine-stitched. Use small basting stitches or backstitches; keep the two thicknesses separated until just before reaching the presser foot in machine stitching. (See Chapter VI for complete sewing directions.) Use no tailor basting, no pad stitching, no top stitching, no outside stitching. Use longer-than-average machine stitches—10 to 12 per inch. Use a "walking foot." Adjust the presser bar so there is not too much pressure on the pile.

Face velvet with chiffon, taffeta, or silk to avoid two layers of pile. Tack the facings and the hems invisibly to the backing.

Steam-press, preferably against a needle board. If this is not available, use the alternate methods described in Chapter VII.

Crepe, faille, matelassé; blistered, puckered, or crinkled fabric: The problem with all of these fabrics is *stretch.* If possible, avoid bias cuts; if they are used, fit with great care.

Press over Turkish toweling or terry cloth to preserve the surface interest (see Chapter VII for pressing directions). *Don't overpress* or you may eliminate the special effect. You may also find yourself with a garment several sizes too big for you. In the case of crepe—it may turn out to be several sizes too small for you.

Chiffon—the dream fabric: Like a dream, it is the most elusive of fabrics. Holding on to this gossamer stuff is the real problem.

To prevent slipping: cover the cutting table with tissue paper. Pin the chiffon to the tissue paper. Place the pattern over it. Use two rows of sharp pins placed close together, one row on either side of the cutting line. Cut with sharp shears through all three layers—tissue paper, chiffon, paper. Mark with chalk or tailor's tacks. Dressmaker's carbon and tracing wheel leave undesirable permanent and visible marking.

Use silk thread and a fine machine needle. Stitch slowly over strips of tissue paper which are torn away after stitching. Use 15 to 18 stitches per inch.

The transparency of chiffon creates difficulty with seams, facings, and hems. French seams are classic but a double row of stitching trimmed close to the stitching line is less prominent. Avoid stitched facings wherever possible; use a double fold of fabric instead. Edges may also be finished with a bias binding of chiffon.

Allow skirts to "hang out" for at least 24 hours before setting the hem. Hems in chiffon are never in between. They may be tiny, rolled hems or so deep they are almost double the fabric. Stay-stitch the hem before rolling it. If the skirt is lined, the lining should be hemmed separately. If the skirt is circular, don't ever expect it to be even; it dips outrageously.

Use a moderately warm iron and, of course, the inevitable press cloth. In this case, the cloth could be tissue paper.

For double- or triple-layered chiffon: Cut each layer separately. Mark only one—the bottom layer. Place the identical sections one over the other, matching the grain lines and the centers. Baste them together through the center. Press each side of the center, smoothing the fabric toward the outer edges. Baste once more a few inches away from the first line of basting on both sides. Press again. Keep this up until all the layers are joined as one. Proceed as if this were a new single layer of fabric.

Lace: This lovely, ladylike fabric looks best when cut on simple lines with beautiful shaping. It needs no more. If possible, plan to use the shaped self-edge as a finish at the neckline and hems.

Lace is generally underlined with net, organza, marquisette, or tulle. It may also be underlined with taffeta or any other silk, depending on the desired effect. Underlining eliminates the necessity for facings which would be disfiguring if they were made of self-fabric. Should facings be necessary, use any of the above underlining materials.

Plan the cutting so that the lace can be cut around design motifs, which are lapped and appliquéd over an adjoining area. By this method there are no regulation straight seams. The irregular joining is done as invisibly as possible by hand so the over-all-design effect is preserved.

Cut around the design motifs leaving ⅛" seam allowance which is turned under. Lap the motifs over the adjoining areas. Join by overhanding. Trim away any excess fabric on the underside. Use a No. 10 crewel needle.

Press on the wrong side over a thick padding of Turkish towels to preserve the raised surface. Use a steam iron and a dry press cloth.

Foreign Beauties: Even stay-at-homes can now enjoy the luxury of these foreign beauties—shantung, Italian pesante, Japanese brocaded silks, Thai silk, and Indian raw silks, to mention but a few. While these are not difficult to sew, they require special handling, too. The handwoven ones among these fabrics are apt to fray easily. They should be worked quickly before the fabric ravels and you are left with only a memory. Stay-stitch immediately on removal from the pattern. Overcast all edges.

The shantungs, pesantes, and Thai silks need plenty of ease; they have no "give." All of these need underlining to prevent seam slippage. (Shantung is the worst offender in this respect.)

Press on the wrong side, using a moderately dry iron and a dry press cloth or a steam iron and a press cloth. Be sure to test a scrap of the fabric first. (See Chapter VII for directions on pressing silks.)

Since the colors and the textures of these fabrics are so overwhelmingly beautiful, they look best when made simply but superbly.

Brave-New-World Fabrics

Laminates, the brand-new fabrics are made of urethane foam bonded to the wrong side of either knit or woven cloth. They give warmth without weight, and insulation against the weather. This is a great, new concept in fabric which has exciting possibilities. As fabrics go, this one is still in its infancy and there are a few kinks that need to be ironed out.

It does have advantages. It doesn't need interfacing, since the foam gives it permanent shape. It doesn't need interlining, since the foam acts as insulation. The resilience of the foam makes it uncrushable. It requires little fitting and little by way of tailoring technique.

Choose a simple unfitted design with few pattern pieces and few details. Gathering or easing the fabric is impossible because of its thickness. Choose patterns that do not include these operations.

Sponging is unnecessary. Trim away the tissue of the pattern at the cutting line. It is easier to cut beside the line rather than through it. Fold the fabric with the foam sides together so the fabric won't slip. There is this also: the grain is clearly visible on the cloth side and not at all on the foam side. In addition, the foam resists pinning which is easy to do on the cloth. The tracing wheel will ruin the foam, and tailor's chalk will mar the right side of the coat. Tailor's tacks are the safest marking.

Use matching plain fabric for facings to avoid two thicknesses of the foam. Reinforce the buttonhole area with iron-on interfacing.

Use a fine machine needle, loose tension, an adjusted presser bar for minimum pressure, 10 stitches to the inch. Strips of tissue paper directly under and over the stitching line will prevent the foam from sticking to the feeder and the presser foot. Bring the needle down into the fabric before lowering the presser foot. Stitch at a moderate speed. Welt seaming is good on foam fabrics both for appearance and structure. Use either single- or double-stitched seams. Bias seams may be taped with bias or plain seam binding to prevent stretching.

Slash the darts. Trim back anything that will produce the least possible bulk.

This fabric requires little pressing. Press the seams and darts open with the finger first. Use moderate heat, a dry iron, and a damp press cloth or use the steam iron and a dry cloth.

Don't overfit, because strain weakens the foam. Since hand stitching will pull away from the foam, all hemming must go through the foam to the fabric.

Fake furs: While man hasn't quite caught up with the animals in the production of fur, these new fabrics are certainly "a reasonable facsimile thereof." They have nap, sheen and realistic color, shading and markings. Since they are meant to be used like fur, they must be treated like fur. Choose a design with lines and details one would commonly find in a fur coat or jacket. Choose a pattern with simple lines, few seams or darts, and little detail.

The layout of the pattern is that for napped fabric. If there are shadings or markings in the "fur," match these at all seams. Cut with sharp shears. Mark with tailor's chalk. Stitch all inside seams by machine. (Avoid outside stitching.) Use a light tension, a medium machine needle, 8 to 10 stitches per inch. Work the pile out of the seams on the right side with a blunt needle. A special technique to reduce all bulk at the seam follows: first shave off the fur for ⅜" of the ⅝" seam allowance. Use a razor or an Exacto knife. Then stitch a regulation seam. Interface and tape as for any tailored garment. Tack all facings and hem to the backing of the fabric.

Fur fabric requires little pressing. Press the seam allowances open over a needle board or self-fabric. Use a steam iron. Press lightly. Brush up the nap after pressing.

Fasten as one would a fur coat. Use furrier's hooks and rings or braid loops and buttons, rather than buttonholes and buttons.

Waterproofed fabrics: By newly developed processes, most any fabric can now be waterproofed. This means that you can make your own raincoat of some unusual fabric in a style you cannot ordinarily find in ready-to-wear raincoats. (When you do find them, they cost a small fortune.)

Some waterproofed fabrics are now available for purchase. There is considerably more selection in fabrics to be waterproofed. Most satisfactory of all is to make the raincoat first, then have the entire coat waterproofed—lining, trimming, and all. Most cleaning services can have this done for you.

Choose a style that is easy to get on and off. Deep armscyes, raglan, or kimono sleeves are best. Remember that you are just as likely to wear the raincoat over a suit as over a dress.

For obvious reasons choose a color-fast fabric. Sponge it before waterproofing. If you are working with fabric that has already been waterproofed, avoid any marking or stitching, both machine and hand, that will pierce or cut into it. These tiny holes can spoil the waterproofing. Use a machine needle and stitch size that is suitable for the fabric. Press with the steam iron.

Interfacing is generally muslin or wigan, though it can be any interfacing appropriate to the design and the fabric.

Raincoats should be at least partially lined. It is nice to have some extra protection from the rain across the shoulders. If you are caught in the rain, this is the area most likely to get wet. Finish the inside of a partially lined coat as if it were an unlined one.

If the raincoat is fully lined, stitch the entire lining together before inserting it. Tack it with loose bastings down the side seams. Attach it to all the facing edges with slipstitching.

Provide enough fastening down the front of the coat so that you are really protected from the rain. Consider making a matching hood or hat.

This section has dealt only with those fabrics other than wool that are currently in vogue for suits, coats, and ensembles. Cottons and linens were not included, though they certainly are so used. They do not generally present any special problems and do not need special handling. When they do—naps, weaves, sheen, texture, surface, weight, etc.—they are treated in the same way as similar fabrics of other fibers. Unless otherwise noted, use all the familiar tailoring techniques and adapt them to your particular fabric.

DOUBLE EXPOSURE—
HOW TO MAKE A REVERSIBLE COAT

There are two types of reversibles: those made with two separate but identical coats that are joined and worn on either side or those made of a single but "two-faced" fabric that can be worn on either side. You buy a "two-faced" fabric because you love what is already there. The kind of "double exposure" that you can create is an exciting challenge to the imagination. Almost any two fabrics can go together. They can either blend or contrast in color, texture, and function. A reversible can be practical on one side and glamorous on the other.

Almost any simple pattern can be used as a reversible even if it is not designated as such. The best choice is unfitted and has no intricate seaming or detail. Omit the facings. Use only one thickness throughout.

The Two-Identical-Coats Type

Use the same pattern for both coats. Seams may be plain, welt, or lapped. Stitch all seams and darts as usual since they will be concealed. Interface as usual. Apply the interfacing and the tape to the front edge of the coat *usually* to be worn on the outside (you'll have to make a decision here). If the coat has a collar, stitch one thickness of collar to each coat. The same would be true of cuffs.

A coat without fastenings is a coat without problems. If you are determined to use buttons and buttonholes, use your ingenuity to devise a method of fastening which is reversible. One method is to make buttonholes on each front of each coat. These are made before the two are joined. Use a set of link buttons (Fig. 264a) which can be changed over and reversed so that the coat will button correctly, right over left, on either side. Another way of handling the buttonholes is to make them on the side usually to be worn outside and finish them on the second coat by the facing method described on page 302.

Slash the darts, trim, and press them open. Shape the bust area. Press all seam allowances open; clip, notch, and grade as necessary.

For an untrimmed edge, place the right sides of both completed coats together. Pin carefully. Stitch all except the hem edges. Press open, trim, and grade the seam allowances; clipping and notching as necessary. Turn to the right side. Finger-press so that the seam line is directly at the edge. Baste the edges together. Make one or two rows of decorative top stitching to hold everything in place.

Join the sleeve and side seams of both coats with long, loose basting stitches. Turn up both hems to the same height. Finish each separately. Allow them to hang free of each other but join them with a series of French tacks. Mark each sleeve at the same length. Turn under the seam allowances of both and slipstitch them together. Top-stitch the edge of the sleeve to match the front edges.

For a trimmed edge: The edges of a reversible coat may be trimmed with ribbon, braid, or bias binding. With wrong sides together and right sides outside, stitch the two coats together on the seam line. Trim the seam allowance close to the stitching. Stitch the ribbon, braid, or bias binding to the edges (page 399). Be sure to make the trim wide enough to completely cover the stitching on both sides.

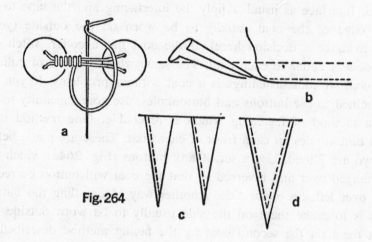

Fig. 264

The Single Fabric "Two-Faced" Type

In these fabrics all seam and dart stitching is exposed. It is a good idea to utilize this structural seaming as decoration.

1. Decide which side is to be worn outside usually.
2. Stitch all seams and darts on the other side.
3. Trim one seam allowance to a narrow width.
4. Fold under the edge of the wider seam allowance. Bring it over the trimmed edge, enclosing it. Stitch along the fold (Fig. 264b).
5. Press the darts toward the center. Stitch the folded edge down to the fabric (Fig. 264c). If the dart is wide, flatten it over the stitching line and stitch both sides of the dart along the folds (Fig. 264d).

Kimono-sleeved styles are simplest to handle. Set-in sleeves may be treated like men's shirt sleeves. First stitch the sleeve into the armhole, then stitch the side and underarm sleeve seam in one operation.

If pockets are used, make them patch pockets. Any slash in the fabric will make an ugly gash on one side or disclose an equally ugly pouch. That is, unless you invent some ingenious pocket arrangement.

The edges of the single-fabric reversible may be bound with ribbon, braid, or bias b'nding. If the fabric does not ravel, the edge may be turned to one side and held in place with several rows of close, decorative top stitching.

TRIMMINGS AND TOUCHES

The possibilities for trimmings and touches are infinite. The following discussion is limited to a few suggestions that can be used with interest (and taste) on present styles.

Velvet for collars: Practically no fabric comes near velvet in its air of elegance and luxury. Even a little of it for a trim adds this touch. The depth of the pile, its sheen and shadow, make it a dramatic contrast to any texture near which it is placed. It is a flatterer. For this reason it has long been a favorite for collars.

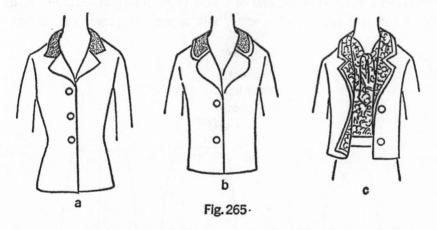

a   b   c

Fig. 265.

There are several ways of using velvet for a collar.

STYLE I—Fig. 265a

1. Complete the collar of garment fabric.

2. Cut another top collar of the velvet. Cut it large enough to permit it to fit easily without pulling up the collar beneath.

3. Fold under the seam allowance on all edges. Miter the corners.

4. Slipstitch the velvet collar to the seam line of the under collar.

STYLE II—Fig. 265b

This is a variation of Style I. The velvet is applied so that a margin of the original fabric is left to show.

STYLE III

If the garment fabric is heavy or bulky, the addition of a third layer of fabric will be too much. Use the velvet *instead* of the upper collar. Slipstitch the upper velvet collar to the under fabric collar.

Lining fabric as trim (Fig. 265c) can be used for collar and lapels to give a very interesting effect, particularly if the accompanying blouse matches.

Embroidered arrowhead or crow's foot is a classic finishing touch. Either can be used at the end of a dart (Fig. 266a), at each end of a bound pocket (Fig. 266b), or to hold a pleat in place (Fig. 266c).

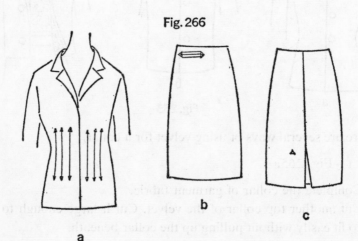

Fig. 266

a

b

c

ARROWHEAD

Fig. 267

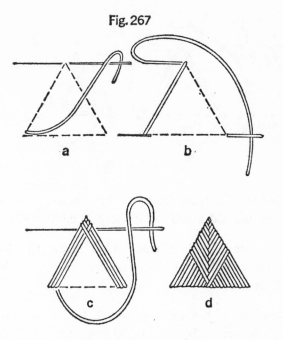

Arrowhead:

1. Mark the triangle. Fasten the thread on the underside. Bring the needle out at the left-hand point (Fig. 267a).

2. Take a small stitch from right to left at the upper point of the triangle. (Fig. 267a).

3. Put the needle in at the right point and bring it up beside the first stitch at the left (Fig. 267b).

4. Continue working down the sides and across the bottom (Fig. 267c) until the triangle is completely filled in (Fig. 267d). Place the stitches close to each other.

Crow's foot:

1. Mark the triangle with indented sides (Fig. 268a). Fasten the thread on the underside and bring the thread out at any point.

2. Take a small stitch at each point of the triangle (Fig. 268b). Turn the work to make it easier, if you like.

CROW'S FOOT

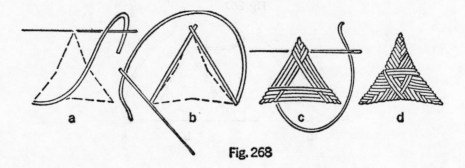

a   b   c   d

Fig. 268

3. Work around the triangle, following the indented outline (Fig. 268c), until all the sides are completely filled in (Fig. 268d).

Beautiful bindings: While Chanel didn't invent this form of trim she has certainly popularized it. No edge is too sacred for its bit of ribbon, braid, or bias.

Braid as binding: If not already folded, fold it in half lengthwise and press. Attach it either by hand or by machine.

To attach braid by hand:

1. Slip the stitched and trimmed edge of the garment into the fold of the braid. Stretch on outside curves, ease on inside curves, miter all corners.

2. Cut the braid ½″ beyond the planned end of the trimming. To prevent the cut end from spreading, stay-stitch it by hand immediately upon cutting. Use small stitches. Turn under the ½″ seam allowance.

3. Pin and baste carefully through all the thicknesses.

4. Slipstitch the edge of the braid to the garment on both outside and underside.

To attach braid by machine:

The method for placement of the braid is the same as for hand stitching, except that one side is stitched at a time.

1. Machine-stitch close to the edge of the braid on the outside.

2. Slipstitch the edge of the braid on the underside.

Alternate method: Machine stitching through all thicknesses close to the edge of the braid is a little risky but can be done if your stitching is accurate. Set the braid as for hand stitching.

Bias binding: The contrast between the bias of the binding and the straight of the garment makes this a very decorative trim, even of self-fabric.

To make the bias binding:

1. Cut a strip of true bias twice as wide as the finished binding plus narrow seam allowances. The binding may be as wide or as narrow as seems consistent with the design. Join bias strips on the straight of the goods to make the called-for length.

2. Press the bias in half lengthwise with the right side outside.

3. Turn under the seam allowances on both edges. Press.

To attach the bias binding:

Apply the bias binding in the same way as the braid binding was attached or by the following method.

1. Pin the right side of one edge of the binding to the right side of the garment. Match the fold of the binding to the seam line of the garment. Stretch on outside curves. Ease on inside curves. Miter all corners.

2. Machine-stitch along the fold. Trim the garment edge if necessary.

3. Roll the binding over the edge of the garment enclosing it.

4. Slipstitch the bias binding to the garment on the underside along the fold.

Consider the decorative possibilities of *hand crocheted trimmings and bindings* in colors that pick-up or contrast with the color of the fabric.

Ribbon trim makes an interesting finish, too. It is best used in straight bands. Most ribbon cannot be swirled. Place it along the edge to be trimmed. Miter the corners. Either top-stitch each edge of the ribbon to the garment by machine or slipstitch by hand. Braid may also be applied in this manner.

Pipings are "hot": A corded piping can make any seam appear purposeful instead of merely necessary. See Chapter VI for directions.

A SUEDE SUIT OR COAT—LUXURY ITEM

The new suedes and skins are so light and supple, the new sewing machines so capable of anything, that a once-undreamed-of luxury has become a real possibility for the home sewer. Leathers and suedes have been big news this year and understandably so. They offer a fresh look in a period marked by sumptuous fabrics.

Suede, goat, calf, and other small skins are sold by hides. (The larger skins are also sold by the full hide and sometimes by half a hide or a side.) While fabric is measured in yards, hides are measured by square feet. It doesn't quite do to convert the feet into yards by the usual arithmetic. The amount you need will be divided among a number of skins. The pattern placement will depend on the size, color, and shape of each individual skin, as well as the size and shape of each pattern piece. The safest thing to do is to take your pattern with you when you buy the skins.

Choose a style that will lend itself to leather or suede, but don't stick too closely to the expected sports type. Since the skins are small, choose a pattern which is either designed in sections or can be divided into sections to make its own design. (This is the first time in this book you have heard such advice. Usually it is: keep it simple.)

By all means make a trial muslin so that you are sure the pattern fits perfectly before you cut the leather. You would hardly want to rip leather, since all the stitching lines would show.

The wrinkling of the sleeve at the elbow (which becomes permanent in leather) shortens the length of the sleeve. Make the sleeves a little longer to compensate for this. Make any necessary alterations to the muslin and transfer them to the pattern.

Prepare the pattern:

The pattern needs a little preparation before it can be placed on the hides. Leather cannot be cut double or on a fold. Each piece must be cut separately. This means that each half pattern must be converted into a full pattern. Trace the other half and Scotch-Tape it to the original pattern. When the pattern says "Cut two," trace another one. Use wrapping paper, tissue paper, or shelf paper. Be sure to trace all the pattern markings—grain, notches, darts, seam allowances, etc. The seam allowances may be trimmed to ⅜" on the pattern to save on the skins. They will all be trimmed down after they are stitched, anyway. And, as noted before, the hole marks made by the needle will show, so you can't plan to let out a seam. Label each pattern piece as it is to appear in the finished garment—right front, left front, right sleeve, left sleeve, etc. This will determine its placement on the skin whether your layout is on the right or wrong side. You will find that the layout of the pattern on the skins is very much easier when you have a separate pattern piece for every part which must be cut. (This is true, too, when working with fur.)

Lay out, cut and mark the skins:

Like fabric, leather has grain. Also like fabric, the skin has more stretch on the crosswise grain than in the lengthwise grain. The grain of the hide runs with the backbone. The neck is the top of the skin. (You will recognize this by its shape.) All pattern pieces are placed lengthwise with the grain in a directional layout going from neck to hem on the corresponding direction of the skin. The pattern pieces need not follow this sequence; they may be used interchangeably. But the flow must be in the same direction because of the nap and, in some instances, the fur.

Place the pattern on either the right or wrong side of the skin. Make certain the placement will produce a right or a left in the finished garment. If fur is involved, the placement must be from the skin side rather than the hair side (see directions for cutting fur on page 409). The pattern may be pinned to the skins if the pins are kept within the seam allowances. Scotch Tape is a good way to hold the pattern in place and so are weights.

Cut the skins with sharp shears or with an Exacto knife. Cut all the notches *out* from the edge. Mark darts and seam lines with chalk. (The tracing wheel would leave permanent, undesirable marks.)

Stitch the skins:

Stitch the darts and seams, easing the leather slowly through the machine. Stitching is directional—from top to bottom. Use silk thread; 7 to 10 stitches to the inch; medium-size machine needle; adjust the upper tension; adjust the presser bar so there is less pressure. Make a test dart or seam on a scrap of hide to make sure the stitching is correct for the skin. Tie threads to secure them. Stitching back and forth over the same spot tends to cut the leather.

Leather has a tendency to stretch when stitched. Stay the seam to the exact length with preshrunk seam binding stitched into it. Hold the tape in position with a paper clip (Fig. 269a).

Interface the garment:

Because leather has considerable body and because shaping is not as essential as it is in tailoring fabric, interfacing can be kept to a minimum. It is used mainly to reinforce the opening and neck edges. Either woven or nonwoven interfacing may be used.

Trim away ¾" of the outside edge of the interfacing. Lap preshrunk tape or seam binding over the trimmed edge. Stitch the binding to the interfacing close to the edge. Catch the binding in the seam which joins facing to garment.

Fig. 269

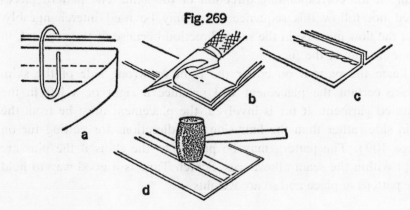

All thicknesses of the leather are generally held in place with top stitching, either hand or machine. Machine top stitching is very decorative when the stitches are large and the thread is buttonhole twist. When top stitching by hand, use either glove or saddle stitching.

Trim, skive, and "press" the skins: Trim the darts leaving a ⅜″ seam allowance. Snip open to the point of the dart. Trim, clip, and notch all seam allowances as necessary. To reduce bulk, skive all seam allowances with an Exacto knife or a single-edged razor blade (Fig. 269b). This beveling corresponds to grading the seam allowances in fabric.

Apply a small amount of rubber cement carefully under each seam allowance (Fig. 269c). Press the seam flat by pounding it with a rawhide mallet or anything which performs like one (Fig. 269d). Lift the seam up again lightly and remove the rubber cement with a "glue ball." This is a ball of dried rubber cement which picks up rubber cement as if it were an eraser. By this method of "pressing," seam allowances fall into place flat.

Leather may be pressed with a warm iron or a steam iron if the skin is protected by a press cloth. If you use the rubber cement correctly this is unnecessary in construction.

Make the buttonholes:

1. Mark the length and width of the buttonhole on the wrong side.

2. Slash through the center of the opening and diagonally to each corner (Fig. 270a).

3. Turn the flaps to the underside to form a rectangular opening (Fig. 270b).

4. Prepare the buttonhole binding. Cut two strips of leather 1″ longer than the length of the buttonhole and at least 2″ wide. Fold the strips lengthwise, making the fold ½″ from one edge (Fig. 270c). Cement the strip lightly in this position.

5. Place the first strip across the opening on the underside as for the finished lip of a buttonhole. The ½″ side is directly against

Fig. 270

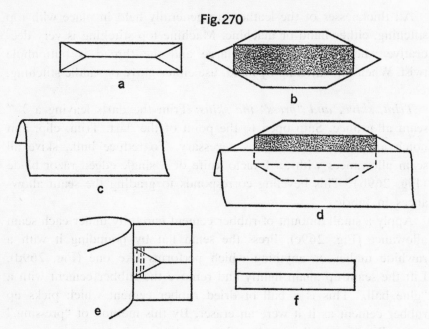

the flap of the rectangular opening. The folded edge is halfway up the opening (Fig. 270d).

6. Stitch the strip to the flap close to the fold line of the flap (Fig. 279d).

7. Trim away and skive the enclosed seam allowances.

8. Place and stitch the second lip of the buttonhole in the same way. Trim and skive the enclosed seam allowances.

9. Fold back each end and stitch the triangle against the strips. Make the several rows of stitching *beside* rather than over each other (Fig. 207e).

10. From the right side the finished leather buttonhole looks like the bound buttonhole in fabric (Fig. 270f).

To finish the buttonhole on the underside: repeat Steps 1 to 3 on the facing; cement the rectangular opening on the facing to the buttonhole or fasten with tiny hemming stitches.

A corded buttonhole can be made with the insertion of string or cord in step No. 4.

Attach the facing and the collar: With right sides together join the facing to the garment. Grade and bevel the seam allowances. Trim at the corners. Clip and notch as necessary. Turn to the right side.

See page 355 for an effective way to attach a notched collar. In general, follow the pattern directions for attaching the collar since in skin garments this is best done by machine.

Set the sleeves: Stitch the sleeve seam and "press" it open. Do *not* gather the cap.

Place the sleeve into its proper position in the armhole. Use rubber cement in place of pins or basting. It will not mar the skins as will pins and needles and it can be easily erased. Should the setting need to be changed the sleeves can simply be pulled away from the armscye and reset.

Start the setting at the shoulder as for a fabric sleeve. Match the shoulder seam of the garment with the shoulder marking at the sleeve cap. Hook your fingers into the garment and sleeve cap so that the cap assumes the outside curve it will have in the finished garment. Grasp with thumb. Holding the sleeve in this position, you will find it easy to ease the cap even without gathers.

Stitch the sleeve into the armscye, starting at the shoulder and continuing down the front armscye to the underarm. Break the thread and tie it. Start at the shoulder once more and stitch down the back armscye to the underarm. Break the thread and tie it.

Set the hems: Once set, the length of the garment can only be shortened, never lengthened. The crease at the hemline is permanent. Turn up the hem and use the rubber cement to "baste" the hem to position rather than pinning it. The hems of many leather garments are considered finished in this state. However, binding can be stitched to the top of the hem and attached by hand to the garment.

The belt:

If possible, cut the belt the desired length and double its width so there need be only one seam. This seam is placed at the middle of the belt on the underside.

Make the skirt and line it:

Gored skirts have the advantage of being able to be cut in sections, making for an economical use of the skins. The fit is easy which is important in leather. Straight skirts should be cut with considerable ease.

The zipper is inserted in the same way as for a fabric skirt. The waistband is attached in the same way as for a fabric skirt. To decrease the bulk, use a single width of the leather. Back with grosgrain ribbon.

All leather skirts should be fully lined. Make the lining like a half slip. Attach it to the skirt at the waistband and the zipper. It, too, is handled in the same way as in a fabric skirt.

Lining the jacket or coat:

Sew bias tape to all facing edges. Lap the tape over the leather and machine-stitch (Fig. 271a). For an extra decorative touch make a corded piping. Place the piping against the facings with the raw edges of both flush. Sew the piping to the facings (Fig. 271b).

Fig. 271

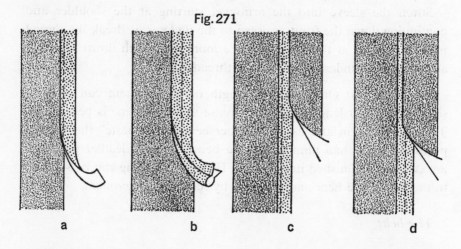

a   b   c   d

Make and apply the lining as for any fabric coat. Slipstitch the edges of the lining to either the seam binding (Fig. 271c) or the piping (Fig. 271d).

Use any of the tailoring techniques for fabric which you may find useful for leather in the course of your work. Anyone who can work with fabric can work with leather.

BE YOUR OWN FURRIER

If Mrs. Cave Woman could do it, so can you! When your friends know you are "clever with your hands," they make you the beneficiary (and often the repository) of all sorts of goodies like Victorian beaded belts, bits of tapestry, old shawls, and even a sleeve or a pocket of fur. What is there to lose but a little time if you try to make a fur hat or a fur collar out of what's left of your Aunt Jane's remodeled fur coat?

Perhaps you've never worked with fur before and every furrier you've ever heard has predicted dreadful consequences if you but dare touch it. You bolster yourself with the thought that if primitive woman, using a crude knife, a bone needle, and strips of hide could make herself a fur coat, you can do it, too.

The furriers try to discourage this activity. They tell you it takes an expert to work with fur. (The tailors will tell you the same thing about tailoring. Has that stopped you from making a suit or coat?)

The problem for most home sewers is not how to make a new fur coat but how to utilize an old one for trimmings, hats, muffs, scarves, and perhaps if one is adventuresome, even a short jacket.

Often the cost of having an old coat remodeled by a furrier is completely out of line with the worth of the fur. Yet it is still too good to discard or to let the children use for dress-up on Halloween. The furriers themselves don't want to be bothered with this small stuff when they could be making and selling a full-length mink in the same time. They leave us no alternative but to do-it-ourselves.

So—let the fur fly! First off, take whatever it is apart. While it is still a coat or a jacket you have grave doubts about cutting into it Once it's apart and flattened out on the table before you, it becomes so much fabric. You are not afraid of fabric!

Equipment for working with fur: Very little more equipment is necessary for working with fur than you already have for tailoring. You will need the following: a single-edge razor blade or an Exacto knife, some thumbtacks or pushpins, fur needles (glover's needles No. 7 are similar to those used for sutures; these pierce the skin without tearing it), and a large enough board on which to block the fur.

How to Make a Fur Jacket Out of an Old Fur Coat

Perhaps you will never want to do this but it does illustrate the techniques used in working with fur. These can be applied to making any of the smaller fur pieces you may be interested in.

Choose a style and a pattern:

Choose a style of simple but subtle lines that is suitable for fur. Choose a pattern with few pattern pieces, few seams, few darts, and one that can be cut from the amount of fur you have.

Make a test muslin:

Make a test muslin of the pattern. Make any necessary changes in it. Transfer the changes to the paper pattern.

Prepare the pattern:

Like leather, fur cannot be cut double or on a fold. Each piece must be cut separately and in its entirety. This means that each half pattern must be converted into a full pattern and each pattern piece which says "Cut two" requires a duplicate.

Trim away all the seam allowances on the pattern. Fur is sewn edge to edge; seam allowances are not necessary. Cut out all the darts in the pattern. It is easier to trace the dart this way.

Examine the fur:

Determine the placement of the pattern on the fur to take advantage of the best parts of it. Consider the shading and spotting which need matching. Examine the fur for any worn, torn, brittle, or broken parts of it which need replacement. Mark any such area in the shape of a triangle with safety pins. Note the direction in which the hair lies. This is the grain of the fur.

Lay out, cut, and mark the fur:

Place the pattern on the fur side to take advantage of the best parts, for color, shading, and spotting of adjoining pieces. Lay the pattern on so the grain of the pattern is parallel to the grain of the fur. For small pieces like collars, the nap of the fur should flow toward the back.

Put enough safety pins around the outside of each pattern piece to locate it on the skin side. Turn to the skin side and replace the pattern within the safety-pin outline. Hold the pattern in place with thumbtacks or pushpins. Trace around the pattern with a soft pencil or chalk (Fig. 272a). Trace the darts. Mark the notches; do not cut them out. Remove the pushpins and the pattern.

To avoid cutting the hair, raise the fur from the cutting surface and cut only the skin with a sharp blade (Fig. 272b). The uncut hair will cover the seam, making the joining invisible.

Not all skins are joined in a straight line. Joinings are less visible on some pile furs if they are cut zigzag. To preserve the flat and the moiré appearances of broadtail, lamb, kid, and pony, cut the joinings in wavy lines (Fig. 272c). Such cutting adds strength to the seams as well as making them less noticeable.

Using the safety pins as a guide, mark any areas that need replacement on the skin side. Cut out the fur triangle. Use the cut-out as a pattern for the replacement. Match the grain, color, shading, and spotting with adjoining areas. Sew the fur patch in place.

Block the pattern into shape:

Trace the pattern of each piece on a large board. Wet the skin side of the fur with a sponge or brush. Place the fur, hair side down, on the board matching the pattern outline. Tack carefully all around the edges with thumbtacks or pushpins (Fig. 272d). Allow the fur to dry thoroughly at least twenty-four hours.

When dry, remove the tacks. Replace the pattern on the skin side of the fur. Re-mark the pattern outline if necessary. Cut on the corrected lines. Cut out the darts.

Fig. 272

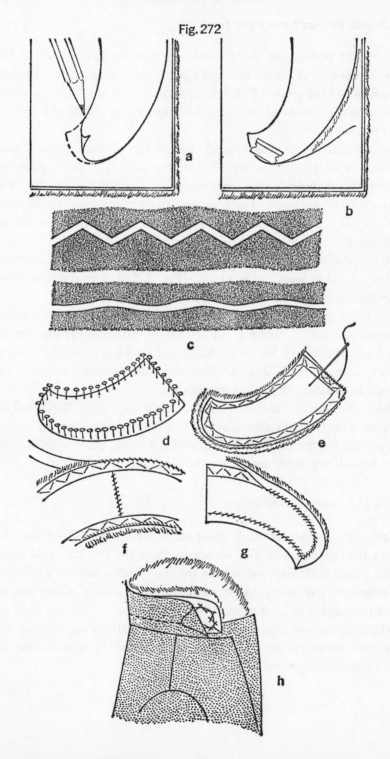

Tape the cut edges:

Place preshrunk tape flat around all edges which need to be joined. Tape both dart legs. The edge of the tape is flush with the edge of the skin. Cut and overlap the tape at corners. Swirl all curved edges. Fasten the tape to the skin with a zigzag hand stitch (Fig. 272e). Taping relieves the strain in weak areas and prevents tearing or ripping at the seams or darts.

Join all seams and darts:

The furrier does this operation speedily by a special machine. You will have to do it by hand—a much slower process.

With fur sides together, join the edges of the pelts only with tiny overhand stitches. Use the fur needle and a single strand of waxed silk or heavy-duty thread (Fig. 272e). Push the hair out of the seam with the point of the needle as you join the edges. Work the hairs out of the seam on the fur side to conceal it.

Join all the seams and darts. Set the sleeve into the armscye and stitch them together.

Back the collar, reinforce the closing edges and hems:

Back the collar with cotton flannel, muslin, or lamb's wool. Use strips of these backing materials to reinforce the closing edges and the hems. Place the center of the strip at the fold line of the fur— that is, the line at which the fur folds back to become the facing or the hem. This gives the turn-back a soft, padded look.

Place tape against the fur side of all outside edges. Miter the corners. Swirl the tape for curved edges. Place the edge of the tape flush with the edge of the skin. Join the tape and skin with overhanding (Fig. 272f). Turn the tape back to the skin side. Where the fur has been backed, turn the tape over the backing. Fasten with hemming, basting, or catch stitches. (Fig. 272g).

Turn up the hem and fasten it. Turn back the facings. It is a nice touch to finish the edges of the facings with a corded piping, braid, or ribbon, which in turn are fastened to the skin.

Make and attach the collar:

If the collar is all fur, make and attach it with overhand stitches. Use any applicable tailoring techniques.

If you have made a fur collar for a cloth coat, slipstitch the cloth under collar to the taped edge of the fur. Run a line of running stitches along the roll line of the under collar. Make it go through to the fur and catch it (Fig. 272h).

If you can get a furrier to do it for you, have him run the garment through the drum of fine sawdust which is standard equipment in all furrier's establishments. This revives the suppleness and pliability of the fur. It also freshens it. If you can't persuade him to do this for you, dampen the fur slightly. Brush it with the grain gently. Fluff it up against the grain lightly. Allow it to dry overnight.

Interlining, if desired, is made and applied in the same way as for a fabric coat. It is attached to the tape. Lining is made and inserted in the same way as in a fabric coat, too. Linings in fur coats are apt to be more sumptuous, in keeping with the luxury character of the fur. Attach the lining to the piping along all the facing edges.

Use furrier's hooks and rings for fastening the coat or jacket.

Basic Techniques Convert Old Fur to New Fashion Items

This basic technique for working with fur can be applied to any fur pieces which you can get out of your worn furs—hats, bags, collars, cuffs, muffs, boas, linings for coats, and so on.

Fur does give an air of luxury to any costume. You needn't be orthodox in your use or in your design. Some of the most creative furriers are not afraid of innovations and not afraid to treat fur as fabric for design. When *you* think of it so, you are on home ground.

HOW TO INTERLINE A COAT

It's fine to "dream of a white Christmas" if your winter coat is sufficiently warm. Interlining will make it so. Interlining will also add weight and bulk to a coat. The trick is to get the coat as warm as possible without any excess weight.

For this purpose lamb's wool interlining is best. (See Chapter I.) It comes in several colors and several weights. Choose that which best suits your personal needs and your fabric. Since everything else in the coat has been sponged, play it safe and sponge the interlining, too.

The pattern:

Lamb's wool comes slightly wider than other wools. Patterns rarely include a pattern for interlining. You will have to work out your own pattern and your own layout. This should not be too difficult because there are so few pattern pieces necessary. Use the lining pattern for an unfitted coat and the coat pattern itself for a fitted coat. The latter will give you an identical shaping which is important.

If you use the lining pattern, some adjustments will have to be made. Eliminate the center-back pleat; place the center back on a fold. Extend the lines of the front shoulder-dart tuck until they converge making a shoulder dart. This will be a long dart. End it 1″ above the high point of the bust.

Make any pattern alterations on the interlining that were made on the coat. One-piece sleeves may be completely underlined (Fig. 273a). In a two-piece sleeve, only the upper sleeve is generally interlined (Fig. 273b). Gussets are not interlined. If piecing of the material is necessary, cut an additional piece on the same grain.

Place the pattern on the interlining, observing the grain. Cut with sharp shears. Mark all seams and darts with dressmaker's carbon paper and the tracing wheel. The seam lines are very important for the construction and the insertion of the interlining.

A variety of methods:

There are a number of ways in which the interlining can be made and inserted into the garment. These are an all-hand method, an all-machine method, and various combinations of the two.

METHOD I—Fig. 273c: Join all sections of the entire interlining with machine stitching. Attach the coat by hand stitching. This is obviously the easiest and the fastest method of all. It is the least perfect unless the garment is still an unaltered, unfitted standard size.

METHOD II—Fig. 273d: Join all the vertical seams and darts by machine just as you would for a lining. Insert and join the rest by hand stitching. This is a simple, easy method which provides some leeway for adjustment.

METHOD III—Fig. 273e: Place each piece of the interlining separately into the coat.

Lap the seams over each other and catch-stitch to the seam allowance. This hand method gives a great deal more chance for adjustment. If, by now, you have forgotten just what changes you did make in fitting your coat, this is a good method for precision setting.

METHOD IV—Fig. 273f: Place each piece separately into the coat. Trim the interlining away so that it just meets the edges of the seam allowances and the facings. Join these with catch stitching. In effect, this interlining acts like an underlining—it backs each piece of the original fabric. By this method there is never any place on the garment that has more than two thicknesses of fabric.

Method IV is the most work but gives the least bulk. Perhaps it does seem to carry things a bit to extremes but it has this advantage: it is often easier to handle one piece at a time than to insert another great mass of wool into an already-voluminous coat.

METHOD V—Fig. 273g: Tailor-baste the interlining to the lining so they are "laminated." (There is such a commercial fabric on the market.) Stitch the darts and seams through all four thicknesses. Trim and grade the seam allowances. Attach the interlining-lining in one operation. This is the least amount of work but produces the greatest amount of bulk. It would do for a loose coat but is unsatisfactory for a fitted one.

Which method you choose depends on the particular coat that you are making and in how much of a hurry you are to complete it.

How to stitch the interlining:

In all except Method V, lap and stitch all seams and darts as in the interfacing. Use a longer stitch and a looser tension, since inter-

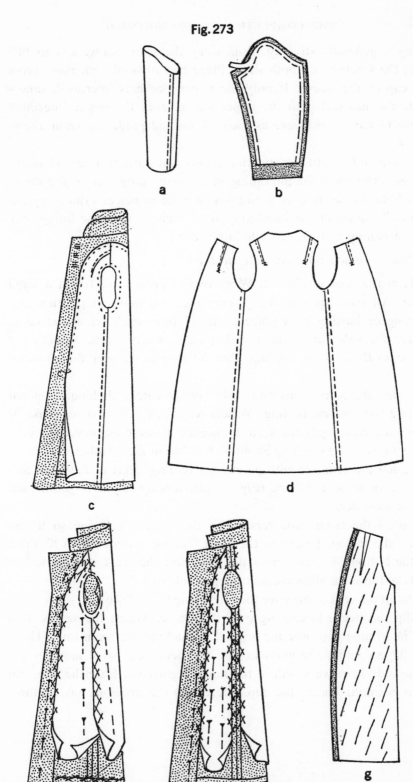

Fig. 273

a

b

c

d

g

lining is generally stretchy. Trim away the seam allowances to ¼" from the stitching on both sides. Place two rows of gathering across the cap of the sleeve. If only the upper sleeve is interlined, tailor-baste the interlining to the upper sleeve. Join the upper interlined sleeve to the under sleeve as usual. Trim and grade the seam allowances.

In Method V, stitch regulation seams and darts through all thicknesses. Trim away the interlining at the seam allowance of the sleeve cap. Fold the lining over it and pin or baste in place. Trim away the seam allowance of the interlining at all facings. Fold the lining over the interlining and pin or baste in place.

How to attach the interlining to the coat:

Turn the coat inside out. Work over a dress form or on a large table. All methods start by placing the interlining in position and pinning or basting it in place 2" to 3" from each seam and edge. Match the side seams and the shaping seams or darts. Smooth the fabric so there is no rippling. Put the interlining over the shoulder pad.

Fasten the side seams first, using either catch stitching, diagonal basting, or uneven basting. Whichever stitch you choose, make it loose and catch only the seam allowance of the coat, never the coat beneath. Stop the stitching about 6" to 8" from the hemline.

Fasten the armhole with permanent basting. Start at the front and work around to the back (Fig. 274a), leaving about 3" unstitched at the shoulder.

Fasten the front shoulders. Trim the front interfacing so it just meets the facing. Fasten to the front facings, leaving 6" to 8" open at the bottom. Fasten across the neck and the back shoulders.

Trim the seam allowances at the armhole to ¼".

Put in the coat lining over the interlining (Fig. 274b).

Slip the sleeve interlining over the sleeve. Match the seams. Lap the interlining cap over the armhole, matching the seam lines. Hook the fingers under the garment and the sleeve cap so it assumes the same outside curve it will in the finished garment. Ease the cap. Pin it to position. Fasten the cap securely to the armhole, taking three

Fig. 274

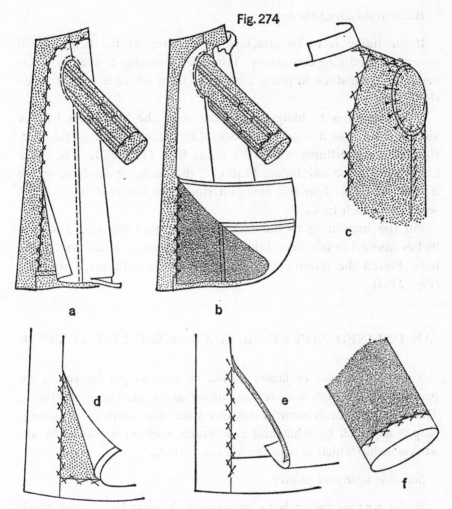

a   b   c

d   e   f

tiny running stitches and a backstitch. Trim the seam allowance to
¼" (Fig. 274c).

Slip the sleeve lining over the interlining and fasten.

Let the interlining hang out before trimming it to the proper
length.

Pin the interlining to the coat fabric about 6" to 8" above the hemline and parallel to it. Decide the hem finish and trim accordingly.

What to do about the hem:

If the lining is to be attached to the coat at the hem, it will cover the interlining completely. Trim the interlining to the top of the hem and catch-stitch in place. Finish the front where it was left open (Fig. 274d).

If the lining is to hang free of the coat, the interlining will be visible. Trim it so it is one inch shorter than the hemline of the coat. Enclose the interlining within the lining hem (Fig. 274e). Hem the lining hem to the interlining. Finish off the facing at the front where it was left open. Join the lining-interlining to the coat hem with a series of French tacks.

Pin the interlining to the coat fabric around the sleeve several inches above the hemline. Trim off the interlining at the top of the hem. Fasten the interlining to the sleeve hem with catch stitching (Fig. 274f).

AN UNLINED JACKET OR COAT—SOME LIKE IT COLD

This kind of coat or jacket should be easy as pie for you, compared to all the work involved in putting in an interlining and lining. This is a type rarely seen in this day when the worth of clothing is judged as much by what and how much goes on inside as by the workmanship which is apparent on the surface.

Suitable style and fabric:

If the coat or jacket is to be unlined, it must be of such fabric that the weight and body of it alone can carry the lines and shaping. For there is very little interfacing used. What little there is must be cut so that it is concealed under the facings and hems. It should be of a soft material so there is not too much difference between faced and unfaced parts. Choose a simple style so that as few seams and darts as possible will show on the wrong side. Choose patch pockets rather than those set in a slash of the garment. The pocket pouch of the latter is not a particularly decorative asset.

"Pretty-ing up" the exposed underside:

Leave the darts uncut. If they must be cut they should be bound. Bias binding is best for this.

All seam allowances are bound, too. Bias binding looks best here, too. Only flat-felled or welt seams remain unbound.

If there is no back facing, turn under the seam allowance of the upper collar and fasten it at the neckline with slipstitching.

If there is a back neck facing, stitch it to the front facing at the shoulders. Attach the back neck facing to the upper collar. Clip the seam allowances and press them open. Tack at the neck seam. Bind the edges of all facings.

Bind the armholes. Finish the hem with binding.

If shoulder pads are used, they should be covered with the garment fabric or a matching silk.

Any and every part of it which is exposed should be finished off so that no raw edges show.

A LINED JACKET OR COAT

So much loving care and so many thousands of hand stitches (count 'em) have gone into the making of your coat or jacket that your reluctance to cover up your handiwork with a mere lining is quite understandable. It is to be hoped that your lining is so beautiful that it will compensate for your loss.

The lining pattern:

Use the pattern for the lining which came with the garment pattern. This generally does a good job of eliminating unnecessary details and stitching. It also shifts the dart control into a soft fold at the shoulder which provides a little more ease to the lining.

If you wish to make a lining when none was included in the pattern this is how to do it: Use the pattern of the coat or jacket. Allow a one-inch pleat at the center back. Trace the facing on the pattern front. Cut away the facing but add seam allowance to the cut edge.

Cut off the pattern at the hemline of the jacket and the sleeve. Make a coat lining 1″ shorter than the coat but add 2½″ for a hem. The original shaping may be retained or the dart control may be shifted to a shoulder-dart tuck laid in a soft fold. Make the same alterations on the lining as were made on the garment.

Cut, mark, and stitch the lining:

Cut, mark, and stay-stitch the lining with the same care and precision as the outer fabric. Stitch all the seams and sections that complete the lining front and the lining back. Stitch front and back linings together at all vertical seams. Leave the shoulders open. Lay a soft fold at the shoulder front and pin. Lay a soft fold at the center back and pin (Fig. 275a). The fold is directly on center back—the pleat on the right side of the garment.

Fig. 275

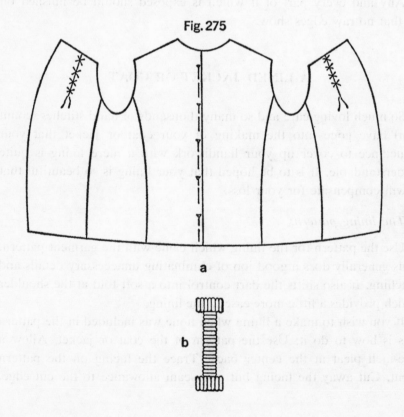

a

b

Note: Darts and dart tucks may be stitched by machine but in fine custom work these are generally laid in soft folds and fastened with either cross-stitches or bar tacks* to a depth of about 1″ to 1½″.

Stitch the sleeve seams. Place two rows of gathering across the cap of the sleeve.

Press all the seam allowances open. Press the lining.

Attach the lining to the garment:

Turn the jacket or coat inside out. Place it over some curved surface. A dress form is ideal. A tailor's ham will do. Don't work on a flat surface or you will eliminate the ease which is derived from inserting the lining in a curve opposite to that in which it will be worn.

The lining must have plenty of ease to prevent drawing or pulling. It must also be attached to the garment in enough places so that it won't twist or slip out of place.

Do the same operation on both sides before going on to the next step.

1. Match the open seam allowances of the side seams of the lining and the garment. If there is no side seam use a side-front or side-back seam instead. Permanently baste the seam allowances together close to the stitching line. Leave the bottom of a jacket lining free 4″ to 5″ from the bottom, and a coat lining free 8″ to 10″ from the bottom (Fig. 276a).

2. Baste the lining firmly to the armhole, starting at the underarm and working toward the shoulder, first at the front and then at the back. Leave the back armhole free for about 2″ from the shoulder (Fig. 276a).

3. Turn under the seam allowance at the front edge of the lining. Pin it in place over the facing, raw edges matching. Slipstitch it, leaving the bottom free for about 3″ to 4″ from the hemline of a jacket and 5″ to 6″ from the hemline of a coat (Fig. 276a).

4. Permanently baste the front shoulder.

---

* A bar tack resembles the bar at the end of a worked buttonhole. It goes through all the material to be held in place. Each end of the bar tack may be finished with a smaller bar tack (Fig. 275b).

Fig. 276

5. Clip the curve at the back of the neck. Fold under the seam allowance of the lining at both back shoulders and across the back of the neck.

6. Pin this folded edge in place over the front shoulders and the neck. Work from both ends of the shoulders toward the center of the back. Fold any surplus lining into the center-back fold (Fig. 276b).

7. Fasten the center-back fold of fabric in place at the neck, waistline, and hem with cross-stitches or bar tacks for about 1″ to 1½″ (Fig. 276c).

8. Slipstitch the back shoulders and neck to the garment.

Attaching the sleeve lining in a set-in sleeve:

1. Clip the seam allowance of the lining underarm both of the sleeve and of the coat or jacket.

2. Slip the lining over the sleeve wrong sides together. Baste one sleeve seam of the lining to the corresponding sleeve seam of the fabric.

3. Pull up the gathers to form a cap to fit the sleeve cap.

4. Turn under the seam allowance and lap the lining over the armscye of the sleeve, matching the underarm, the shoulder, and any sleeve seams.

5. Slipstitch the sleeve lining to the sleeve around the armhole (Fig. 276d). There is a great deal of stress on the underarm of the lining and it often comes apart. To avoid this, use buttonhole twist or heavy-duty thread of a matching color. If the coat or jacket is to get a great deal of wear, use tiny whipping stitches instead of slipstitching.

To complete the hems of jacket, coat, and sleeves:

Let the garment hang so that the lining settles before finishing the hem. Then pin the lining to the fabric several inches above the hemline of jacket, coat, and sleeves. Place the pins parallel to the hemline (Fig. 277a and 277b).

Jacket-lining hem:

1. Cut off any lining which shows below the bottom of the jacket (Fig. 277a).

2. Turn under the seam allowance of the lining and pin it over the top of the hem, raw edges matching. Note the small tuck which provides the lengthwise ease. Slipstitch.

3. Finish the remaining front edge which was left open by slipstitching.

Coat-lining hem:

1. Mark the lining at the bottom of the coat with a line of pins (Fig. 277b).

Fig. 277

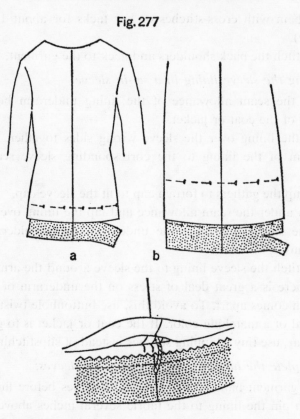

a   b

c

2. Cut off the lining 1½″ below this (Fig. 277b).

3. Turn up the coat lining to make a 2½″ hem. This makes the coat lining 1″ shorter than the coat. Use any suitable hem finish.

4. Slipstitch the remaining front edge which was left open.

5. Place a French tack between the hem of the lining and the hem of the coat at the side seams (Fig. 277c).

Sleeve-lining hem:

The sleeve-lining hems of both coat and jacket are done in the same way.

1. Pin the lining to the sleeve several inches above the hemline.

2. Trim away any lining which shows below the finished edge of the sleeve.

3. Turn under the seam allowance of the lining.

4. Pin the lining over the top of the sleeve hem, raw edges matching.

5. Slipstitch the lining to the top of the sleeve hem.

Lining a kimono-sleeved style:

1. Stitch together the entire lining except for the shoulder-sleeve seams.

2. Press the lining; press open all seam allowances; clip where necessary.

3. Lay folds at the front shoulder and the center back just as for the set-in sleeve style.

4. Match the open seam allowances of both lining and fabric at the side seams and continue along the undersleeve seam. Stop the same distance from the bottom of sleeve and garment as for the set-in sleeve. Permanently baste the seam allowances.

5. Turn under the seam allowance at the front edge and slipstitch to the facing.

6. Pin the lining front in place across the entire front shoulder and sleeve, making any necessary adjustments. Fasten with permanent basting. Trim away any surplus fabric.

7. Turn under the seam allowances of the back shoulder and sleeve seams. Pin in place making any necessary adjustments. Trim away any surplus material.

8. Clip the curve at the back of the neck. Turn under the seam allowance and pin across the back. Start at the shoulders and work toward the center back. Fold the extra fabric into the center-back pleat and cross-stitch in place.

9. Slipstitch the shoulder-sleeve seams and the neck back.

10. Finish the hems in the same way as suggested for the set-in sleeve styles.

The above methods of inserting a lining give an opportunity to make any adjustments in the lining which were made in fitting the garment. Machine-made garments don't observe such niceties for they depend on standard sizes.

Press the lining:

The lining should be pressed lightly on the right side. Be sure to use a dry press cloth.

Press a slight roll to hide the stitching along the facing and hem edges. If a coat lining hangs free of the coat, press the hem separately. Press the pleat at the center back.

Turn the sleeve inside out and slip it over the sleeve board. The cap should rest over the end of the board. Press from hem to cap.

Right side touch-up for the coat or suit:

Give the coat or suit a touch-up pressing from the right side. See Chapter VII.

A weighty matter:

You may just want to weight the bottom of the jacket or coat so it hangs well. Use a covered weight tacked to the upper edge of the hem at the side seams (Fig. 278a). Or, use Chanel's very own method for weighting her jackets. This is a length of chain stitched in full view from facing to facing across the hem (Fig. 278b).

Fig. 278

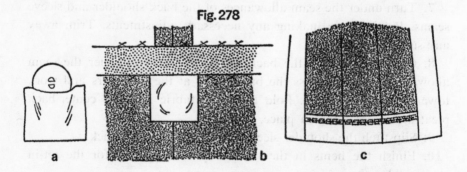

These are the final touches. Your coat or suit is completed at last.

The Master Signs His Work

It's been long and you have worked hard. It is to be hoped that you are proud of what you have created. When the picture is done the master signs it. The final touch is your signature. This could be your initials embroidered on the lining a few inches above the hipline. Or a label which you can make for yourself of your favorite color of ribbon. Embroider your name or initials. Cross-stitch it in place at the center back of your lining 1″ to 2″ below the neckline (Fig. 279). It will write Finish with a flourish.

Fig. 279

My wish for you is the one with which my family always greeted me when I appeared in something new—

"WEAR IT IN THE BEST OF HEALTH!"

Index